First World War
and Army of Occupation
War Diary
France, Belgium and Germany

23 DIVISION
68 Infantry Brigade
Northumberland Fusiliers
11th Battalion
10 January 1915 - 31 October 1917

WO95/2182/4

The Naval & Military Press Ltd
www.nmarchive.com
Published in association with The National Archives

Published by

The Naval & Military Press Ltd

Unit 10 Ridgewood Industrial Park,

Uckfield, East Sussex,

TN22 5QE England

Tel: +44 (0) 1825 749494

www.naval-military-press.com

www.nmarchive.com

This diary has been reprinted in facsimile from the original. Any imperfections are inevitably reproduced and the quality may fall short of modern type and cartographic standards.

© **Crown Copyright**
Images reproduced by permission of The National Archives, London, England, 2015.

Contents

Document type	Place/Title	Date From	Date To
Heading	WO95/2182/4 11 Bn N'berland Fus Aug 1915-Oct 1917		
Heading	23rd Division 68th Infy Bde 11th Bn North'D Fus. Aug 1915-1917 Oct To Italy.		
Heading	23rd Division II Northland Fus. Vol I Aug To Oct 15		
War Diary	Bramshott Camp.	24/08/1915	25/08/1915
War Diary	Ostrohove Camp.	26/08/1915	26/08/1915
War Diary	Eperleques	27/08/1915	06/09/1915
War Diary	Hazebrouck	07/09/1915	07/09/1915
War Diary	School, Steenje.	08/09/1915	08/09/1915
War Diary	Laventie	09/09/1915	17/09/1915
War Diary	Erquinghem Lys. Fort. Rompu.	18/09/1915	26/09/1915
War Diary	Estaires	27/09/1915	27/09/1915
War Diary	Fort Rompu	28/09/1915	28/09/1915
War Diary	Estaires.	29/09/1915	04/10/1915
War Diary	Bois Grenier Line.	05/10/1915	12/10/1915
War Diary	Billets in Rue Du Biez and Rue De Lettre "D" Position	13/10/1915	15/10/1915
War Diary	Firing Line "A" Position	16/10/1915	19/10/1915
War Diary	Support Trenches	20/10/1915	24/10/1915
War Diary	Firing Line. in A Position	25/10/1915	29/10/1915
War Diary	D Position Billets In Rue De Lettre.	30/10/1915	31/10/1915
Heading	23rd Division 4th Northumb: Fus: Vol: 4 Nov 15		
War Diary	D Position	01/11/1915	01/11/1915
War Diary	C Position Bois Grenier Line.	02/11/1915	06/11/1915
War Diary	A Position	06/11/1915	09/11/1915
War Diary	D Position	10/11/1915	13/11/1915
War Diary	A Position.	14/11/1915	16/11/1915
War Diary	Fort Rompu.	17/11/1915	23/11/1915
War Diary	C Position	24/11/1915	24/11/1915
War Diary	Rue Marle.	25/11/1915	25/11/1915
War Diary	C Position	26/11/1915	26/11/1915
War Diary	Rue Marle	26/11/1915	28/11/1915
War Diary	A Position	29/11/1915	30/11/1915
Heading	23rd Div 11th Northumb Fus. Vol. B 5		
War Diary	A Position.	01/12/1915	02/12/1915
War Diary	Rue Marle	02/12/1915	02/12/1915
War Diary	D Position.	03/12/1915	06/12/1915
War Diary	A Position	07/12/1915	10/12/1915
War Diary	C Position	11/12/1915	14/12/1915
War Diary	Hallobeau (Div Reserve).	15/12/1915	18/12/1915
War Diary	Hallobeau	19/12/1915	21/12/1915
War Diary	B Bn. Right Section.	22/12/1915	26/12/1915
War Diary	D Position.	27/12/1915	29/12/1915
War Diary	B Position	30/12/1915	31/12/1915
Heading	11th Northland Position Vol 6 Jan 16		
War Diary	B Place.	01/01/1916	02/01/1916
War Diary	C Position	03/01/1916	05/01/1916
War Diary	Rue Domoire.	06/01/1916	07/01/1916
War Diary	H.9.a.0.3	08/01/1916	08/01/1916
War Diary	Brigade Reserve.	08/01/1916	09/01/1916

Type	Description	Start	End
War Diary	Rue Domoire.	10/01/1915	14/01/1915
War Diary	A Position Left Sector Trenches 3.26.5	15/01/1915	16/01/1915
War Diary	9.21.1. (inclusive.)	17/01/1915	19/01/1915
War Diary	Rue. Marle H.6.d.6.5	20/01/1916	21/01/1916
War Diary	A Battn	22/01/1916	27/01/1916
War Diary	Rue Marle. "C"	28/01/1916	31/01/1916
Miscellaneous		29/01/1916	29/01/1916
War Diary	Jesus Farm B.26.d.4.1	01/02/1916	06/02/1916
War Diary	Jesus Farm.	07/02/1916	08/02/1916
War Diary	B Battalion Right Sector.	08/02/1916	17/02/1916
War Diary	B Battn.	18/02/1916	21/02/1916
War Diary	Rue Domoire	22/02/1916	24/02/1916
War Diary	Sailly.	25/02/1916	26/02/1916
War Diary	Morbecque.	26/02/1916	28/02/1916
War Diary	Marle Des-Mines.	29/02/1916	29/02/1916
War Diary	Marle-Les-Mines	01/03/1916	07/03/1916
War Diary	Fresnicourt.	08/03/1916	11/03/1916
War Diary	Fresnicourt. Q.25.b.	12/03/1916	15/03/1916
War Diary	Hersin Q.5.d.	16/03/1916	16/03/1916
War Diary	Bully Grenay. R.11.a.	17/03/1916	18/03/1916
War Diary	D Position	18/03/1916	20/03/1916
War Diary	Front Line Trenches	21/03/1916	21/03/1916
War Diary	A Position	22/03/1916	24/03/1916
War Diary	A Battn.	25/03/1916	25/03/1916
War Diary	Calonne.	25/03/1916	25/03/1916
War Diary	C Position.	25/03/1916	28/03/1916
War Diary	A Battn.	29/03/1916	31/03/1916
Miscellaneous	Battalion Operation Orders For 17th March 1916	17/03/1916	17/03/1916
Miscellaneous	To/-O.C., O.C. Coy.	20/03/1916	20/03/1916
Miscellaneous	Battalion Operation Orders For March 21st.	20/03/1916	20/03/1916
Miscellaneous	To/-O.C., O.C. Coy.	21/03/1916	21/03/1916
Miscellaneous	Battalion Operation Orders For 25th March 1916	25/03/1916	25/03/1916
Miscellaneous	Battalion Operation Orders For 29th March 1916	29/03/1916	29/03/1916
War Diary	A Battn. Calonne Section	01/04/1916	02/04/1916
War Diary	Bully Grenay	03/04/1916	03/04/1916
War Diary	D Battn.	04/04/1916	05/04/1916
War Diary	A Battn.	06/04/1916	07/04/1916
War Diary	Calonne. Section	08/04/1916	10/04/1916
War Diary	A Battn. Fire Trench.	10/04/1916	11/04/1916
War Diary	C Battn. Supports Billets Calonne.	12/04/1916	14/04/1916
War Diary	A Battn. Fire Trench.	15/04/1916	15/04/1916
War Diary	A Position in Calonne.	16/04/1916	18/04/1916
War Diary	Hersin.	18/04/1916	22/04/1916
War Diary	St. Georges Day	23/04/1916	24/04/1916
War Diary	Hersin.	25/04/1916	26/04/1916
War Diary	Divion I.24.b.36.B	26/04/1916	30/04/1916
Miscellaneous	Battalion Operation Orders For 2nd April 1916	02/04/1916	02/04/1916
Miscellaneous	Daily Working Parties In "D" Position.	03/04/1916	03/04/1916
Miscellaneous	G. Beaton.		
Miscellaneous	After Orders.	05/04/1916	05/04/1916
Miscellaneous	A Form. Messages And Signals.		
Miscellaneous	Battalion Operation Orders For 6th April 1916	06/04/1916	06/04/1916
Miscellaneous	To/O.C. Coy	06/04/1916	06/04/1916
Miscellaneous	Battalion Operation Orders For 10th April 1916	10/04/1916	10/04/1916
Miscellaneous	Daily Working Parties to Be Found by the Battalion in "C" Position.	09/04/1916	09/04/1916

Miscellaneous	Battalion Operation Orders For 15th April 1916	15/04/1916	15/04/1916
Miscellaneous	A Form. Messages And Signals.		
Miscellaneous	B.O.O. For 15th April Sheet 2	14/04/1916	14/04/1916
Miscellaneous	Advance Battalion Operation Orders For 18th April 1916	18/04/1916	18/04/1916
Miscellaneous	Battalion Operation Orders For 18th April 1916	18/04/1916	18/04/1916
Miscellaneous	Battalion Operation Orders For 26th April 1916	26/04/1916	26/04/1916
War Diary	Divion	01/05/1916	05/05/1916
War Diary	Beaumetz Lez Aire	06/05/1916	18/05/1916
War Diary	Barlin.	19/05/1916	19/05/1916
War Diary	Souchez Sector	20/05/1916	20/05/1916
War Diary	D Bn.	21/05/1916	24/05/1916
War Diary	A Battn Souchez I S.1.b. 9/3/4.a.	25/05/1916	25/05/1916
War Diary	Front Line.	26/05/1916	28/05/1916
War Diary	C Battn. X.10.b.5.1	29/05/1916	30/05/1916
War Diary	C Position N.D. de Lorette.	31/05/1916	31/05/1916
Miscellaneous	Battalion Operation Orders For 3rd May 1916	03/05/1916	03/05/1916
Miscellaneous	Battalion Operation Orders For 19th And 20th May 1916	20/05/1916	20/05/1916
Miscellaneous	To/-O.C., O.C. Company	18/05/1916	18/05/1916
Miscellaneous	Battalion Operation Orders For 20th May 1916	20/05/1916	20/05/1916
Miscellaneous	Battalion Operation Orders For 25th May 1916	25/05/1916	25/05/1916
Miscellaneous	Battalion Operation Order For 30th May 1916	30/05/1916	30/05/1916
War Diary	C Battn.	01/06/1915	01/06/1915
War Diary	N.D. De Lorette.	02/06/1915	04/06/1915
War Diary	A Battn.	05/06/1915	09/06/1915
War Diary	Fus 10	10/06/1916	11/06/1916
War Diary	Bowers.	12/06/1916	12/06/1916
War Diary	Verchin	13/06/1916	15/06/1916
War Diary	Coyecque	16/06/1916	24/06/1916
War Diary	Picquigny	25/06/1916	29/06/1916
War Diary	Poulainville.	30/06/1916	30/06/1916
Heading	68th Bde. 23rd Div. War Diary Brigade temporarily under orders of 34th Division 10th to 20th July. 11th Battalion Northumberland Fusiliers. July 1916		
Miscellaneous	War Diary of 11th Service Battn. Northumberland Fusiliers	22/08/1916	22/08/1916
Miscellaneous	A Form. Messages And Signals.		
War Diary	Poulainville.	01/07/1916	01/07/1916
War Diary	Franvillers	02/07/1916	02/07/1916
War Diary	Millencourt Albert	03/07/1916	05/07/1916
War Diary	Front Line System	06/07/1916	07/07/1916
War Diary	Trenches.	08/07/1916	10/07/1916
War Diary	Albert.	10/07/1916	13/07/1916
War Diary	Dernacourt	14/07/1916	14/07/1916
War Diary	Becourt Wood	15/07/1916	15/07/1916
War Diary	Trenches	16/07/1916	18/07/1916
War Diary	Albert	19/07/1916	19/07/1916
War Diary	Franvillers	20/07/1916	25/07/1916
War Diary	Peake Wood	26/07/1916	27/07/1916
War Diary	Nr Becourt Wood	28/07/1916	29/07/1916
War Diary	Becourt Wood	30/07/1916	31/07/1916
Miscellaneous	11th Northumberland Fusiliers. 97 P F	13/07/1916	13/07/1916
Miscellaneous	O.C. 11th N.F.	08/07/1916	08/07/1916
Miscellaneous	And Signals.		
Miscellaneous	A Form. Messages And Signals.		

Miscellaneous	To all Units 68th Brigade.	11/07/1916	11/07/1916
Miscellaneous	Special Order of The Day By Major General J.M. Babington, C.B., C.M.G.	18/07/1916	18/07/1916
Heading	68th Brigade 23rd Division. 1/11th Battalion Northumberland Fusiliers August 1916		
War Diary	Support Line O.G.1 & 2. Near Mametz And Bazentin Le Petit Woods.	01/08/1916	04/08/1916
War Diary	Front Line Opposite Intermediate Line & Switch.	05/08/1916	07/08/1916
War Diary	Becourt	07/08/1916	07/08/1916
War Diary	Behencourt	08/08/1916	11/08/1916
War Diary	Ailly-Le Haut Clocher	12/08/1916	13/08/1916
War Diary	Fletre Q.30.d.2.5	13/08/1916	14/08/1916
War Diary	Steenwerck Area.	15/08/1916	16/08/1916
War Diary	Le Bizet.	17/08/1916	24/08/1916
War Diary	Front Line Trench.	25/08/1916	31/08/1916
Miscellaneous	Battn. O.O. for August 7th	07/08/1916	07/08/1916
War Diary	Front Line Trenches 99-111	01/09/1916	03/09/1916
War Diary	Bailleul District	03/09/1916	05/09/1916
War Diary	Nordasques	05/09/1916	09/09/1916
War Diary	Molliens Au Bois	10/09/1916	12/09/1916
War Diary	Millencourt.	12/09/1916	18/09/1916
War Diary	Support Trenches Martinpuich	19/09/1916	20/09/1916
War Diary	L Contalmaison	20/09/1916	22/09/1916
War Diary	Front Line	23/09/1916	24/09/1916
War Diary	Front Line Trenches Martin Puich	25/09/1916	26/09/1916
War Diary	Support Trenches	26/09/1916	26/09/1916
War Diary	Camp Near Fricourt	27/09/1916	30/09/1916
War Diary	Lozenge Wood.	01/10/1916	01/10/1916
War Diary	Contalmaison	02/10/1916	02/10/1916
War Diary	Le. Sars.	03/10/1916	08/10/1916
War Diary	Becourt Wood	09/10/1916	11/10/1916
War Diary	Ailly Le Haut Clocher.	12/10/1916	12/10/1916
War Diary	St. Riquier	13/10/1916	15/10/1916
War Diary	Erie Camp. Sheet. 28. Belgium & France G.11.c.b.2	15/10/1916	17/10/1916
War Diary	Ypres.	18/10/1916	19/10/1916
War Diary	Front Line	20/10/1916	23/10/1916
War Diary	Poperinghe.	24/10/1916	28/10/1916
War Diary	The Bund Zillebeke.	29/10/1916	31/10/1916
Miscellaneous	The Attached Is The War Diary of The 11th (Service) Battalion Northumberland Fusiliers For The Month Of November 1916	04/12/1916	04/12/1916
War Diary	Bund. Zillebeke.	01/11/1916	01/11/1916
War Diary	Trenches. A. Battn Right. Bde.	02/11/1916	06/11/1916
War Diary	Hospice Ypres.	07/11/1916	09/11/1916
War Diary	A & B Coy & H.Q.	10/11/1916	10/11/1916
War Diary	Toronto Camp.	11/11/1916	11/11/1916
War Diary	C & D. Coy Erie Camp.	12/11/1916	15/11/1916
War Diary	A Battn Left Sector HQ at Willeries	16/11/1916	20/11/1916
War Diary	Infantry Barracks. Ypres.	21/11/1916	24/11/1916
War Diary	A Battn. Left Sector Bn H.Q. at Tuilleries.	25/11/1916	30/11/1916
War Diary	Toronto Camp	01/12/1916	07/12/1916
War Diary	Hospice Ypres	08/12/1916	10/12/1916
War Diary	A Battn. Right Bde.	11/12/1916	16/12/1916
War Diary	Zillebeke Bund.	17/12/1916	20/12/1916
War Diary	A Position Right Bde Sector I. 30. I to 1.30.9	21/12/1916	23/12/1916
War Diary	Toronto Camp	24/12/1916	31/12/1916

Type	Description	From	To
Miscellaneous	The attached is the War Diary Of the 11th (Service) Battalion Northumberland Fusiliers, for the month of January 1917	03/02/1917	03/02/1917
War Diary	Infantry Barracks Ypres	01/01/1917	03/01/1917
War Diary	A. Battn. Right Bde. Sector.	04/01/1917	08/01/1917
War Diary	Barracks. Ypres.	09/01/1917	11/01/1917
War Diary	A. Battn. Left. Bde.	12/01/1917	16/01/1917
War Diary	Toronto Camp	17/01/1917	26/01/1917
War Diary	Bund.	27/01/1917	28/01/1917
War Diary	B. Position	29/01/1917	29/01/1917
War Diary	Right Sector	30/01/1917	31/01/1917
Miscellaneous	The Attached Is The War Diary Of The 11th (Service) Battalion Northumberland Fusiliers, For The Month Of February 1917		
War Diary	C Position.	01/02/1917	05/02/1917
War Diary	B. Position	05/02/1917	09/02/1917
War Diary	Toronto Camp.	10/02/1917	16/02/1917
War Diary	Infantry Barracks Ypres.	17/02/1917	26/02/1917
War Diary	E. Camp. A. 30.A.5.5	27/02/1917	27/02/1917
War Diary	Belgium 28.N.W.	28/02/1917	28/02/1917
Miscellaneous	The Attached Is The War Diary Of The 11th (Service) Battalion Northumberland Fusiliers For The Month Of March 1917	01/04/1917	01/04/1917
War Diary	Bollezeele.	01/03/1917	19/03/1917
War Diary	Houtkerque.	20/03/1917	20/03/1917
War Diary	P. Camp.	21/03/1917	21/03/1917
War Diary	X. Camp.	22/03/1917	31/03/1917
Operation(al) Order(s)	11th Northumberland Fusiliers-Order No. 1	18/03/1917	18/03/1917
Operation(al) Order(s)	11th Northumberland Fusiliers-Order No. 2	19/03/1917	19/03/1917
Operation(al) Order(s)	11th Northumberland Fusiliers-Order No. 3	21/03/1917	21/03/1917
War Diary	X. Camp. A.1b.c.4.16	01/04/1917	01/04/1917
War Diary	Belgium 28.N.W.	02/04/1917	04/04/1917
War Diary	Bolzeele	04/04/1917	12/04/1917
War Diary	G.12.c.4.0	13/04/1917	14/04/1917
War Diary	Hooge. Sector.	15/04/1917	15/04/1917
War Diary	Centre. Subsection (Front-Bois)	15/04/1917	16/04/1917
War Diary	Centre. Sub. Sector Hooge	17/04/1917	17/04/1917
War Diary	Support Battalion	18/04/1917	22/04/1917
War Diary	Left Battalion (Front Line) Map.	23/04/1917	23/04/1917
War Diary	Zillebeke. 28.N.W. & N.E. 1/10000	24/04/1917	24/04/1917
War Diary	Left-Battn. (Front Line.) Zillibeke 1/10,000	25/04/1917	30/04/1917
Operation(al) Order(s)	11th Northumberland Fusiliers Order No. 4	03/04/1917	03/04/1917
Operation(al) Order(s)	11th Northumberland Fusiliers Advance Order No. 4	03/04/1917	03/04/1917
Operation(al) Order(s)	11th Northumberland Fusiliers-Order No. 5	12/04/1917	12/04/1917
Operation(al) Order(s)	11th Northumberland Fusiliers-Order No. 6	14/04/1917	14/04/1917
Operation(al) Order(s)	11th Northumberland Fusiliers-Order No. 7	22/04/1917	22/04/1917
Operation(al) Order(s)	11th Northumberland Fusiliers-Order No. 8	30/04/1917	30/04/1917
War Diary	Steenvorde Area	01/05/1917	08/05/1917
War Diary	Toronto Camp.	09/05/1917	10/05/1917
War Diary	Reserve Battn of Right Brigade	11/05/1917	13/05/1917
War Diary	Left Front Battn of Divisional Front.	14/03/1917	18/03/1917
War Diary	Scottish Lines	19/05/1917	31/05/1917
Operation(al) Order(s)	11th Northumberland Fusiliers Order No. 9	08/05/1917	08/05/1917
Operation(al) Order(s)	11th Northumberland Fusiliers Order No. 10	09/05/1917	09/05/1917
Operation(al) Order(s)	11th Northumberland Fusiliers Order No. 11	13/05/1917	13/05/1917
Miscellaneous	Headquarters, 23rd Division.	14/05/1917	14/05/1917

Type	Description	Date 1	Date 2
Operation(al) Order(s)	Right Group. 23rd Divisional Artillery. Operation Order No. 1	15/05/1917	15/05/1917
Miscellaneous	Table "A"		
Miscellaneous	Code to be used on night of May 16	15/05/1917	15/05/1917
Operation(al) Order(s)	11th Northumberland Fusiliers Order No. 12	15/05/1917	15/05/1917
Operation(al) Order(s)	11th N.F. Order No. 12	15/05/1917	15/05/1917
Operation(al) Order(s)	Additional Instructions To 11th N.F. Order No. 12	16/05/1917	16/05/1917
Miscellaneous	C.O.		
Operation(al) Order(s)	Additional Instructions To 11th. N.F. Order No. 12	16/05/1917	16/05/1917
Miscellaneous	O.C. 11th N.F. Notes On Your Raid Orders.	16/05/1917	16/05/1917
Miscellaneous	G.124/1/8. Reference Trench Map Zillebeke 28 N.W.4 and N.E.3 (parts of).	16/05/1917	16/05/1917
Miscellaneous	Table "A"		
Operation(al) Order(s)	To/2nd Lt. Hunter. O.C. No. 2. Patrol.	16/05/1917	16/05/1917
Miscellaneous	To/O.C. Coy.	16/05/1917	16/05/1917
Miscellaneous	To/O.C. C. Coy	16/05/1917	16/05/1917
Miscellaneous	To Adjutant 11th N.F. No. 1 Raiding Party.	17/05/1917	17/05/1917
Miscellaneous	To Adjutant 11th N. Fus.		
Miscellaneous	From Capt Adamson to Adjt.		
Operation(al) Order(s)	11th Northumberland Fusiliers-Order No. 13	16/05/1917	16/05/1917
Miscellaneous	C.O.		
Miscellaneous	To:- Headquarters, 68th Infantry Brigade.	17/05/1917	17/05/1917
Operation(al) Order(s)	11th Northumberland Fusiliers-Order No. 14	27/05/1917	27/05/1917
Miscellaneous	C.O.		
Operation(al) Order(s)	11th Northumberland Fusiliers-Order No. 15	30/05/1917	30/05/1917
Miscellaneous	Table "B"	30/05/1917	30/05/1917
Miscellaneous	To/-O.C., O.C. Coy	30/05/1917	30/05/1917
War Diary	Centre Sub Sector	01/06/1917	06/06/1917
War Diary	Hill 60 Sector Zillibeke 28.N.W.	07/06/1917	08/06/1917
War Diary	Attack on Hill 60	09/06/1917	09/06/1917
War Diary	Camp. O.	10/06/1917	12/06/1917
War Diary	Thieshouk	13/06/1917	13/06/1917
War Diary	Q.35.b. 3.3	14/06/1917	14/06/1917
War Diary	Neay 27 SE	14/06/1917	18/06/1917
War Diary	Thieshouk Q.35.b.3.3	19/06/1917	28/06/1917
War Diary	Thieshouk	29/06/1917	29/06/1917
War Diary	Micmac Camp. H.31.b. St. Hupertushoek	30/06/1917	30/06/1917
Operation(al) Order(s)	11th Northumberland Fusiliers Order No. 16	06/06/1917	06/06/1917
Operation(al) Order(s)	11th Northumberland Fusiliers-Order No. 17	10/06/1917	10/06/1917
Operation(al) Order(s)	11th Northumberland Fusiliers-Order No. 18	12/06/1917	12/06/1917
Miscellaneous	To/-O.C., O.C. Coy.	12/06/1917	12/06/1917
Operation(al) Order(s)	11th Northumberland Fusiliers-Order No. 19	20/06/1917	20/06/1917
Operation(al) Order(s)	11th Northumberland Fusiliers-Order No. 20	28/06/1917	28/06/1917
Map	1st Objective-Red 2nd-Blue Final-Black Battn Boundys Yellow.		
Miscellaneous	The Attached Is The War Diary Of The 11th (Service) Battalion Northumberland Fusiliers For The Month Of July Of July 1917	31/07/1917	31/07/1917
War Diary	Micmac Camp. H.31.b. Sheet 28 N.W.	01/07/1917	05/07/1917
War Diary	Left Battn Div. Front. HQ. Hedge. St	05/07/1917	09/07/1917
War Diary	Support Battn.	10/07/1917	13/07/1917
War Diary	Camp At N.1.a.7.8. Sheet 28.S.W.	14/07/1917	23/07/1917
War Diary	Thieushouk.	24/07/1917	30/07/1917
War Diary	Quelmes	31/07/1917	31/07/1917
Operation(al) Order(s)	11th Northumberland Fusiliers-Order No. 21	04/07/1917	04/07/1917
Operation(al) Order(s)	11th Northumberland Fusiliers-Order No. 21. (A).	08/07/1917	08/07/1917

Type	Description	Date From	Date To
Operation(al) Order(s)	11th Northumberland Fusiliers-Order No. 22	12/07/1917	12/07/1917
Operation(al) Order(s)	11th Northumberland Fusiliers-Order No. 23	20/07/1917	20/07/1917
Operation(al) Order(s)	11th Northumberland Fusiliers-Order No. 24	28/07/1917	28/07/1917
Operation(al) Order(s)	11th Northumberland Fusiliers-Order No. 25	29/07/1917	29/07/1917
War Diary	Quelmes W.13.b. Map 27A. S.E.	01/08/1917	07/08/1917
War Diary	Quelmes	08/08/1917	08/08/1917
War Diary	Serques.	09/08/1917	23/08/1917
War Diary	Micmac Camp	24/08/1917	28/08/1917
War Diary	H.33.a.7.3	29/08/1917	29/08/1917
War Diary	Dickebusch H.33.a.7.3	30/08/1917	31/08/1917
Operation(al) Order(s)	11th Northumberland Fusiliers Order No. 26	08/08/1917	08/08/1917
Operation(al) Order(s)	11th Northumberland Fusiliers-Order No. X.	13/08/1917	13/08/1917
Operation(al) Order(s)	11th Northumberland Fusiliers-Order No. Y	20/08/1917	20/08/1917
Miscellaneous	Copy No. 1-Bde. H.Q.		
Operation(al) Order(s)	Amendment To Para. 4 of 11th Northd. Fusiliers Order No. Y.	21/08/1917	21/08/1917
Operation(al) Order(s)	11th Northumberland Fusiliers Order No. 27	23/08/1917	23/08/1917
Operation(al) Order(s)	11th Northumberland Fusiliers Order No. 28	29/08/1917	29/08/1917
Heading	War Diary. of 11th (S) Battalion, Northumberland Fusiliers. From Sept. 1st 1917. To. Sept. 30th 1917. Vol. 24		
War Diary	Dickebusch H.33.a.7.3	01/09/1917	01/09/1917
War Diary	Dallington Camp 4.35.a.9.a.	02/09/1917	02/09/1917
War Diary	Steenvorde Area.	03/09/1917	04/09/1917
War Diary	Nordpeene Area.	05/09/1917	12/09/1917
War Diary	Steenvorde Area	13/09/1917	13/09/1917
War Diary	Murrumbige Camp	14/09/1917	15/09/1917
War Diary	J. Camp H.28.d.5.5	16/09/1917	17/09/1917
War Diary	Torr Top Tunnels	18/09/1917	18/09/1917
War Diary	Front Line	19/09/1917	19/09/1917
War Diary	The Battle of the Menin Road	20/09/1917	22/09/1917
War Diary	J. Camp Dickebusch.	23/09/1917	23/09/1917
War Diary	Westoutre	24/09/1917	24/09/1917
War Diary	Thunderer Camp M.8.a.3.2	25/09/1917	27/09/1917
War Diary	Ridge. Wood Camp	28/09/1917	28/09/1917
War Diary	N.5. Central	29/09/1917	30/09/1917
Operation(al) Order(s)	11th Northumberland Fusiliers-Order No. 30	01/09/1917	01/09/1917
Operation(al) Order(s)	11th Northumberland Fusiliers-Order No. 31		
Operation(al) Order(s)	11th Northumberland Fusiliers-Order No. 32	10/09/1917	10/09/1917
Operation(al) Order(s)	Xth Corps Offensive. Corrigenda To 11th Northumberland Fusiliers Order No. 32	15/09/1917	15/09/1917
Operation(al) Order(s)	Xth Corps Offensive. 11th Northumberland Fusiliers Order No. 32	17/09/1917	17/09/1917
Miscellaneous	Plan of Assembly At Zero Hour.		
Operation(al) Order(s)	11th Northumberland Fusiliers Order No. 33	12/09/1917	12/09/1917
Operation(al) Order(s)	11th Northumberland Fusiliers Order No. 34	13/09/1917	13/09/1917
Miscellaneous	Xth Corps Offensive. 11th Northumberland Fusiliers Instructions No. 1	14/09/1917	14/09/1917
Miscellaneous	Xth Corps Offensive. 11th Northumberland Fusiliers Instructions No. 2	14/09/1917	14/09/1917
Miscellaneous	To/-O.C., O.C. Coy. With Reference To 11th N.F. Instructions No. 1:-	14/09/1917	14/09/1917
Operation(al) Order(s)	11th Northumberland Fusiliers-Order No. 35	15/09/1917	15/09/1917
Miscellaneous	Xth Corps Offensive. 11th Northumberland Fusiliers Instructions No. 4. Signals.	17/09/1917	17/09/1917

Type	Description	Date From	Date To
Miscellaneous	Xth Corps Offensive. 11th Northumberland Fusiliers Instructions No. 5	17/09/1917	17/09/1917
Miscellaneous	Xth Corps Offensive. 11th Northumberland Fusiliers Instructions No. 6. Reinforcement Arrangements.	15/09/1917	15/09/1917
Miscellaneous	Xth Corps Offensive. 11th Northumberland Fusiliers Instructions No. 7. Contact Aeroplanes.	15/09/1917	15/09/1917
Miscellaneous	Xth Corps Offensive. 11th Northumberland Fusiliers Instructions No. 8. Machine Guns.	15/09/1917	15/09/1917
Miscellaneous	To/-O.C., O.C. Coy.	17/09/1917	17/09/1917
Miscellaneous	Reference : Zillebeke 1/10000. Report On Reconnaissance Of Ground In J. 20. a. Carried Out By A Patrol Under 2nd Lieut. Lyone on The Morning Of 17th Sept. 1917	17/09/1917	17/09/1917
Operation(al) Order(s)	11th Northumberland Fusiliers-Order No. 36	18/09/1917	18/09/1917
Miscellaneous	The O.C. 11th Northumberland Fusiliers	23/09/1917	23/09/1917
Operation(al) Order(s)	11th Northumberland Fusiliers-Order No. 37	23/09/1917	23/09/1917
Operation(al) Order(s)	11th Northumberland Fusiliers-Order No. 38	27/09/1917	27/09/1917
Operation(al) Order(s)	11th Northumberland Fusiliers-Order No. 39	30/09/1917	30/09/1917
Miscellaneous	Special Order.		
Miscellaneous	The Attached Is The War Diary Of The 11th (Service) Battalion, Northumberland Fusiliers, For The Month Of October 1917	31/10/1917	31/10/1917
War Diary	Phincboom X.8. Central	01/10/1917	01/10/1917
War Diary	Thieushouk Q.35.d.3.3	02/10/1917	05/10/1917
War Diary	Thieushouk	06/10/1917	07/10/1917
War Diary	Curragh Camp M.16.c.6.7	08/10/1917	08/10/1917
War Diary	Ontario Camp	09/10/1917	09/10/1917
War Diary	Dickebusch Camp	10/10/1917	10/10/1917
War Diary	N.2.b.6.2. Railway Dugouts	11/10/1917	11/10/1917
War Diary	Front Line	12/10/1917	15/10/1917
War Diary	Brewery Camp H.28.d.7.5	16/10/1917	19/10/1917
War Diary	St Martin Au-Laert.	20/10/1917	31/10/1917
Miscellaneous		02/10/1917	02/10/1917
Operation(al) Order(s)	11th Northumberland Fusiliers-Order No. 40	02/10/1917	02/10/1917
Operation(al) Order(s)	11th Northumberland Fusiliers-Order No. 41	07/10/1917	07/10/1917
Operation(al) Order(s)	11th Northumberland Fusiliers-Order No. 42	09/10/1917	09/10/1917
Operation(al) Order(s)	11th Northumberland Fusiliers-Order No. 43	10/10/1917	10/10/1917
Operation(al) Order(s)	11th Northumberland Fusiliers-Order No. 44	19/10/1917	19/10/1917

WO95/2182/4

11 Bn N'berland Fus

Aug 1915 - Oct 1917

23RD DIVISION
68TH INFY BDE

11TH BN NORTH'D FUS!
AUG 1915-MAR 1919
917 OCT

TO ITALY

11th Workman's Pro.
Vol: I

121/7761

23rd Kwaun

Aug 6 Oct 15
Nov '14

Army Form C. 2118.

WAR DIARY
or
INTELLIGENCE SUMMARY.
(Erase heading not required.)

Instructions regarding War Diaries and Intelligence Summaries are contained in F. S. Regs., Part II. and the Staff Manual respectively. Title pages will be prepared in manuscript.

Place	Date	Hour	Summary of Events and Information	Remarks and references to Appendices
Bramshott Camp.	24/8/15.	3a.m	Advance party, strength 3 Officers & 130 men, marched to Liphook Station, entrained for Southampton 5.55 a.m.. Transport and Advance party conveyed to Havre. One man admitted to Hospital at Havre	Re Mayor
	25/8/15.	4p.m.	Entrained by half Battalions at Liphook Station for Folkestone. Together with Divisional Staff embarked on the QUEEN and sailed at 10 p.m. Strength 28 Officers & 856 men. Landed Boulogne 11.45 p.m. marched to Ostrohove Camp.	Re Mayor
Ostrohove Camp.	26/8/15.	3.30p.m.	Rest all day. Parade 3.30 p.m. Orderly Room Sergt. left behind for Base. Interpreter taken on strength. Marched to Pont de Briques Station. Entrained, meeting Advance party and Transport on train at 5 p.m. Detrained at WATTEN Station and marched to billets in EPERLEQUES. Arrived 11 p.m. Strength 31 Officers & 985 men.	Re Mayor
Eperleques	27/8/15.		Rest day. Visited by G.O.C.Division and Brigade. Headquarters and Transport formed into separate units. 800 letters passed by Regimental Censor.	Re Mayor
	28/8/15.		Companies had 2 hours route march and bathing parade. Strength 31 Officers & 988 men and 5 attached. 750 letters censored.	Re Mayor
	29/8/15.		Church of England Parade at HOULLE. Strength 31 Officers & 988 men and 5 attached. 600 letters censored.	Re Mayor
	30/8/15.		Companies paraded for practising bomb throwing, Bayonet Fighting and final assault, respirator work, etc. Machine Gun Class for Officers commenced. Strength 31 Officers & 988 men, & 5 attached. 561 letters.	Re Mayor
	31/8/15		Machine Gun Course at Wisques for C.O., 2nd in Command, M.G.Officer. Range Finding class started. Companies continued training. 525 letters. Strength 31 Officers & 988 men & 5 attached.	Re Mayor
	1/9/15		Divisional Exercise. Parade at 5.30 a.m. Route march via HOULLE, IMLINGHEM, NOLINGHEM, MOULLE, SERQUES. Parade state 29 Officers, 961 men. Return about 12.30 p.m. Strength 31 Officers & 990 men and 5 attached. Fighting strength return rendered up to 6 p.m. 31st. 350 letters censored.	Re Mayor
	2/9/15		Companies had early morning route march from 5 a.m. to 7 a.m. Strength 31 Officers & 990 men & 5 attached. Machine Gun, Range Finding and Grenadier Courses. 3 Machine Gun Officers proceeded to Wisques for lectures. 500 letters censored.	Re Mayor
	3/9/15.		Brigade Day cancelled owing to rain. Strength 31 Officers & 990 men & 5 attached. G.O.C. Brigade lectured to all Senior Officers on Secret Information of Attack. 977 letters censored.(207 Field postcards & 57 G.)	Re Mayor
	4/9/15		Working party Strength 8 Officers, 30 N.C.O's, 572 men to dig defensive trenches, Parade 6 a.m. Rendezvous with similar party from 10th N.F. at TILQUES.Reserve section of Machine Gun Officers classes fired table 1 of course. 649 letters censored.	Re Mayor

Army Form C. 2118.

WAR DIARY
or
INTELLIGENCE SUMMARY.
(Erase heading not required.)

Instructions regarding War Diaries and Intelligence Summaries are contained in F.S. Regs., Part II and the Staff Manual respectively. Title pages will be prepared in manuscript.

Place	Date	Hour	Summary of Events and Information	Remarks and references to Appendices
	5/9/15		Orders for move of Division came. Day spent cleaning up etc. No letters censored.	R.E. Moyan
	6/9/15		Brigade started at 6 a.m. and marched to HAZEBROUCK arriving about 4 p.m. and were billeted in Rue BAILLEUL. 13 men fell out on line of march but all rejoined before night. About 30 letters censored.	R.E. Moyan
HAZEBROUCK	7/0/15	9 a.m.	The Brigade started at 9 a.m. and marched to School Near BAILLEUL arriving about 1.45 p.m. 38 men fell out on line of march, 3 men had not rejoined by night. From the other three Bns 759 fell out. One heavy draught horse was left behind. Battalion was billeted in the village occupied by Brigade Headquarters. Post of about 100 letters censored. Pte. Sewell died of pneumonia in Hospital at Havre. 1st casualty.	R.E. Moyan
SCHOOL, STEENJB.	8/9/15		The Battn. was inspected by General Pulteney i/c 3rd Corps - the Division now forming part of that Corps of 1st Army. Preparations for move of Battn. Number of letters censored 1600, including Field Postcards 325, Green envelopes 205.	R.E. Moyan
LAVENTIE	9/9/15	3 p.m.	Marched as a Battn to ESTAIRES - attached to 10th K.R.R. in billets in LAVENTIE.	R.E. Moyan
	10/9/15		Companies attached to corresponding Companies of 10th K.R.R. Working parties furnished. All special-ist Officers taken over for instruction - M.G.Section and Signallers marched up to trenches at 3p.m. Headquarters 10th R.B. at PICANTIN. A & B Coys attached to 11th K.R.R. in trenches - C & D Coys to 10th R.B. 2nd Machine Gun Officer, Signalling Officer & M.G. reserve section struck off Company duties from this date. Heavy firing at aeroplanes throughout the day - 1 German plane brought down. Battalion H.Q. attached to 10th R.B. at PICANTIN. Line of trench held Map 36 S.W.1 Square N.8.c.8.- 13.b.1.1. - 1 man of "D" Coy shot in head - wounded.	R.E. Moyan
	10/9/15		Battalion in trenches all day - nothing special happened - relieved by 10th N.F. relief completed by 10 p.m. billeted in Laventie.	R.E. Moyan
	12/9/15		Battalion went into trenches with 10th R.B. & 11th K.R.R. in the evening.	R.E. Moyan
	13/9/15		Company inspections in morning.	R.E. Moyan
	14/9/15		One man of "C" Coy shot through head at 4.17 a.m. when on sentry - Battn relieved by 10th N.F. and marched to LAVENTIE.	R.E. Moyan
	15/9/15		Battn in trenches all day. Trench Mortar killed one man of "B" Coy and wounded 3 men of "B" Coy. They were working outside the parapet. The Battn withdrew to billets in Laventie.	R.E. Moyan
	16/9/15		Battn rested in billets all day. Large post. Strength 31 Officers and 975 men.	R.E. Moyan
	17/9/15		Battn started at 3 a.m. and marched with 10 minute intervals between Companies to a farm N. of ERQUINGHEM-LYS where they bivouacked in tents taken over from 2nd Cameronians. The 23rd Division	R.E. Moyan

Army Form C. 2118.

WAR DIARY
or
INTELLIGENCE SUMMARY.
(Erase heading not required.)

Instructions regarding War Diaries and Intelligence Summaries are contained in F. S. Regs., Part II. and the Staff Manual respectively. Title pages will be prepared in manuscript.

Place	Date	Hour	Summary of Events and Information	Remarks and references to Appendices
ERQUINGHEM LYS.	18/9/15		having taken over its portion of the line, the 69th & 70th Brigades were in the firing trench and the 68th in reserve. Brigade H.Q. at STEENWERCK.	Re hayai
FORT ROMPU	19/9/15.		Battn moved to FORT ROMPU. March off at 11 a.m. Coys following at 15 mins interval. S.Staffs took over camp at ERQUINGHEM-LYS. Coys bathed in Divnl baths. Strength 31 Officers & 970 men.	Re hayah
	20/9/15.		Church of England & R.C.Parades. A Coy found fatigue of 40 men for work at Coal Depot from 12 till 4 p.m. B & C Coys found 100 men each for work from 6.30 p.m. till 10.45 at LA VESEE(I.19.B.1.9) and RUE FLEURIE (I.17.b.1.8) Three Officers went round trenches taken over by 23rd Division. Two Companies bathed in Divisional baths at ERQUINGHEM. 1 Officer & 50 men did Coal fatigue at Depot of 3rd Corps. Three Officers visited trenches taken over by 23rd Division. 2 men wounded, slightly, at duty. Shrapnel fell from firing at aeroplanes. Strength 31 Officers & 979 men.	Re hayah Re hayah Re hayah
	21st		Coal Field by fatigue party. 8 Officers visited Division trenches – bombardment of enemy's trenches commenced in the morning. Battn received orders to hold itself in readiness to proceed to any part of line at an hour's notice in battle order. Strength 31 Officers & 979 men.	Re hayah
	22nd		Bn. practise alarm- Bn. on parade within 1 hour-Transport 2 hours-Coal fatigue-3 fatigues of 100 men at night to Fire Station(I.9.c.3.4) Strength 31 Officers and 979 men.	Re hayah
	23rd		Coal fatigues-spare kit and overcoats of men conveyed to Bde H.Q. at Steenwerck.	Re hayah
	24th		Bn.to hold itself in readiness to move at 30 mins notice-blankets conveyed to H.Q.Steenwerck- Officers kits and mess kit loaded-Conference of Officers at Bde H.Q.	Re hayah
	25th		Urgent message received at 4.50 a.m. "Rouse your Battalion and get them fed". Battalion stood by. Advance was made by 8th and Meerut Divisions.	Re hayah
	26th		Orders received to fetch greatcoats in the morning from Steenwerck-orders received at noon to march to Estaires and to be affiliated temporarily to 20th Division-Battn moved off at 3.30 p.m. and was billeted in the town.	Re hayah
ESTAIRES	27th		Six men of "B" Coy severely wounded by accidental explosion of bomb during class of instruction. Battn received orders to retur to billets in 23rd Division area- left Estaires at 5.30 p.m.	Re hayah
FORT ROMPU	28th		Battn billeted at Fort Rompu by 8 p.m.- No orders as to where Bde H.Q. situated. Orders received to return to billets evacuated in Estaires. Bn billeted by 6 p.m.	Re hayah
ESTAIRES	29th		Bn rest all day-affiliated to 20th Division as reserve - Brigade M.G. Course commenced.	Re hayah
	30th		Companies did route marches in the morning - paid out in the afternoon.	Re hayah

Army Form C. 2118.

WAR DIARY
or
INTELLIGENCE SUMMARY.
(Erase heading not required.)

Instructions regarding War Diaries and Intelligence Summaries are contained in F. S. Regs. Part II. and the Staff Manual respectively. Title pages will be prepared in manuscript.

Place	Date	Hour	Summary of Events and Information	Remarks and references to Appendices
ESTAIRES.	1/10/15		Battalion billeted in Estaires as reserve to 20th Division-2 Officers and 75 men attached temporarily to 173rd Mining Coy for tunnelling purposes.	Re Mayor
	2/10/15		Fatigue of 400 men found to dig reserve line of trenches at LE DRUMEZ-half the Brigade relieved half of 69th Brigade.	Re Mayor
	3/10/15		Church of England parade-Battn Trench Routine orders issued by Lieut.Col.I.Thord-Gray.	Re Mayor
	4/10/15		Battn moved from ESTAIRES at 9.20 a.m. Halted and lunched at FORT ROMPU-advance party proceeded in afternoon to take over billets and posts in BOIS GRENIER Line. A & C Coys took over trenches from two Coys of 10th West Riding – B & D Coys under Major Blackden took over billets in Rue de Lettre. Col.Gray in command of BOIS GRENIER LINE. 1 Coy of S.Staffs and 1 Coy Motor Machine Gun Section attached. Signal communication between H.Q. & Bde good- with Coys bad. Battn.H.Q. at 36 N.W.Sheet 4.I.19.c.5.8. Advance Brigade dugout.	Re Mayor
BOIS GRENIER LINE.	5/10/15		System of communication between Coys improved-Battn Advance H.Q.at I.19.d.2.8. H.Q.Coy divided. Clerks, Signallers, Runners at Bn.H.Q. Pioneers etc at Advance H.Q. Weather very bad. Wind northerly.	Re Mayor
	6/10/15	11.45 p.m.	Advance party proceeded to take over trenches from 10th N.F. Relief in order D.A.B.C. completed 52, 53, 54 & S.S. 54 taken over. Quiet night. One man of A Coy slightly wounded in the head. Trenches 52, 53, 54 & S.S. 54 taken over. Quiet night. Battn on our left, 12th D.L.I. used M.G. to no purpose apparently. One man wounded.	Re Mayor
	7/10/15	2.15 p.m. 3.15 p.m.	Quiet day. Artillery ranging about 2.15 p.m. Working party observed at I.26.c.8.1. at 3.15 p.m. No casualties. Lieut.Harding on patrol returned with piece of German wire.D Coy's patrol sniped at heavily.	Re Mayor
	8/10/15		Quiet day. M.G.Section claims to have hit sniper. Strength 30 Officers & 970 men. Lieut.Powell, R.A.M.C. changed for Capt. Russell, R.A.M.C.	Re Mayor
	9/10/15		Quiet day. M.G.Section fired at enemy's working party. One man slightly wounded.	Re Mayor
	10/10/15.	11.30 a.m. 2 p.m. 3.30 p.m.	Enemy's Artillery bombarded T.53 occupied by B Coy at 11.30 a.m., 2 p.m., 3.30 p.m. Latrine blown up. 1 man killed, and 2 wounded. Enemy manned their parapet as though for an advance. S.O.S. sent. Enemy retired on opening of Artillery fire.	Re Mayor
	11/10/15	9 a.m. 11 a.	Enemy shelled T.52, 53, 54 heavily between 9 a.m., 11 a., 2nd Lt.W.K.Maclachlan wounded in the leg, two other men wounded. Considerable damage done to parapet but repaired at night. Situation very quiet after noon. Enemy's aeroplane brought down.	Re Mayor
	12/10/15		T.52, 53 shelled slightly – one man accidentally wounded- Battn relieved by 10th N.F. and billeted in "D" position along RUE DU BIEZ and RUE DE LETTRE.	Re Mayor

Army Form C. 2118.

WAR DIARY
or
INTELLIGENCE SUMMARY.
(Erase heading not required.)

Instructions regarding War Diaries and Intelligence Summaries are contained in F.S. Regs., Part II. and the Staff Manual respectively. Title pages will be prepared in manuscript.

Place	Date	Hour	Summary of Events and Information	Remarks and references to Appendices
Billets in RUB DU BIEZ and RUE DE LETTRE "D" Position	13/10/15		A & B Coys accommodated in billets in RUE DU BIEZ and C & D in huts in RUE DE LETTRE. H.Q. in RUE DU BIEZ. Divisions on our right and left made feint attacks. Men sttod by. 200 men on fatigue.	Re hayes
	14/10/15		Machine Gun & Bombing classes. All the Battn bathed in Divisional baths. 200 men on fatigue at Shaftesbury Avenue and TRAMWAY FARM.	Re hayes
	15/10/15		A & B Coys fired 15 rounds (10 individual and 5 rapid) on range in RUE DU BIEZ. Inter Company Football matches. 210 men on fatigue at ANCARDARIE in SHAFTESBURY AVENUE.	Re hayes Re hayes
Firing Line "A" position	16/10/15		Battn finished the range practice and relieved the 10th N.F. in trenches— A Coy T.52, C Coy T.53, D Coy T.54, B Coy S.S. T.54. Relief completed by 7.30 p.m.	Re hayes
	17/10/15		Very quiet day— misty & no artillery or aerial observation — 5 Two Officers of Divisional Yeomanry attached for instruction.	Re hayes
	18/10/15		Very quiet morning— slight Artillery duel in early afternoon— German rifle fire at aeroplanes— retaliated with our Machine guns.	Re hayes
	19/10/15		Enemy's artillery fired on T.I.32, Bn. H.Q. & Shaftesbury Avenue between 2.15 p.m. and 4 p.m.— no damage done. One man of A Coy and one man of D Coy wounded by rifle fire.	Re hayes
Support Trenches	20/10/15		Quiet day— one man of A Coy wounded. Battn relieved by 10th N.F. composed of 2 Coys 10th N.F. & 2 Coys Sherwood Foresters. Relief completed about 8 p.m. Battn occupied "C" position.	Re hayes
	21/10/15.		Battn had the use of the Divisional baths all day (order D.A.B.C.) No large working parties. A & C Coys in support trenches and B & D Coys in billets.	Re hayes
	22/10/15		Working parties all day— shelled in the morning— 1 man of D Coy wounded. Enemy's M.G. very busy in BOIS GRENIER ROAD at night. 11th N.F. defeated R.F.A. A.103 by 3 – NIL.	Re hayes
	23/10/15		Working parties from B & D Coys on the TRAMWAY Breastwork and support trenches. A & C Coys work on parados and dugouts. 2nd.Lt. E.St.C.Tulloch joined Bn from Hospital.	Re hayes
	24/10/15		Church parade attended by 5 Officers and 15 men from Artillery. Working parties on TRAMWAY Breastwork and support trenches. Strength 28 Officers & 951 other ranks.	Re hayes
FIRING Line.	25/10/15		The Bn relieved the composite Bn of 10th N.F. & 1st Sherwood Foresters in "A" position. Relief completed by 7.45 p.m.	Re hayes
In A Position	26/10/15		Very quiet day. Artillery duel between ourselves and enemy. No shells dropped in our area. 1 man of D Coy wounded in the wrist. Trenches very wet and muddy. New Bn.H.Q. dugouts occupied.	Re hayes
	27/10/15		Very quiet day—Some Artillery & aeroplane work. Two shells dropped in rear of our support trench. Trenches very wet and muddy. Morning very quiet. Artillery could be heard South about 2.15 p.m.	Re hayes
	28/10/15.		Enemy's artillery opened on Bn H.Q. & Shaftesbury Avenue—our guns quited them down. About 3.30 p.m. they opened on JOCK'S JOY and XXXXX T.26.1, T.26.2 T.26.1 2 men of B Coy killed & 2 wounded. 5 Howitzers replied but eventually curled up & fire ceased covering trench T.32 T.26.1 & T.26.2 at 5.15 p.m.	Re hayes

Army Form C. 2118.

WAR DIARY
or
INTELLIGENCE SUMMARY.
(Erase heading not required.)

Place	Date	Hour	Summary of Events and Information	Remarks and references to Appendices
	29/10/15		Enemy shelled I.32 but did no damage. Battn relieved by 10th N.F. Relief completed by 7.15 p.m. Battn took over billets in D Position in RUE DU BIEZ AND RUE DE LETTRE.	R E Mayer
D POSITION BILLETS IN RUE DE LETTRE.	30/10/15		Officer & 25 men of 21st Siege Battery attached temporarily. Battn had fatigue of 200 men to find for work on new breastwork— found by A & D Coys.	R E Mayer
	31/10/15		Battn had the use of the Divisional baths all day. Church of England parades in New Soldiers' Club in RUE DE LETTRE. Fatigue of 200 men required for breastwork furnished by B & C Coys.	R E Mayer

Instructions regarding War Diaries and Intelligence Summaries are contained in F. S. Regs., Part II. and the Staff Manual respectively. Title pages will be prepared in manuscript.

23rd Strauss

Mr Wollhuck: Fur:
Vol: 4

121/7693

Nov. 15.

Army Form C. 2118.

WAR DIARY
or
INTELLIGENCE SUMMARY.
(Erase heading not required.)

Instructions regarding War Diaries and Intelligence
Summaries are contained in F.S. Regs., Part II
and the Staff Manual respectively. Title pages
will be prepared in manuscript.

Place	Date	Hour	Summary of Events and Information	Remarks and references to Appendices
"D" Position	1/11/15		Fatigue of 100 men for heartwork found by C & D positions - weather very bad - Strength 28 Officers & 943 other ranks.	R.C. Hayall
"C" Position - BOIS GRENIER LINE.	2/11/15		Very bad weather - 1st Battalion relieved the 1st Sherwood Foresters in "C" Position - B and D Coys in the Reserve Trenches and A and C in billets in RVE du LETTRE - Relief completed 7.15 pm - Telephone communication very bad	R.C. Hayall
	3/11/15		B and A Coys employed in drawing teem our lines and in refacing SHAFTESBURY and PARK ROW AVENUES - A and C Coys sent working parties into Trench 53 in A position and to B position - New loopholes in "C" Position started at Bn HQ	R.C. Hayall
	4/11/15		Bombproof at Bn. HQ continued - working parties sent for drainage B Battalion) drawn from A & C Companies - improvements in wet weather	R.C. Hayall
	5/11/15		Engineers covered fatigue of 100 men from B Coy in right sector of reserve trenches - dug-out at Bn. HQ. Continued - Very heavy artillery fire all day - about 4 new concentrates enemys fire on L'Annie - Machine Guns on Bois GRENIER Road about 8.30 pm.	R.C. Hayall
"A" Position	6/11/15		Engineers conducted fatigue of 110 men from B Coy in right sects of reserve trenches - The Bn relieved the 1st Sherwood Foresters in "A" position - relief completed by 8 pm - Strength 28 Officers and 943 other ranks.	R.C. Hayall
	7/11/15		Very quiet day due probably to misty weather.	R.C. Hayall
	8/11/15		Sec. Lieut. J.S. Handley "B" Coy shot at 6.45 am in trench 111 g.26.2. It was probably stunned by enemy sniper leaning over parapet - one man of "B" Coy wounded in leg - one man of "B" Coy killed	R.C. Hayall
	9/11/15		Cutting wood - A fatigue of 80 men from ammunition park was sent forward to collect. Very quiet day - practically no artillery or sniping activity - in evening on lines ammunition left behind by battalions relieved.	R.C. Hayall
"D" Position	10/11/15		Enemy put about 10 shells into an area at 9.30 am - one man of "D" Coy wounded now - later shelved by 10th M.F about 1 pm.	R.C. Hayall
	11/11/15		Battn had more of letters in afternoon "C & D" Coys - rest all day - Enemy shelled GRIS POT.	R.C. Hayall
	12/11/15		Battalion rested all day.	
	13/11/15		Battalion had one of the Battn in its afternoon - relieved the 10th NF in "A" position - A Coy in g.32 - B in g.26.1 - C in SS.54 - A in g.26.2	

Army Form C. 2118.

WAR DIARY
or
INTELLIGENCE SUMMARY.
(Erase heading not required.)

Instructions regarding War Diaries and Intelligence Summaries are contained in F. S. Regs., Part II. and the Staff Manual respectively. Title pages will be prepared in manuscript.

Place	Date	Hour	Summary of Events and Information	Remarks and references to Appendices
"A" Postur.	14/11/15		10 Cadets from Salone at ST OMER were attached to Batts. for 24 hours — Relief completed 6.30pm. Commanding Officer went into Rest Hospital at STEENWERCK.	R.E. Mayall.
	15/11/15		Weather improved — aeroplane observation active in morning — very quiet day.	R.E. Mayall.
	16/11/15		Aeroplane observation very active — artillery active — advance party of 1st Worcesters Regt. came to join Trenches — one man slightly wounded at duty. Morning fairly and mainly — battalion relieved by the 1st Worcestershire Regt. — relief completed 7.15 p.m. Batt. proceeded to huts in FORT ROMPU. — complete 10 pm	R.E. Mayall. R.E. Mayall.
FORT ROMPU.	17/11/15		Battalion rested and cleaned up — during the 4 days the battalion has been in the line — 2 days in "A" portion — 7 days in "C" portion — 11 days in "D" portion, during the period casualties were — one officer killed, one wounded — and five killed and 19 wounded.	R.E. Mayall. R.E. Mayall.
	18/11/15		Battalion rested — Coal fatigue of 100 men found for Corps Depot at BAC ST. MAUR. Officers instruction in close order drill — Physical Exercises in early morning started — Route March	R.E. Mayall
	19/11/15		3 hours for each company — Fatigue of 100 men from "B" Coy for R.E. in left sector.	R.C. Mayall
	20/11/15		Strength of battalion 27 officers + 937 other ranks — Companies had close order drill	R.E. Mayall
	21/11/15		Church of England parade at LA DOR NOIR — 476 men on parade — Baths cleaned up for G.O.C. Inspection.	R.E. Mayall
	22/11/15		Inspection by G.O.C. Brigade from 9.30am to 12.30 p. — Inspected by companies and then followed by company & platoon drill.	R.E. Mayall
	23/11/15		Advance party sent on to visit "C" Postur. in left Section — HQ in RUE MARLE — B+D Coys in billets in RUE MARLE — A Coy in billets in CHAPELLE D'ARMENTIERS — C Coy in trenches in BOIS GRENIER — M.G. in firing line with "A" Battalion. Lieut Col. J. Hunt-Grey Crummers Major Coffin 9th Yorks afforded	R.E. Mayall R.E. Mayall
"C" Postur.	24/11/15		its battalion in order to proceed forthwith to England.	
RUE MARLE			Battalion had to furnish fatigues to SAILLY Bridge and SAILLY Brickfields — also to Corps Coal at BAC ST. MAUR. — Battalion relieved by "C" portion Left Sector relieving 10th West Riding Regiment. — Relief completed 8 pm	R.E. Mayall
MARLE	25/11/15		Permanent working party of 50 men from under R.E. — from D. Coy. Lt. Drop off 8 men arrived and time Battalion Cambrin indian hostel to the old Company. 6 + A 16 C 1 K B.	R.E. Mayar

2353 Wt. W3441/1454 700,000 5/15 D. D. & L. A.D.S.S./Forms/C. 2118.

Army Form C. 2118.

WAR DIARY
or
INTELLIGENCE SUMMARY.
(Erase heading not required.)

Instructions regarding War Diaries and Intelligence Summaries are contained in F. S. Regs., Part II. and the Staff Manual respectively. Title pages will be prepared in manuscript.

Place	Date	Hour	Summary of Events and Information	Remarks and references to Appendices
"C" Position RUE MARLE	26/11/15	6pm	Strength of Battalion 27 Officers and 943 other ranks. At 6pm Headquarters Staff's Band. D. Coy. stood to in gas helmets for 15 minutes. NO/UP 87 Pte. J. Eady died answered at 5pm in Shrapnel Corner Trench.	W. Alterin
"	27/11/15		Received orders from Brigade for Relief of 10th Battn NF in A position, the Battalion less a Concert at B.H.H which was attended by the Divisional General and Brigadier.	hal turin
"	28/11/15		Advance party proceeded to Trenches. Take over from 10th NF. Relief carried out and completed at 7.9 pm.	A. Alterin
A Position	29/11/15		An Artillery Bombardment was carried out at 11.70am and again in the afternoon about 30 shells exploded in the 40 yds Trench, one entering mine Acifical and Dugout marking the two trenches and leading down the Parason in front of 2nd Command Dugout.	hal turin
"	30/11/15		One of our Aeroplanes was brought down by Enemy fire just at its being taken on the Sabine. It was flying very low having apparently been hit by Shrapnel. When nearing the Enemy Trenches a Gun line of Enemy machine hand on and it was to our camp.	hal turin

11ᵗʰ Northumb: Fus:
Vol: B 5
124/7936

23ʳᵈ 10/7/17

Army Form C. 2118.

WAR DIARY
or
INTELLIGENCE SUMMARY.
(Erase heading not required.)

Instructions regarding War Diaries and Intelligence Summaries are contained in F. S. Regs., Part II. and the Staff Manual respectively. Title pages will be prepared in manuscript.

Place	Date	Hour	Summary of Events and Information	Remarks and references to Appendices
"A" Position.	1.12.15		A very quiet day. A mine was exploded in the Salient near the C.O. of "A" Company's dugout upon investigation by an Engineer Officer however the was found the explosive.	W. Adkin ?
	2.12.15		At 3.20 q/10 of our Aeroplanes returned from German lines and were heavily shelled upon near Rue Rd. 31 in dought then went for a Ronde and were returning. The Battalion HQrs relieved by the 10th N.F. and proceeded to "D" posting in Rue Marle. Capt. unfurled at 8.20pm. At q/about a few shells were dropped in Road immediately outside to pr. On entrance in Pery one Ry hqs office damaged the Poisching the casualty no casualties. Rats hops in the some trivery Major E.G. Coffin was her Commanding Officer join the Battalion in the trenches	Re Morgall
Rue Marle. "D" Position.	3.12.15		The Battalion was relieved in "A" position by 10th N.F. and proceeded to "D" position in RUE MARLE – Companies rested all day and cleaned up.	Re Morgall
	4.12.15		Battalion had the use of (14) Divisional Baths all day – the Boches shelled RUE MARLF about 4-4.5pm – Killed the driver and horses of the water cart – also killed seven Pioneers and wounded several – the Battalion lost 15 from cellar accommodation for all ranks.	Re Royall
	5.12.15		Voluntary Church Parade in Soldiers Club. Both "slept in cellars again.	Re Morgan
"A" Position.	6.12.15		Advance parties proceeded in morning to take over trenches in "A" position – Bn. relieved 10th N.F. in "A" position – Relief completed 7.5 pm – Very quiet night	Re Morgan
	7.12.15		very quiet day - an artillery strafe during breakfast from 11.30am - 12.30pm - Enemy retaliated on RUE MARLE and batteries.	Re Royall
	8.12.15		Quiet day – Sergt Spencer shot in Salient – considerable artillery activity by our guns	Re Royall Re hrap

2533 Wt W3344/1454 700,000 5/15 D, D&L A.D.S.S./Forms/C. 2118.

WAR DIARY
or
INTELLIGENCE SUMMARY.

(Erase heading not required.)

Army Form C. 2118.

Place	Date	Hour	Summary of Events and Information	Remarks and references to Appendices
"A" Position	9/12/15		Quiet day – our artillery shelled enemy's parapet opposite salient between 3 pm – 4.30 pm – enemy machine guns fired on parapets through the night.	R.E. Wagner
	10/12/15		Enemy Shelled Bn Hd – PARK ROW AVENUE pt. J.26.5 – J.20.1 - J.20.2 from 9.15 am – 11.15 am – with H.E. Shrapnel – large shell – no casualties – Considerable damage done to communicating trenches – one near O.P. C.oy billet – communication with artillery broken – signallers kept eventually gone – Bn relieved by 10th N.F.	R.E. Wagner
"C" Position	11/12/15		Battalion billetted in RUE MARLE in "C" Position – B Coy in BOIS GRENIER fin – A Coy in CHAPELLE D'ARMENTIÈRES – A.c.c in RUE MARLE – Quiet aerts	R.E. Wagner
	12/12/15		Voluntary Church Parades – quiet day.	R.E. Wagner
	13/12/15		Battalion billetting area altered – B Coy moved its RUE MARLE – quarters	R.E. Wagner
	14/12/15		Battalion relieved by 2nd Northants and proceeded to 17th over night – Horses started 5 pm, completed	R.E. Wagner
HALLO-BEAU Div (reserve)	15/12/15	9.45 am	Billets at HALLOBEAU H.1.b.1.8 – horses started 5 pm, completed 9.45 am. Commanding Officer Inspection of Camp in morning – Refitting cleaning hosetco – Company route marches.	R.E. Wagner
	16/12/15		Training under Company arrangements – Regt Sgt Maj Close to New Watering Party of 200 men fr 12th R.E at RUE MALF – 30 men fr D.A.C	R.E. Wagner
	17/12/15		Companies employed on musketry, bombing and route marches	R.E. Wagner
	18/12/15		Musketry and close order drill.	R.E. Wagner

WAR DIARY
or
INTELLIGENCE SUMMARY.
(Erase heading not required.)

Army Form C. 2118.

Instructions regarding War Diaries and Intelligence Summaries are contained in F. S. Regs. Part II. and the Staff Manual respectively. Title pages will be prepared in manuscript.

Place	Date	Hour	Summary of Events and Information	Remarks and references to Appendices
HALLOBEAU	19/12/15		No church parades. — Final of Inter-Company Football Tournament between C. Coy v M.G. won by C. Coy	Re Hayes
	20/12/15		Party of officers went over left battalion of right sector of 23rd Div line.	Re Hayes
	21/12/15		Wet day — all working parties cancelled	Re Hayes
"B" Bn. Right Sector	22/12/15		Battalion was relieved by 9th Yorks and took over trenches 9.32 to J.26.4 from 8th Yorks. C. Coy on the right — one platoon of A. Coy — D. Coy in the left — B & A. Coys in BOIS GRENIER LINE — relief completed 7 pm. One N.C.O of Transport killed and one man of C. Coy wounded	Re Hayes
	23/12/15		Considerable artillery activity all day — enemy shelled TUCKS JOY — SHAFTESBURY AVENUE — SS guns from 11 am to 2 pm — Considerable damage done to communication trenches.	Re Hayes
	24/12/15		At 5.30 am enemy hit 12 shells in rear of Tucks Joy — at 11.30 am again about 40 shells were fired around SS guns — our artillery was very active	Re Hayes
	25/12/15		There was considerable artillery activity on both sides — our guns bombarded enemy's parapet at J.26.b.d. — their guns did little damage proving a few shells in near of T.J.26.3. — Xmas Day	Re Hayes
	26/12/15		There was continuous artillery activity and to left of T.J.26.4 was shelled at 2.30 pm — Hun dug outs were smashed in its citadel by shells H.E. — retaliation was called for and the enemy fire severer to become more intense to our Support lines — Relieved by 10th N.F. — Proceeded to B Picture	Re Hayes

WAR DIARY
or
INTELLIGENCE SUMMARY.
(Erase heading not required.)

Army Form C. 2118.

Place	Date	Hour	Summary of Events and Information	Remarks and references to Appendices
"D" position	27/12/15		The Battalion had the use of the baths in the morning – HQ at LA ROLANDERIE FARM. A, B and C Coys in RUE de LETTRÉ and D Coy & M.G. in RUE du BIEZ – 9 Snrs of B Coy in BOIS GRENIER line.	RE fatigue
	28/12/15		C. & D. Coys had their Christmas Dinners (got up by officers subscription) – all fatigue parties for R.E. and SHAFTESBURY AV. found by A & B Coys – 9 Snrs of A Coy relieved 9 Snrs of B Coy in BOIS GRENIER line.	RE fatigue
	29/12/15		A & B Coys HQ & M.G. had Christmas Dinners – Fatigue parties for R.E. and 10"NF	RE fatigue
"B" Position	30/12/15		Advance parties proceeded to trenches to take over. – A Coy in T.9.32 in T.9.26. C Coy (1 platoon) T.9.26.1, B Coy T.9.26.2, 9.26.3, 9.26.4 – C (3 platoons) and A Coy in BOIS GRENIER line. – Relief complete. – C. Coy moved up to left of B Coy – one man wounded (A Coy)	RE fatigue
	31/12/15		Quiet day – two men of Battn. wounded – one man of C. Coy wounded (died) one man of D Coy – very heavy rifle and M.G. fire throughout evening & to midnight	RE fatigue

1131 Household Auxilius.

Vol III 6
Pau 16

23

WAR DIARY or INTELLIGENCE SUMMARY

Army Form C. 2118.

Place	Date	Hour	Summary of Events and Information	Remarks and references to Appendices
"B" Place.	1/1/16	1.30am	A party of 10th N.F. attempted to raid the enemy's trench at S.26.c.8.1. — they were seen by the enemy and fired on heavily — enemy's artillery opened quickly and continued to bombard our trenches until about 2.30 p.m. — our casualties were one killed and 5 wounded — estimate of casualties of 10th N.F. killed unknown. Enemy's searchlight and star shell were very much alive. 15 to 20 aeroplanes afternoon. 3 a.m. The day passed off quietly.	R.E. Mayal
	2/1/16		Enemy shelled our trenches between 11am and 2pm — between 12 & 3pm shot was 9 pm from Joe's Joy and Bn Hq were shelled very heavily with H.E. — no one was wounded — our field guns and Howitzers retaliated effectively — afternoon was quiet and night.	R.E. Mayal
"C" Position	3/1/16		Morning very quiet — considerable shelling on our right in the afternoon — relieved by 10th N.F. and proceeded to "C" position. Bn Hq. H.17.d.1.0. — A. Coy (2 Platoons) RUE DES CHARLES and (2 Platoons) CEMETERY POST. B Coy (2 Platoons) RUE DE LETTRÉ and (2 Platoons) RUE TOULETTE — C Coy COMMAND POST A Coy BOIS GRENIER line. — Quiet day.	R.E. Mayal
	4/1/16			R.E. Mayal
	5/1/16		Quiet day — in evening big gun brought up to staffs — was put under cover but no retaliation.	R.E. Mayal
RUE DOMOIRE.	6/1/16		Orders for relief by 1st Worcester Regt — received 15 Coys. — quiet day.	R.E. Mayal
	7/1/16		Battalion relieved by 1st Worcester Regt — moved to RUE DOMOIRE in Brigade Reserve. Relief complete 7.50 p.m.	R.E. Mayal
H.q.a.0.3.	8/1/16		Quiet day — refitting and cleaning — parades — parts for emergency defence scheme recouped — 100 men (50 B. 50 C) on fatigue.	R.E. Mayal
Brigade Reserve.	9/1/16		Church Parade for all denominations — working party orders for 10th N.F.	R.E. Mayal

WAR DIARY or **INTELLIGENCE SUMMARY**

Army Form C. 2118.

Place	Date	Hour	Summary of Events and Information	Remarks and references to Appendices
RUE DORMOIRE	10/1/15		Working parties of 638 men found for SHAFTESBURY AVENUE – BOIS GRENIER LINE and front line. 68 deficient.	Re Mayall
	11/1/15		Companies did close order drill, route marches etc. – "B" Coy inspected by CO.	Re Mayall
	12/1/15		Battalion had the use of the baths – 650 men sent. – A. Coy inspected by CO.	Re Mayall
	13/1/15		Close order drill, route marches etc. – C & D Coys inspected by CO. – relief orders received.	Re Mayall
	14/1/15		Company drill etc. – Officers went to take over trenches in left sub-sector.	Re Mayall
"A" Position left	15/1/15		The Battalion relieved the 8th Yorkshire Regt. 69th Brigade in trenches of right subsector of left sub-sector.	Re Mayall
Sector Trenches G.26.5			D Coy T.9.21.1 (60) – T.9.21.2 (61) – C. Coy was in BOIS GRENIER Line and support platoon. A Coy Divisional Area – A. Coy held T. G. 26.5 (57) and T.9 20.1 (58) – B. Coy T.9 20.2 and 116 men 16 S.S. line G. 26.5. – Relief under felt 7.5 p.m. – Quiet night – Strength of Battalion (14th) down in establishment – one Rifleman wounded in working parties.	Re Mayall
	16/1/15		Very quiet day – artillery on both sides was silent. – Solitary sniper active at times. Our artillery fist morning were opposite G.20.2 between 10.30 a.m. and 12.15 p.m. – answered.	Re Mayall
G.21.1. 17/1/15 (Withdrawn)			Range was obtained – enemy retaliated on rear of G.26.5 and top of TANK ROW Nr. Pte Colley of A Coy while aiming through loophole in G. 26.5 had a German bullet shot clean down the Barrel of his rifle – the breech and bolt were only slightly damaged and the man although knocked off his footstep by enemy sniper – about 7.35 p.m. enemy put about 20 large shells into ARMENTIERS and to G35 and went over to ERQUINGHEM. –	Re Mayall
	18/1/15		Two men of A. Coy wounded in solitary sniping over a parapet to listening post. Very quiet day – artillery duel on our right all afternoon – Sergt Liddell of "B" Coy shot through the head while visiting listening post. – Draft of other Rgts. 3 offs. and 7 men from the Base taken on our strength.	Re Mayall
	19/1/15		12.30 p.m. enemy began to shell the entrenchment in Trench G.21.1 – retaliation was ordered. Enemy sent shrapnel over G. 26.5. – enemy began again on G. 21.1 with heavy stuff – a heavy artillery duel followed and considerable damage was done on both sides. Relieved in A section by 10th N.F. – HQ in RUE MARLE – C. Coy in BOIS GRENIER f... A. Coy in ARMENTIERS. ERQUINGHEM Rd – B & D Coys in RUE MARLE	Re Mayall

Army Form C. 2118.

WAR DIARY
or
INTELLIGENCE SUMMARY.
(Erase heading not required.)

Instructions regarding War Diaries and Intelligence Summaries are contained in F. S. Regs., Part II. and the Staff Manual respectively. Title pages will be prepared in manuscript.

Place	Date	Hour	Summary of Events and Information	Remarks and references to Appendices
RUE MARLE H.6.d.65	20/1/16		Working parties of 60 men each furnished by Band D Coys sent to 10th NF in A'tières – also 50 men guide to R.E. – Relief of "A" Company rounded in Erculogescoled.	Re Mayall
	21/1/16		Working parties of 60 men each furnished at 10am and 6pm by A & B Coys sent to 10th NF in A'tières – also 50 men in morning to R.E. and 100 of A Coy in evening – B Coy relieved C Coy in BOIS GRENIER Line.	Re Mayall
	22/1/16		Nothing parties to 10th NF in morning and evening – R.E. working party enrolled	
"A" Battn.	23/1/16		No working parties furnished – relieved 10th NF in "A" tières – D Coy in J.26.5 and J.20.1. – E Coy J.20.2 and J.21.1 and A Coy in J.21.2 – B Coy in Bois GRENIER R line "TRAMWAY" FME to DOG'S LEG RP. – Relief complete at 8pm – Bn HQ shelter at 8pm and at 10.45pm.	Re Mayer
	24/1/16		Quiet day – artillery cut wire in morning and evening retaliation very slight – no men of "A" Coy (N.G.) wounded.	Re Mayer
	25/1/16		Our artillery carried out a scheme – enemys artillery was active throughout the day but did little damage –	Re Mayer
	26/1/16		Enemies Artillery very active – shelled Bn Hd. – S. Line and BOIS GRENIER Line consistently from 10am – 3pm – Very little damage – no wounded – man on listening post, native of "C" Coy on Salient was accidentally shot by one of from listening post.	Re Mayer
	27/1/16		Kaisers Birthday – enemy shelled constantly all day on S. Line and BOIS GRENIER Line – very little damage and no casualties – C Company – Company relieved by 10th NF, 1st Royal Scots attacked Re Mayer A & D Companies in BOIS GRENIER Line – B Company fireway to RUE MARLE – ARMENTIÈRES – C Coy RUE MARLE – Heavy Shelling from 11.15 pm to 12am.	

2353 Wt. W2311/1454 700,000 5/15 D. D. & L. A.D.S.S./Forms/C. 2118.

Army Form C. 2118.

WAR DIARY
or
INTELLIGENCE SUMMARY.
(Erase heading not required.)

Instructions regarding War Diaries and Intelligence Summaries are contained in F. S. Regs., Part II. and the Staff Manual respectively. Title pages will be prepared in manuscript.

Place	Date	Hour	Summary of Events and Information	Remarks and references to Appendices
RUE MARLE. "C"	28/1/16		Officers & N.C.O.'s of "C" Coy gave instruction to C. Coy 1st Royal Scots in trenches — C Coy found working parties of 50 men with 25% of attached company — in evening "A" Coy 1st Royal Scots relieved C. Coy R.S. — all four Platoons billetted in RUE MARLE	RE Hoyall
	29/1/16.		"A" Coy 1st Royal Scots was relieved by "A" Coy 1st Royal Scots in evening — morning working party of 50 men for R.E.	RE Hoyall
	30/1/16		Church & Eng Cadre Parade for "C" Coy — Company and attached company in Billets. Working party of 30 men in afternoon for R.E. and 100 men at night — B Coy 1st R.S. relieved A Coy	RE Hoyall
	31/1/16		Advance parties proceeded to JESUS FARM to take over billets for 8 days in Divisional Reserve — C & D Coys 1st Royal Scots attached in the night - Relieved in "C" written by 13th Worcestershire Regiment — took over from 2nd East Lancs. — Strength of Battalion 29 officers + 857 other ranks.	RE Hoyall

1/2/16.

RE Hoyall
Captain Adjutant for
O.C. 11 Northumberland Fusiliers

No.11/24061 Pte. F.Colley, of "A" Company, 11th Northumberland Fusiliers, while aiming through a loop-hole in the parapet of Trench I.26.5 had a German bullet shot clean down the barrel of his rifle before he had fired his own round. The man, although knocked off the fire step was practically uninjured.

The bolt mechanism of the rifle was intact. There is an obstruction in the barrel, presumably the two bullets. The Brass case of the cartridge is in the chamber, the end being driven out and ground to powder, a great deal of which was ingrained on the head of the bolt. It is presumed that the bolt head was driven back sufficiently to allow of the escape of the gas.

29/1/16.

Lt.Colonel,
Commanding
11th(S)Bn.Northumberland Fusiliers.

Army Form C. 2118.

WAR DIARY
or
INTELLIGENCE SUMMARY.
(Erase heading not required.)

Instructions regarding War Diaries and Intelligence Summaries are contained in F. S. Regs., Part II. and the Staff Manual respectively. Title pages will be prepared in manuscript.

Place	Date	Hour	Summary of Events and Information	Remarks and references to Appendices
JESUS FARM B.26.d.4.	1/2/16		Major H. Beale assumed Temporary Command of Battalion during absence on leave of Lieut-Col E.G. Capper – Capt. W. Godfrey appointed 2nd in Command of 9th Welsh Regt. – Commanding Officer inspected billets – Battalion cleaned up and refitting handed.	RE Mayall
	2/2/16		All Officers and N.C.O's inspected by G.O.C. Division at HALLOBEAU – his remarks summary of great lack of uniformity in dress and equipment. Company Commanders Conference – Companies having Section Commanders Conferences – too commands – 10th Welsh Batt attached & fed etc for the handles.	RE Mayall
	3/2/16		Companies had route marches and grenade training at ERQUINGHEM – Capt. W. Godfrey left for his new regiment – Classes for NCOs – MG – Signallers	RE Mayall
	4/2/16		Battalion used the use of baths for 400 men (each company 90, HQ 29, MG 20) – also rifle range at ERQUINGHEM – B. Coy fired 90 men in morning and A Coy 90 in afternoon – N.G. up to 9.30 am – G.O.C. Brigade inspects transport at 11 am in training. Record of Casualties up to date – Killed 20 (including one officer) – Wounded 60 (including one officer) – of the 60 wounded 25 have rejoined the unit reported 35 – Sick (officers) – Evacuated Sick 130 – killed 20 – wounded and yet to embarkation to date – Officers 30 – O.R. 158. – Leave figures from time of Major H. Beale transferred 10 Command: increased & Capt. The Earl of Dundee assumed Infantry Command.	RE Mayall
	5/2/16		Battalion found working parties for R.E. – 500 men all day – A Coy had two men killed in B.15 GRENIER Rue by a shell.	RE Mayall
	6/2/16		Church Parades all morning – G.O.C. Brigade inspected the transport in the morning – Strength of Battalion 27 Officers and 859 O.R.	RE Mayall

WAR DIARY or INTELLIGENCE SUMMARY

Army Form C. 2118.

Place	Date	Hour	Summary of Events and Information	Remarks and references to Appendices
JESUS FARM.	7/2/16.		Two companies of 10th Lincolns billetted at JESUS FMF for the night — grenade training — patrols went to visit trenches — Inspection for G.O.C. Inspection cancelled.	RCMayer
	8/2/16		G.O.C. inspection cancelled — the Battalion relieved the 10th West Riding in "B" Batt: Right Sector — H.Q. JOCK'S JOY — B Coy trenches S 32.1 and S 26.2 and S 26.3 — D Coy S 26.3 — S 26.4. — C. Coy Bois GRENIER line — each company made up to 160 strong. — 2 Coys of 24 NF. billetted at JESUS FMF.	RCMayer
"B" Battalion Right Sector	9/2/16		Very quiet night. Lieut A.C. Pritchard was hit by a bullet on the finger but did not leave the trenches. Fine frosty morning. Private Beals 'A' Co killed during the morning. B Company 25th NF came in for instruction in the trenches. Very quiet night.	RCMayer
	10/2/16		Fine frosty. Lt J.T. MacDouall hit by a whizzbang. On the whole very quiet. Brig Gen Pyge Croft came round the trenches, also Colonel of 25th NF. D Co 25th NF attaches to us. Col Coffin returned from leave. Very quiet night. Pte Hey D, Co hit on patrol & died of wounds. Very wet day. Col REAO was flooded — damned at 5th trench. Patrol from D Co find no patrols of enemy looking for reason of flood. Rain ceased about 10 pm but still cold. D Co 25th NF gone to B Co trenches again.	RCMayer
	11/2/16			RCMayer

WAR DIARY
or
INTELLIGENCE SUMMARY.

Army Form C. 2118.

Place	Date	Hour	Summary of Events and Information	Remarks and references to Appendices
	12/2/16	—	The Enemy started shelling about 9am & continued all morning shelling S.S.1 and Jocks Toy. HQ. LONDON BRIDGE & BOIS GRENIER line. At 12.45 his bombardment became very severe & stopped about 2pm. Our artillery retaliated well. The trench gun going off 2 secs after being asked for. 1 man killed & 4 wounded in A Co & 1 killed & 2 wounded of the 25th N.F. Aerial torpedoes made their first appearance & did a lot of damage. The 12th N.F. relieved the battalion about 7.30 pm & we moved to D position.	R.E. Mayer
	13/2/16		Enemy were again active shelling most of battery positions. Over 60 heavy shells were counted. 2/Lt Haynes reported for duty from 16th Lancashires posted to 'B' Company. A second company of 25th N.F. was attached & we were very crowded in billets.	
	14/2/16		Three working parties were supplied of 180 men altogether. The battalion had three ways of baths. 2/Lt Emmerson & 2/Lt Britton reported for duty & were attached to B & D companies respectively. Had to send a M.G. to 13 DLI owing to their being out of order.	R.E. Mayer
	15/2/16		Two working parties supplied totalling 150 men. Baths. All companies busy drawing tracks & cleaning up. Col Sir J. Laidlie Griffiths arrives here attached for 14 days. Draft of 41 McCD R.Chayor arrives. 13 posted to their old companies - 10 to A & 18 to B.Co. all except 1 have been out there before. Looks a good lot. Major Fray. Scottish Horse came over. Col Griffiths.	R.C.Mayor
	16/2/16		Very quiet day. Two working parties totalling 150 men supplied. Started training billets.	R.C.Mayor
	17/2/16		Relieved 10 R.N.F. Relief completed 7.20. Very quiet day.	R.C.Mayor

WAR DIARY or INTELLIGENCE SUMMARY.

Army Form C. 2118.

(Erase heading not required.)

Place	Date	Hour	Summary of Events and Information	Remarks and references to Appendices
"B" Bn.Hn.	18.2.16		Very quiet & very wet day. At night good deal of work was done on our wire. A hostile patrol came up to our wire. Two four patrols chased it back but failed to catch it. Lt. Major Beale GSO extension of trench to 20th. 18 men attached to battalion HQ.	R.E. Mayall
	19.2.16		Fine day & warmer. Enemy shelled BOIS GRENIER & trench up line. Otherwise very quiet. Capt. & Adjt Mayall returned from leave.	R.E. Mayall
	20.2.16		Very quiet day – C.O. & Adjt of 11th Suffolk Regt. came to MOAT FMS & assemble arrangements for relief – enemy shelled BOIS GRENIER line.	R.E. Mayall
	21.2.16		Enemy shelled BOIS GRENIER line constantly all day – fifteen men of MOAT FMS damaged – one man of A Coy wounded – Battalion relieved by 11th Suffolk Regt. 101st Brigade – 34th Division – relief complete 8.25 p.m. Battalion went into Reserve Billets at RUE DOMOIRE	R.E. Mayall
RUE DOMOIRF	22.2.16		Very quiet day – orders for move to Corps Reserve cancelled – Battalion was off in billets for 4 hours and also changes 300 long rifles for 300 short ones. Only 12 short rifles necessary to complete fit out – 60 steel helmets for Coy issued – ordered 20 H.Q. –	R.E. Mayall
	23.2.16		Training Programme for week issued – orders to hold in readiness – working party of 160 men to R.E. in Corps Reserve again cancelled.	R.E. Mayall
RUE MARLE	24.2.16		Training Programme begun – Orders received for move to SAILLY on 25th Sous on Grande – Commandant duties for Groups Officers & NCOs.	R.E. Mayall

Army Form C. 2118.

WAR DIARY
or
INTELLIGENCE SUMMARY.
(Erase heading not required.)

Instructions regarding War Diaries and Intelligence Summaries are contained in F.S. Regs., Part II. and the Staff Manual respectively. Title pages will be prepared in manuscript.

Place	Date	Hour	Summary of Events and Information	Remarks and references to Appendices
SAILLY	25/5		Orders received for march to SAILLY in morning and issued to companies about 12 midnight – gas alarm – battalion marched from 10.40am from ERQUINGHEM Bridge – no blankets or kits for the men arrived	R E Strayall
MORBECQUE	26"		Orders received for march to MORBECQUE about 3am – issued to companies about 6am – Battalion marched off at 9.45am via ESTAIRES-NEUF BERQUIN – VIEUX-BERQUIN – VIERHOUCK – LA MOTTE – STEENBECQUE – arrived at MORBECQUE 6pm – no casualties on the march – Transport arrived late – Officers kits after midnight	R E Strayall
	27"		Battalion rested all day. cleaned up camp – Shoes on ground all day	R E Strayall
	28"		Battalion paraded under Company arrangements in the morning – in evening orders received and issued for move to area of BRUAY – orders issued 10.30pm.	R E Strayall
MARLE-DES-MINES	29"		All transport proceeded by road under the Brigade Transport Officer at 8.15am – all kits etc were taken to STEENBECQUE Station by motor lorry in the morning – the battalion entrained at STEENBECQUE at 2pm and detrained at CALONNE – RICQUART at 4.15pm – battalion then marched to MARLE-LES-MINES and was billetted there by 8pm.	R E Strayall
			During the month the following officers have left the battalion: Capt Godfrey; Capt Gatehouse; Lieut Dr Rowland; 2 Lt Macwaland Capt Graham. The following officers have joined the battalion 2/Lieuts Haynes, Edmuson, Wilson, Maddison. Strength of battalion 31 Officers – 856 O.R.	R E Strayall Capt Adjt

Army Form C. 2118.

WAR DIARY
or
INTELLIGENCE SUMMARY.
(Erase heading not required.)

Instructions regarding War Diaries and Intelligence Summaries are contained in F. S. Regs., Part II. and the Staff Manual respectively. Title pages will be prepared in manuscript.

Place	Date	Hour	Summary of Events and Information	Remarks and references to Appendices
MARLES-LES-MINES	1/3/16		2/Lt. Edmison despatched to CARLONNE – RICQUART Station to superintend unloading and transport of kits – Battalion proceeded on route march at 11.30am in afternoon. Companies paraded under their own arrangements.	RE Krayale
	2/3/16		The Brigade was inspected by Lt General H. Wilson K.C.B. D.S.O. in command of 4th Corps – in afternoon companies had lectures from Company officers.	RE Krayale
	3/3/16		Owing to wet weather battalion parade in morning postponed – Companies had lectures and paraded under their own arrangements – Major H. Beale left the battalion for duty as instructor at 23rd Div. Infantry Base ETAPLES – afternoon battalion parade.	RE Krayale
	4/3/16		Q.2. Mr. Sergt Warner proceeded to England on course at Aldershot – was presented all parades in morning – Lecture to officers at BRVAY in afternoon by Col Carrickan.	RE Krayale
	5/3/16		Church parade in school yard behind Mairie – 2 hours drill by Companies – Heavy snow on the ground – Companies did rapid loading practice and route marches.	RE Krayale
	6/3/16			RE Krayale
	7/3/16		Battalion parade in morning and bombing practice – orders received for move into Divisional Area – 29 officers – 863 O.R. – 132 O.R. Regimen.	RE. Krayn
FRESNI-COURT	8/3/16		Battalion paraded ready to move off at 8.40 am – arrived FRESNICOURT at 12.30 pm. Accommodation very limited for officers and men – relieved French sentries.	RE Krayale
	9/3/16		Companies paraded under their own arrangements – classes for NCOs under Regl Sergt Major	RE Krayale
	10/3/16		Companies paraded under their own arrangements – bombing parade under Grenadier officer. – Draft of 41 NCOs & OR arrived from Base	RE Krayale
	11/3/16		Morning lectures under company arrangements – Battalion parade – Lecture to all officers of battalion by Brigadier in evening.	RE Krayale

Army Form C. 2118.

WAR DIARY
or
INTELLIGENCE SUMMARY.
(Erase heading not required.)

Instructions regarding War Diaries and Intelligence Summaries are contained in F. S. Regs., Part II. and the Staff Manual respectively. Title pages will be prepared in manuscript.

Place	Date	Hour	Summary of Events and Information	Remarks and references to Appendices
FRESNICOURT Q.2.5.b.	12/3/16		Orders received that movement of troops into trenches on 16th cancelled - Remain in Camp - 2nd Lt. W.K. MacLellan and 2nd Lt. W.M. Tipton reported for duty on arrival from England.	R. Hayes
	13/3/16		Battalion continued baths in the camp - Its whole bn. except details completed. - Parades under Company arrangements.	R. Hayes
	14/3/16		Companies paraded under their own arrangements - operation orders for move on 16th. - Party of five officers proceeded to inspect CALONNE Section.	R. Hayes
	15/3/16		Second party of five officers proceeded to trenches in CALONNE Section to trenches under their own arrangements in its morning - Battalion to take over from 22nd London Regt. First party under 2nd Lt Lindsey proceeded to HERSIN to take over from 22nd London Regt.	Billeting R. Hayes
HERSIN Q.5.d.	16/3/16		The Battalion paraded ready to move off at 9 am - Companies marched with 10 minutes interval between platoons - The battalion was billetted in HERSIN by 12.30 pm. - HQ. was at Q.5.d.8.8. (Ref 36 A S.E.)	R.E. Hayes
BULLY GRENAY R.11.a.	17/3/16		Advance parties proceeded to BULLY GRENAY to take over billets ('A' bn.) from 13th Essex Regt. in the CALONNE Section & 1st bn. Devon of the 4th Coys - 1st in Trenches proceeded to renovate lines. Left Brigade of the Left at FOSSE 10 (Q.17.A.6.0.) - Battalion started from HERSIN at 2 pm and marched with ten minute intervals between companies and 100 yards distance between platoons. order (B.E.D.A., M.G. H.Q. 1st Line) - Route FOSSE No 3, MAZINGARBE - LES BREBIS - BULLY GRENAY.	R.E. Hayes R.E. Hayes

WAR DIARY
or
INTELLIGENCE SUMMARY.

(Erase heading not required.)

Army Form C. 2118.

Place	Date	Hour	Summary of Events and Information	Remarks and references to Appendices
~~HERNI~~ BULLY GRENAY. "D" Position.	17th (cont.)		Battalion was billeted in BULLY GRENAY by 5.30 p.m. – Battn. HQ situated at R.11.a.4.4. Transport Lines at R.B.b.9.8.	Re Hayes
	18th		2nd Lieut A.G. Lane (8th N.F.) joined for duty with battalion and posted to "C" Company – "A" Coy found working party of 2 platoons on communication trench to CALONNE 8 a.m. – 12 noon – "B" and "C" Coys had to find 125 men each for evening working party – Strength of Battalion 30 Officers and 905 O.R. (AFW 213) – Total number of men employed on working parties between and 400 O.R. – 2nd Lt. N.Y. Wilson, shot in the groin on working party.	Re Hayall
	19th		Battalion found 5 Officers and 375 O.R. in Working Parties – Parties proceeded on to the trenches all day – Capt. the Hon. Sidney Toley Adjutant 10th N.F. Killed. Relief orders for 21st issued in the morning – working parties of 4 officers and 350 O.R.	Re Hayall. Re Hayall.
Front Line Trenches "A" Position	20th			
	21st		Battalion relieved the 10th N.F. in "A" position taking over the line from M.20 & 2.45 on its right to M.21.a.2.9. – A Company took over right company – D Coy centre company – B Coy left company – C Company in Support in CALONNE at M.14.d.4.8. – Battn HQ at M.14.d.2.4 – Relief complete at 9.15 pm – one man killed and four wounded. By shell in CALONNE Square about 9.30 pm.	Re Hayall
	22nd		Very quiet day – one man of A Coy wounded in arm by bullet while lying retired in Sap. – Occasional grenade throwing on either side.	Re Hayell.
	23rd		Very quiet morning – enemy shelled trench mortar batteries in afternoon without doing any damage – two men wounded by rifle grenade.	Re Hayal
	24th		Quiet morning – Enemy shelled left of the line about 3 p.m. with shrapnel and CALONNE about 5.30 pm with H.E. 2nd Lt. T. Haynes killed and Sergt Hervey wounded by premature explosion of one of our own rifle grenades.	Re Hayes

WAR DIARY
or
INTELLIGENCE SUMMARY.
(Erase heading not required.)

Army Form C. 2118.

Place	Date	Hour	Summary of Events and Information	Remarks and references to Appendices
"A" Batt."	25/3/16.		Very quiet morning - from 2.15pm to 8.45pm enemy shelled our right of its centre company with shrapnel, H.E. and whizz bangs - two men of "D" Company wounded - relieved by 10th R.F. in evening - relief complete 8.30pm - proceeded to close support billets in CALONNE - Companies billeted and alarm posts arranged by 10pm.	R.E. Kayall
CALONNE "hostun"	26/3/16.		At 2 pm all our Trench Mortar Batteries, Torpedo Guns, M.G. and Rifle Grenades fired heavily on the enemy's trench - our batteries opened also - no apparent damage - we lost one man killed and one Corporal wounded - 2 Lt. E.G. Barron and 16 of our grenadiers fired rifle grenades into enemy trench from the left. - a man of B. Coy wounded by shell shock	R.E. Kayall
	27/3/16		Quiet day - men working parties provided for R.E. 2nd Leans party proceeded to England.	R.E. Hayes
	28/3/16		Quiet day - all men under cover at 8 pm to shuffle by 8th Yorks on our right - relief orders issued.	R.E. Kayall
	29/3/16		The Battalion relieved the 10th N.F. in "A" position - started at 2.30pm and came up by sections with 100 yards interval - Sergt. Major Sheflett of "A" Company wounded by shrapnel - Enemy swept roads with M.G. fire throughout the day - considerable bombing activity throughout the night. - Capt. S.C. Well joined for duty from England.	R.E. Kayall
"A" Batt."	30/3/16.		Enemy shelled the neighbourhood of Battalion HQ at intervals all through the day - ennonniaide aerial activity - 9 aeroplanes attacked for the enemy. - A Coy on right, D Coy in centre, C Coy on left and B Coy in support - enemy shelled its right and centre Companies at 8.15pm with whizzbangs. - One man of C Coy slightly wounded by rifle grenade.	R.E. Kayall
	31/3/16.		8th Yorks on our right bombarded enemys trenches from 5.10 and enemy shelled RUE DE TEMPLE, CALONNE and centre company with whizz-bangs throughout the morning - third leave party proceeded to transport lines.	R.E. Kayall

31/3/16

R.E. Kayall
Captain Adjutant
for O.C. 11th Yorks Fusrs

S E C R E T.

Battalion Operation Orders for 17th March 1916.

1. The 68th Brigade will relieve the 6th Brigade in the CALONNE Section of the Defences, on the 17th inst., 11th N.F. taking over "D" position in BULLY GRENAY from 13th ESSEX REGT.

2. A Billeting party, consisting of 1 Officer and 4 N.C.O's per Company, 1 Officer and 1 N.C.O. for Headquarters, 1 N.C.O. for Machine Gun and 1 N.C.O. for Transport and 1 N.C.O. for Qr.Mr's Dept., will report at the Headquarters, 13th ESSEX at 10 a.m. on 17th inst.

3. All Trench Stores, bombs and S.A.A. will be taken over by daylight on 17th inst.

4. 1st Line Transport Lines are at FOSSE 10.

5. Billeting parties of the 6th Brigade (2nd.S.Staffs) will report at our Battalion H.Q. at 10 a.m.

6. The Battalion will march to billets in the following order- Starting point Headquarter Mess - B, C, D, A, Machine Gun, Headquarters.
    TIMES OF STARTING. "B"Coy at 2 p.m., "C" Coy at 2.10 p.m., "D" Coy at 2.20 p.m., "A" Coy at 2.30 p.m., Machine Gun and Headquarters at 2.40 p.m.
    Platoons will march at intervals of 100 yards.

7. Machine Gun Limbers will accompany the M.G. Section.

8. TRANSPORT. 1st Line Transport, unless otherwise ordered, will follow in rear of the Battalion.
    Officers' valises of "A", "D", Headquarters & M.G. will be stacked at the H.Q. Mess by 1 p.m., and those of "B" & "C" Coys at "C" Coy's mess by the same hour.
    The Transport Officer will arrange to send the baggage wagons to collect these. The Mess cart will collect the Officers' Mess kits at 2 p.m.
    Arrangements for carrying spare kits and blankets will be notified later.
    1 blanket per man will be carried rolled on top of the valise.

9. ROUTE. FOSSE 2, RAILWAY CROSSING L.21.c., MAZINGARBE, LES BREBIS, BULLY GRENAY.

10. The advance parties will meet their platoons at the entrance into BULLY GRENAY.

R C Mayall

16th March 1916.

Capt. & Adjutant,
11th Northd. Fusiliers.

To/- O.C.,
" " Coy.

20th March 1916.

Reference Relief Orders the time of commencement of relief has been changed from 3 p.m. to 6 p.m. Companies will therefore move off by platoons, with intervals of 100 yards between platoons, at the following times:-

"A" Coy. - 6 p.m.
"D" : - 6.15 p.m.
"B" : - 6.30 p.m.
"C" : - 6.45 p.m.

Headquarters will follow in rear of "C" Coy.

"C" Company will not take blankets.

R.C. Mayne
Capt. & Adjutant,
11th Northd. Fusiliers.

S E C R E T.

BATTALION OPERATION ORDERS FOR MARCH 21ST.

1. The 11th N.F. will relieve 10th N.F. in "A" position, 10th N.F. proceeding to "D" position.

2. DISPOSITION.
   Right Company — "A" Coy.
   Centre Company — "D" Coy.
   Left Company — "B" Coy.
   Support — "C" Coy.

3. Companies will leave their billets in BULLY GRENAY at the following times:—
   "A" Coy — 3 p.m.
   "D" Coy — 3.20 p.m.
   "B" Coy — 3.40 p.m.
   "C" Coy — 4 p.m.

Companies will march in sections in single file at intervals of 50 yards between sections. Guides from 10th N.F. will be met at xxxxxx the SQUARE in CALONNE. The 11th N.F. will move up to the trenches via the CALONNE NORD Trench and the 10th N.F. will proceed to "D" position via the CALONNE SUD Trench.

4. O.C. Lewis Detachment will make his own arrangements for relieving by 1 p.m. on 21st inst.

5. Advanced Parties, consisting of 1 Officer & 4 N.C.O's per Company, will proceed to the trenches to take over trench stores on the morning of the 21st. The Signalling Officer will detail a party to take over the lines during the morning.
The Grenadier Officer will arrange to take over all Bomb Stores during the morning.

6. O.C. Companies will report to Battalion H.Q. by wire and by orderly immediately relief is complete.

7. TRANSPORT. (i) The Transport Officer will send the field kitchens and watercarts up to CALONNE SQUARE.
(ii) All Blankets and Officers' spare kits and spare mess kits will be stacked in a heap at Company Headquarters and a loading party and guard left in charge until the arrival of the Transport.
(iii) All Officers' Trench Kits, mess kits and Company Stores for the trenches will be stacked in a separate heap at Company Headquarters, with loading party as guard.
   A reliable N.C.O. of each Company will be left in charge of (ii) & (iii).

Capt. & Adjutant,
11th Northd. Fusiliers.

20th March 1916.

To/- O.C., " " Coy.

21st March 1916.

The following Bombers will be required for posts while the Battalion is in the front line and should be detailed at once. They will march up to the trenches in front of the first platoon of their Companies and will relieve the grenadiers of the 10th N.F. on their arrival:-

"A" Coy. 1 Sgt., 2 Cpls., and 23 bombers.
"B" Coy. & 1st Post. 1 Sgt., 1 Cpl., & 16 bombers.
          2nd. Post. The Grenadier Sergt (Sgt. Robinson "A" Coy) 1 Cpl., and 25 men. (This post is in the mine area.)
"D" Coy. 1st Post. 2 N.C.O's & 10 bombers.
          2nd. Post. 1 Sgt., 1 Cpl., and 26 bombers. (This post is in the mine area.)

The following grenadiers will be drawn from "C" Coy and will be attached temporarily while the Battalion is in the trenches to Companies as stated:-
    "B" Coy - 1 N.C.O. and 10 grenadiers.
    "D" Coy - 1 N.C.O. and 10 grenadiers.

These parties should report to "B" and "D" Companies respectively at 5.30 p.m. this evening.

Arrangements must be made by Companies for the rationing of these men.

RC Mogale
Capt. & Adjutant,
11th Northd. Fusiliers.

S E C R E T.

BATTALION OPERATION ORDERS FOR 25TH MARCH 1916.

1. The 11th N.F. will be relieved in "A" position by 10th N.F. and will proceed to "C" position, taking over from 13th D.L.I. from corresponding Companies.

2. The 10th N.F. will commence to leave billets at 6 p.m. using the CALONNE SUD Trench. Platoons of the 11th N.F. on relief will proceed to their billets by the CALONNE NORD Trench.

3. Lewis Guns will be relieved before 1 p.m.

4. Advance parties of 1 Officer and 4 N.C.O's per Company will proceed to billets to take over billets and billet fixtures before noon on the 25th inst. These parties will return to their Companies and act as Platoon guides.

5. No Trench will be vacated by relieved Company until occupied by relieving Company.

6. The Signalling Officer will arrange to take over lines in "C" position during the afternoon.
   The Grenadier Officer will arrange to take over all Bomb Stores during the afternoon.
   The Regimental Sergt. Major will arrange to relieve all Guards of "C" Battalion during the afternoon.

7. All Officers' kits, mess kits and Company stores will be manhandled from the trenches to billets.

8. O.C. Companies will detail parties to report to the Regtl. Sergt. Major at Battalion H.Q. as soon after relief as possible for the purpose of unloading blankets, rations etc.

9. With reference to para. 3 of the 68th Inf. Bde Defence Scheme the following instructions are issued in case of alarm:-
   (a) "C" Company will provide the four Platoons for the specified posts.
   (b) "A" Company will stand to behind the houses at Battalion Alarm Post.
   (c) "B" and "D" Companies will stand to in cellars.
   (d) 2nd. Lt. R.W. Taylor is detailed as Officer in charge of Details and should reconnoitre the post indicated before relief.

10. With reference to para. 6 of the 68th Inf. Bde Defence Scheme O.C. Companies will furnish a certificate immediately after the relief is complete that the instructions therein have been complied with.

11. With reference to para. 7 of the 68th Inf. Bde Defence Scheme the Grenadier Officer will detail the party therein required.

R.C. Mayall

24th March 1916.

Capt. & Adjutant,
11th Northd. Fusiliers.

SECRET.

BATTALION OPERATION ORDERS FOR MARCH 29TH 1916.

1. 11th N.F. will relieve the 10th N.F. in "A" position, 10th N.F. proceeding to "C" position.

2. DISPOSITION.   Right Company -   "A".
                  Centre Company -   "D"
                  Left Company   -   "C"
                  Support Company - "B"

3. Companies will start from their billets at the following times and will proceed by sections via the communication trenches to their allotted posts. A distance of not less than 100 yards must be maintained between sections:-
   "A" Coy - 2.30 p.m.
   "D" Coy - 2.50 p.m.
   "C" Coy - 3.10 p.m.
   "B" Coy - 3.30 p.m.

4. The Grenadier Officer will detail the necessary bombing parties from the Support Company and will arrange the posts in consultation with the O.C. Companies in the front line.

5. Lewis Guns will relieve before 1 p.m.

6. The Signalling Officer and Grenadier Officer will arrange to take over the lines and bomb stores respectively by 1 p.m.

7. Advance parties consisting of 1 Officer and 4 N.C.O's per Company will proceed to the trenches to take over trench stores before noon on the 29th inst. These parties will include a Grenadier N.C.O to take over bomb stores.

8. TRANSPORT. All Trench kit will be man handled.
   Blankets, Officers' spare kit and stores to be returned to Transport Lines will be left stacked at Company Headquarters under the charge of a reliable N.C.O. and a small loading party as a guard. This N.C.O. will be responsible for handing over the blankets etc., to his Company Qr. Mr. Sergt. on arrival of the Transport at night.

9. Ration parties will report to the Regimental Sergeant Major at 7.30 p.m.

R.C. Mayall
Capt. & Adjutant,
11th Northd. Fusiliers.

28th March 1916.

11 Nov
Army Form C. 2118.

7 43
XXIII
9 Vol 3

WAR DIARY
or
INTELLIGENCE SUMMARY.
(Erase heading not required.)

Instructions regarding War Diaries and Intelligence Summaries are contained in F.S. Regs., Part II. and the Staff Manual respectively. Title pages will be prepared in manuscript.

Place	Date	Hour	Summary of Events and Information	Remarks and references to Appendices
"A" Batt.n CALONNE Section	1/4/16		Enemy shelled the RUE du TEMPLE (Bn. HQ) and CALONNE in retaliation – French aeroplane brought down behind the right of our line during the afternoon – at 4.30pm our torpedo guns & Stokes Mortars loosed off our heavy retaliation from its Boche – considerable activity with rifle grenades opposite right of our line throughout the night – Capt. S.C. Wells retired to ETAPLES – relief orders received.	R.E. Waygall
	2/4/16		Enemy shelled the RUE de TEMPLE during the morning – in afternoon heavy rifle grenade fire against our centre company silenced by artillery fire – one killed and S.I. wounded – returned in evening by 10th N.F. by 7pm and proceeded to "D" Position to Bully	R.E. Waygall
BULLY GRENAY	3/4/16		GRENAY found about 550 men for working parties and 60 men for ammunition party at Div. HQ.	R.E. Waygall
"D" Batt.n	4/4/16		Usual working parties amounting to 430 men found by battalion – 450 men battal.	R.E. Waygall
	5/4/16		Working parties of 500 men found for the R.E. – Relief orders issued	R.E. Waygall
"A" Batt.n CALONNE Section	6/4/16		Battalion relieved the 10th N.F. in "A" Junction – A Coy in Support – B Coy on right – D Coy in Centre and C Coy on left – commenced to leave billets at 6.30pm, relief complete 8.57p – Very quiet day – enemy shelled the right company about 5pm, wounding two men of B Coy – enemy again shelled the slag heap about 10pm and retaliation was called for by our left company.	R.E. Waygall
	7/4/16		Enemy shelled the RUE DU TEMPLE all morning – retaliation was tardy and weak – very quiet day in the front line – no casualties	R.E. Waygall
	8/4/16		Enemy artillery active throughout the day – our artillery cut wire – enemy trench mortar very active against its centre company – one killed and five wounded – Q.M.S. Warner returned from his leave from the course in England – left Q.M.S. Warner – Parker wounded slightly.	R.E. Waygall
	9/4/16		At 4.20am our batteries fired two salvoes accompanied by trench mortars and rifle grenades – enemy retaliated about 6am in centre company into trench.	R.E. Waygall

W.25+1/1454 700,000 5/15 D.D.&L. A.D.S.S./Forms/C. 2118.

Army Form C. 2118.

WAR DIARY
or
INTELLIGENCE SUMMARY.
(Erase heading not required.)

Instructions regarding War Diaries and Intelligence Summaries are contained in F.S. Regs., Part II. and the Staff Manual respectively. Title pages will be prepared in manuscript.

Place	Date	Hour	Summary of Events and Information	Remarks and references to Appendices
"A" Batt". Fire Trench.	10/4/16.	(cont.)	At 1.30pm our artillery began a three hour intense bombardment of enemy's lines culminating in an intense bombardment for 10 minutes at 4.30pm — Enemy candles were let off. Sound of gongs, gas and sirens were heard from the enemy lines — our left company was severely damaged several times by enemy retaliation. 10 men of B.3 D.L.I. sent up in its evening to repair item — on casualties were Capt H.M. Ferraio wounded — one man killed, one wounded, one shell shock and one accidentally injured. All of "C" Company — Very quiet night.	R.E. Knoyle.
	11/4/16.		Enemy shelled our left and centre extensively between 1.15 pm & 4.2 pm and again between 12.45 pm at night by 10th N.F. and proceeded to "C" position — our battalion was directed to support B.L.M. in CALONNE taking over from 13th D.L.I. — Relief was complete at 9.50 pm.	R.E. Knoyle.
"C" Batt". Support Billets CALONNE.	12/4/16.		Usual working parties formed for R.E. etc 350 men Supplied. — Orders received that the 14th Instant all ranks ordered to rejoin their battalion and leave stopped from the 14th Instant — 2nd Lieut. Smith joined ready and was attached to "C" Company.	R.E. Knoyle.
	13/4/16.		Usual working parties of 350 men furnished for R.E. and 13th D.L.I. — Capt. Malcolm's leave extended to 19th inst — 29 officers on the battalion from leave — Capt. Malcolm apptd Second in Command of battalion and 891 other ranks.	R.E. Knoyle.
	14/4/16.		Usual working parties of 350 men furnished for R.E. and 13th D.L.I. — Strength return 29 officers 9.18 O.R. (includes details) — Capt. East of temporary hospital) — Relief Battalion received morning working parties formed but all ready vans at 8am and work till 12 noon — Battalion relieved 10th N.F. in "A" Position, starting from Billets in CALONNE at 2.30pm.	R.E. Knoyle.
"A" Batt". Fire Trench.	15/4/16.		and going up, with 1 minute interval between sections — "C" Company on right, "A" Company in centre and "B" Company on left — "D" Company in Support — Platoon, guns released by 12 noon — Relief complete at 4pm — Very quiet night — no casualties	R.E. Knoyle.

2353 Wt. W2544/1454 700,000 5/15 D.D.&L. A.D.S.S./Forms/C. 2118.

Army Form C. 2118.

WAR DIARY
or
INTELLIGENCE SUMMARY.
(Erase heading not required.)

Instructions regarding War Diaries and Intelligence Summaries are contained in F.S. Regs., Part II. and the Staff Manual respectively. Title pages will be prepared in manuscript.

Place	Date	Hour	Summary of Events and Information	Remarks and references to Appendices
"A" Position in	16/4/16		Advance Operation Orders for 18th inst. issued. – Very quiet day – at 11 p.m. we endeavoured to knock out its enemy's Sap at M.21.a.z.7. with six rounds from our torpedo gun, the enemy did not retaliate. – One man killed and one wounded of M.G. Section by Rifle Grenade.	R.E. Mayall
CALONNE.	17/4/16		Very quiet day – enemy shelled 16 Lt.W.F. company with heavy shell in morning and again during the afternoon, apparently searching for the torpedo gun. – Battalion Operation Orders for 18th inst. issued – no casualties.	R.E. Mayall
	18/4/16		Billeting party under 2/Lt. Lindsay started for HERSIN at 8.15 a.m. – Enemy shelled TAMWORTH trench and the slag heap on its left between 4 and 5.30 p.m. and put four heavy trench mortars into centre company – one man of 'A' Coy wounded at duty shell shock – our howitzers retaliated and silenced the enemy – the battalion was relieved by the 2nd South Stafford Regt – relief complete 10.50 p.m. – battalion proceeded to billets in HERSIN – The Battalion was billeted at 2.20 a.m. (19th) – Hq. of Battalion Map. 36.B.S.E. Q.6.c.1.7. – Total Casualties for period in trenches 48 (1 Killed) (11 Killed)	R.E. Mayall
HERSIN	19/4/16		Battalion rested and cleaned up all day. – Lieut Craig and 2.Lt. Watts from 3rd N.F. joined the battalion for duty. – Band began to practise again.	R.E. Mayall
	20/4/16		Battalion provided 300 men for work on SOUCHEZ Sector. – C.O. inspected billets of A&C Coys. – Medical Officers inspected B&D Coys	R.E. Mayall
Church Parade Position	21/4/16		Church Parade – Battalion provided 300 men for work. – C.O. inspected billets of B&D Coy. – Medical officer inspected A Coy.	R.E. Mayall
	22/4/16		Battalion provided 400 men for work in SOUCHEZ trenches but these were cancelled on account of bad weather.	R.E. Mayall
St. GEORGES DAY	23/4/16		Battalion Church Parade in morning. – Played 104th F. at football in afternoon and lead (3-2) – B Coy held the Shrieking Concert. – Capt. R.A.J. Berry joined for duty.	R.E. Mayall
	24/4/16		Enemy shelled HERSIN Station between 6 a.m. and 9 a.m. – G.O.C. Division inspected the Battalion at work at 9.45 a.m. – Two men of reserve battalion wounded by enemy shelling station.	R.E. Mayall

WAR DIARY or INTELLIGENCE SUMMARY

Army Form C. 2118.

Place	Date	Hour	Summary of Events and Information	Remarks and references to Appendices
HERSIN.	25/4/16		Enemy shelled the town in the early morning – the Battalion furnished 370 men for working parties. Capt R.A.J. Berry and 2/Lt. E.C. Clogg joined for duty on 24th – Band played three times	R.E. Heyall
	26/4/16		The Battalion paraded 276 strong at 8.40am to march to DIVION – Order of March Band, A.B. C.D. M.G. H.Q. 1st line transport – 370 men on working parties. Arrived BARLIN, RUITZ & route BARLIN, RUITZ – Arrived 12.30pm, very hot march, 28 men fell out – M.O. followed in motor lorries and arrived about 1.40pm – M.O. began to inoculate the battalion, doing half HQ, M.G. and transport – H.Q. at 36.b.7, 9.24.b.2.6.	R.E. Heyall
DIVION 9.24.b. 36.b.	27/4/16		M.O. inoculated one platoon of each company – Battalion cannot at training according to scheme.	R.E. Heyall
	28/4/16		Battalion found 350 men for working parties all day – Companies had one platoon each resting after inoculation – Lieut Nattcott left for the Base – Capt Malcolm rejoined from leave.	R.E. Heyall
	29/4/16		Companies & squadron in working under their own arrangements – classes and practices the whole battalion went through gas demonstration in afternoon – 2/Lt. Hewitt from the Cottonian Guards joined for duty – 4 platoons inoculated.	R.E. Heyall
	30/4/16		Officers tactical exercise in morning – 31 officers + 905 O.R. – Battalion had Names of the Baths – Officers and N.C.O's paraded at Nemoun to PERNES.	R.E. Heyall

R.E. Heyall
Captain Adjutant
for O.C. 11th North'd Fus'rs

30/4/16

S E C R E T.

BATTALION OPERATION ORDERS FOR 2ND APRIL 1916.

1. The 11th N.F. will be relieved in "A" position by the 10th N.F., and will proceed on relief to "D" position, taking over from 13th D.L.I.
   Companies will take over the same billets as they occupied when the Battalion was last in "D" position.

2. The 10th N.F. will commence to leave billets at 5.30 p.m., and the 11th will withdraw to BULLY via CALONNE SUD.

3. Lewis Guns will be relieved before noon.

4. No trench will be vacated by relieved Battalion until occupied by relieving Battalion.

5. Billeting parties, consisting of 1 Officer and 4 N.C.O's per Company will proceed to billets to take over billet fixtures on the morning of the 2nd. The Grenadier Officer will arrange to take over all bomb stores during the afternoon.
   The Signalling Sergeant will arrange to take over the lines during the afternoon.
   The Regimental Sergeant Major will arrange to relieve the permanent guards in "D" position during the afternoon.

6. All Officers' kits, mess kits, stores etc., will be man handled down the trench to CALONNE SQUARE by 5.30 p.m. An N.C.O. and 4 men per Company will remain in charge of the baggage and will hand it over to their Company Qr.Mr.Sergt. on arrival of the Transport.

7. The Transport Officer will arrange with the Transport Officer of the 10th N.F. to have as few wagons on the road as possible during the relief. For this purpose the blanket wagons which bring our blankets to BULLY could take back the blankets of 10th N.F. from CALONNE, and the 10th N.F. ration carts could take back our stores to BULLY.
   The Transport Officer will arrange to send up the horses to take the field kitchens and water carts from CALONNE SQUARE to BULLY.

R C Mayall
Capt. & Adjutant,
11th Northd. Fusiliers.

1st April 1916.

DAILY WORKING PARTIES IN "D" POSITION.

Item	No.	Coy.	Shovels	Picks	Rendezvous	Time	To	Hours	Work	Remarks
1.	10	M.G.			FOSSE 1. R.5.c.8.8.	10 a.m.	R.E.			
2.	20	M.G.	20	10	R.E.Stores, CALONNE.	8 p.m.	R.E.	4	Water supply.	New supply to ANGRES Section.
3.	9	H.G.			R.11.a.4.8.	6.15 p.m.	R.E.		Loading stores.	
4.	50	"D"			BERTHELOT STREET.	9 a.m.	R.E.	6	Reserve Line.	To be sent up in sections of 12 men each section to file into a house on E. side of road.
5.	50	"D"			BERTHELOT STREET	6 p.m.	R.E.		Reserve Line.	do. do. do. do.
6.	100 100	"A" "B"	200	100	RLY. BRIDGE, M.1.d.7.2.	7 p.m.	R.E.	4	CALONNE NORD.	Cutting Dakening CALONNE NORD
7.	15	"B"	15	5	RLY BRIDGE, M.1.d.7.2.	9 a.m.	R.E.		CALONNE NORD.	Cutting Dakening CALONNE NORD
8.	15	"B"			BULLY MARKET SQUARE R.5.c.8.2.	9 a.m.	R.E.			Report to 25th A.T. Coy. R.E.
9.	20	"B"	20	8	R.E. Stores, CALONNE.	7.30 p.m.	R.E.		SOGNY POST.	Construction of Strong Point.
10.	50	"B"	50	5	WEST END OF BOYAU CHAPTAL	6.30 p.m.	R.E.	4	Clearing trench.	R.E. guide on 1st night only at 7.R.5.c.8.8.

(i) Tools to be drawn from R.E. Store, BULLY GRENAY, R.5.c.8.8.
(ii) An Officer is to accompany each party of 50 or over.

THIS CANCELS ALL PREVIOUS INSTRUCTIONS.

3/4/16.

R C Hayell
Capt. & Adjutant,
11th Northd. Fusiliers.

G. Beaton & Son Ltd
James Sq.
Holland Park Lane.
Contract T/IV 1928.

40/20
From 100 light

SECRET.

AFTER ORDERS.

(i) Reference Relief Orders of this date, the following amendments are made:-

(a) Para.2. "D" Company — Centre.
            "C" Company — Left.

(b) Para.3. "D" Company — 6.45 p.m.
            "C" Company — 7 p.m.

R.C. Mayall
Capt. & Adjutant,
11th Northd. Fusiliers.

5/4/16.

"A" Form.
Army Form C. 2121.

MESSAGES AND SIGNALS.

No. of Message............

Prefix......... Code........... m.	Words	Charge	This message is on a/c of :	Recd. at.............. m.
Office of Origin and Service Instructions.				
....	Sent		.... Service.	Date...............
....	At.............. m.			From...............
....	To..............			
	By..............		(Signature of "Franking Officer.")	By...............

TO {

| * | Sender's Number | Day of Month | In reply to Number | **A A A** |

From				
Place				
Time				

The above may be forwarded as now corrected.   (Z)

....
Censor.   Signature of Addressor or person authorised to telegraph in his name.

* This line should be erased if not required.

(A1) C. Ltd., London— W.14042/M.44. 150,000 Pads. 12/15. Form C.2121.

SECRET.   BATTALION OPERATION ORDERS FOR 6TH APRIL 1916.
───

1. The 11th N.F. will relieve the 10th N.F. in "A" position, 10th N.F. proceeding to "D" position.

2. DISPOSITION.   "B" Company — Right.
                  "C" Company — Centre.
                  "D" Company — Left.
                  "A" Company — Support.

3. Companies will leave their billets at the following times, proceeding to the trenches via CALONNE SUD with intervals between platoons:—
   "B" Coy — 6.30 p.m.
   "C" : — 6.45 p.m.
   "D" : — 7.0 p.m.
   "A" : — 7.15 p.m.

4. Lewis Guns will be relieved after 3 p.m. The teams will proceed up to the trenches via CALONNE SUD, moving in small parties.

5. Advance parties, consisting of 1 Officer & 4 N.C.O's per Company, and Grenadier N.C.O's, will proceed to the trenches to take over trench stores after 3 p.m. on the 6th.
   The Grenadier Officer will arrange to take over all bomb stores after 3 p.m. on the 6th.
   The Regimental Sergt. Major will arrange to relieve all permanent guards, which do not come under Company arrangements, after 3 p.m.
   The Signalling Sergt. will arrange to take over lines after 3 p.m.

6. TRANSPORT. Two dumps will be established at each Company Headquarters, one for stores to be returned to Transport Lines and one for stores for trenches.
   All blankets, Officers' spare kits, etc., will be stacked at the former dump, and Officers' trench kits, etc., at the latter. A reliable N.C.O. and small loading party will be left in charge when the Companies move off, and will hand over to the Company Qr.Mr.Sergt. on arrival of the Transport.

7. The Transport Officer will arrange with the Transport Officer of the 10th N.F. for an interchange of wagons so as to have as little transport on the roads as possible.

8. Ration parties will report to the Regimental Sergeant Major at 8.15 p.m.

9. "Stand to" in the morning will be at 4 a.m. In the evening it is left to the discretion of Company Commanders.

                                        R.C. Mayall.
                                        Capt. & Adjutant,
                                        11th Northd. Fusiliers.
5/4/16.

To./O.C. "A" Coy.   SECRET.

    The following grenadiers of "A" Coy.
will report to "C" and "D" Coy. immediately
after teas this evening. They will be attached
to the respective companies while the Battalion
is in 'A' position for duty on bombing posts.
They should march up to the trenches in
front of the first platoon of the company
to which they are attached. Please arrange
for transferring their rations.

1 Sergt + 10 men to "C" Coy for Stag Post.
1 Cpl + 10 men to "D" Coy for Mine Post.

For information & necessary action

6/4/16
                          R.C. Mayall
                          Capt. Adjutant.

S E C R E T.   BATTALION OPERATION ORDERS FOR 10th APRIL 1916.

1. The 10th N.F. will relieve 11th N.F. in "A" position, 11th N.F. proceeding to "C" position, taking over from 13th D.L.I.
    Companies will occupy the same billets as previously.

2. IN CASE OF ALARM. The Battalion will immediately "stand to" as follows:-
    "A" Company - behind houses at Battalion ALARM POST.
    "B" Company - in their own cellars.
    "C" Company - 2 platoons will occupy the reserve line of defence North of HYDE PARK inclusive and HOUGEMONT HOUSE.
                    1 platoon will occupy HORSE GUARDS AVENUE.
                    1 platoon will occupy trench M.9.c.2½.3. to M.9.c.5.5.
    "D" Company - in their own cellars.

    2nd. Lt. R.W. Taylor is detailed as Officer in charge of details.

    The Orderly Officer will report at ADVANCED BRIGADE HEADQUARTERS.

    The attention of O.C. Companies is drawn to para. 6 of the Defence Scheme. With reference to this paragraph as soon as every platoon knows its own alarm post it should be dismissed for the night without further orders.

3. The 10th N.F. will commence to leave billets at 6.30 p.m., using CALONNE SUD. The 11th N.F. will withdraw to CALONNE via CALONNE NORD.

4. Lewis Guns will be relieved by daylight.

5. No trench will be vacated by relieved Battalion until occupied by relieving Battalion.

6. Advance parties, consisting of 1 Officer & 4 N.C.O's per Company, will proceed to CALONNE on the morning of the 10th to take over billets and billet fixtures.
    The Grenadier Officer will take over bomb stores during daylight.
    The Regimental Sergeant Major will arrange to relieve guards during the afternoon.

7. All Officers' kits, Company stores etc., will be man handled to billets during the afternoon. All fatigue parties of this nature will not leave their trench before 6 p.m., and will be clear of CALONNE SUD by 7 p.m. The CALONNE NORD must not be used for this purpose.

8. The Quartermaster will arrange for the blankets and Officers' spare kits to be brought up to the billets on the evening of the 10th inst.

R.C. Mayall
Capt. & Adjutant,
11th Northd. Fusiliers.

9/4/16.

DAILY WORKING PARTIES TO BE FOUND BY THE BATTALION IN "C" POSITION.

Item	No.	Coy.	Shov.	Picks	Rendezvous	Time	Report to	Hours	Work	Remarks.
1.	46 20	"A"	35	15	HYDE-PARK CORNER	7 p.m.	R.E.	4	TUNNEL TRENCH.	
2.	26 30	"A"	50	20	R.E.Store, CALONNE	9 a.m.	R.E.		TUNNEL TRENCH.	Day party for Item 1.
3.	50	"B"			R.E.Store, CALONNE	7 p.m.	R.E.		HOXTON ROAD.	Clearing, deepening & firestepping HOXTON ROAD.
4.	4.	"B"			R.E.Store, CALONNE	8 a.m.	R.E.	6	Clearing.	As detailed daily.
5.	6	"B"			R.E.Store, CALONNE	7.15 p.m.	R.E.	4	Unloading.	Unloading timber at R.E.Stores.
6.	24	"C"			AMPTHILL TUNNEL	7 p.m.	R.E.	6	Driving tunnel.	Tools on site. Continuous shifts day & night. 1st six at 7 p.m., 2nd at 1 a.m., 3rd at 7 a.m., and 4th at 1 p.m.
7.	20	"C"			R.E.Store, CALONNE	8 p.m.	R.E.	4	M.G.emplacement.	Carrying party for item 13 and observation post.
8.	20	"C"	15	5	R.E.Store, CALONNE	7.30 p.m.	R.E.	4	HYDE PARK	Firestepping HYDE PARK Trench and driving tunnel.
9.	25	"D"			MARBLE TUNNEL, H.Q. CALONNE.	2 p.m.	R.E.	4	Deepening CALONNE NORD.	
10.	6	"D"			MARBLE ARCH	9 a.m.	Pioneers		Labour for Pioneer party revetting & reclaiming WALL STREET.	
11.	20	"D"			MARBLE ARCH	7 p.m.	do.		do.	do.
12.	30	"D"			H.Q., 23rd Div. Tunnelling Coy.; RUE DE TEMPLE, CALONNE.	7 p.m.	Tunnellers			
13.	18	M.G.	15	5	HYDE PARK CORNER	9 a.m.	R.E.	6	M.G.emplacements.	3 reinforced concrete emplacements in reserve-line.
14.	10	M.G.			R.E.Store, CALONNE	6 p.m.	R.E.		M.G.emplacement at SIEGE 5.	
15.	6	H.Q.			R.E.Store, CALONNE	6.30 p.m.	R.E.		AMPTHILL TUNNEL.	Carrying party for Item 6.

(1) An Officer will accompany Items 1 & 3.
(2) The first shift of In Item No.6 will commence work at the first detailed hour after our relief is complete, i.e. 1 a.m.
(3) Headquarters of the East Anglian Coy., R.E. are at M.14.a.5.4.

9/4/16.
R.K. Haynal
Capt. & Adjutant, 11th N.F.

S E C R E T.

BATTALION OPERATION ORDERS FOR 15TH APRIL 1916.

1. The 11th N.F. will relieve the 10th N.F. in "A" position, the 10th N.F. taking over billets in "C" position.

2. DISPOSITION.   Right Company - "C".
   Centre   :   - "A".
   Left   :   - "B".
   Support   :   - "D".

3. Companies will move off at the following times and will maintain an interval of 100 yards between platoons:-

   "C" Coy - 2.30 p.m. via CALONNE SUD.
   "A" : - 2.45 p.m. via CALONNE SUD.
   "B" : - 3 p.m. via CALONNE NORD.
   "D" : - 3.15 p.m. via shortest route.

4. LEWIS GUNS will relieve before noon, proceeding to trenches via CALONNE NORD, relieved teams withdrawing via CALONNE SUD.

5. Advance parties, consisting of 1 Officer, 4 N.C.O's and BOMBING N.C.O. per Company, will proceed to trenches to take over Trench Stores before noon on the 15th.
   The Bombing Officer will arrange to take over all Bomb Stores before noon on the 15th.
   The Signalling Officer will arrange to take over all lines before noon on the 15th.
   The Regimental Sergeant Major will arrange to relieve all Guards by 2.30 p.m. on the 15th.

6. All Officers' kits, mess kits and Trench stores will be man handled and will follow immediately in rear of the Company so as not to block the relieved Battalion.

7. All Officers' spare kits, blankets and stores to be returned to the Transport, will be stacked at Company Headquarters and left under the charge of a reliable N.C.O. and small loading party who will act as guard. The N.C.O. will be responsible for handing over to the Company Qr.Mr. Sergt., on the arrival of the Transport at night.

8. The Transport Officer will arrange with the Transport Officer of the 10th N.F. for an interchange of wagons so as to have as little Transport on the roads as possible.

9. Ration parties will report to the Regimental Sergeant Major in CALONNE SQUARE at 8.30 p.m.

10. "STAND TO" in the morning will be at 3.45 a.m. In the evening it is left to the discretion of Company Commanders.

11. O.C. "D" Company will detail the following Bombing parties for attachment to Companies in the front line:-

    1 Sergt. & 10 men to "B" Company for SLAG POST.
    1 Corpl. & 10 men to "A" Coy for MINE POST.

    Each Company will detail the same two men who were attached to the Brigade Machine Gun Company during the last tour in front line to report to Lieut. Frost for similar duty at 5 p.m. on the 15th.

continued:-

To/- O.C., SECRET.

" " Company.

With reference to para. 6 of Battalion Operation Order for Relief on 10th inst., please note that your Advance Parties will not proceed from the trenches before 11 a.m., as in the event of the Operations postponed today taking place tomorrow, the Relief will not take place until the 11th inst.

R.C. Mayall
Capt. & Adjutant,
11th Northd. Fusiliers.

"A" Form.
MESSAGES AND SIGNALS.

Army Form C. 2121.
No. of Message............

Prefix............ Code............m.	Words	Charge	This message is on a/c of :	Recd. at................... m.
Office of Origin and Service Instructions.				
	Sent		............................Service.	Date........................
	At............................m.			From....................
	To			
	By		(Signature of "Franking Officer.")	By

TO {

| * | Sender's Number | Day of Month | In reply to Number | A A A |

From				
Place				
Time				

The above may be forwarded as now corrected.   **(Z)**

.... Censor.   Signature of Addressor or person authorised to telegraph in his name.

* This line should be erased if not required.
(A1) C. Ltd., London— W.14042/M.44. 150,000 Pads. 12/15. Form C.2121.

B.O.O. FOR 15TH APRIL. SHEET 2.

The Regimental Sergeant Major will detail two men for duty as observers to report to the Intelligence Officer at No.1 Observation Post immediately on completion of relief.

12. O.C. Companies are requested to ensure that the "taking over" returns submitted to Orderly Room on completion of relief are as exact as possible, as these returns will form the basis of the lists to be handed over to the new Brigade at the end of the tour.

14/4/16.

R.C. Mayall.
Capt. & Adjutant,
11th Northd. Fusiliers.

S E C R E T.

ADVANCE BATTALION OPERATION ORDERS FOR 18TH APRIL 1916.

Reference Map 1/40,000 Sheets 36B and 36C.

1. The 68th Brigade will be relieved by 6th Infantry Brigade in CALONNE SECTION on night 18/19th April.

2. The 11th N.F. will be relieved in "A" position by the 2nd. South Staffs., and will proceed on relief via BULLY GRENAY and PETIT SAINS to billets in HERSIN.
   Units of the 6th Brigade will use CALONNE NORD, which will be reserved for traffic to CALONNE only on the 18th. CALONNE SUD will be reserved for traffic from CALONNE.

3. No Company will move before arrival of relieving Company.

4. No movements on the road East of BULLY GRENAY are to be made in larger bodies than sections with 100 yards interval.

5. Platoon Commanders will see that all their Section commanders are made familiar with the route to HERSIN on the map before the 18th.

6. All Trench Stores, maps, photographs and log books will be handed over on relief to the 2nd South Staffs. A receipted copy of the handing over return will be sent in to Battalion Headquarters the following day.

7. Lewis Guns will be relieved by daylight. Time of relief will be given later.

8. All Transport of the 68th Infantry Brigade will be WEST of GRANDE PLACE BULLY GRENAY by 10 p.m. No Transport of the 6th Brigade will be EAST of the above spot until after that hour.

9. The 68th Brigade Headquarters will close at BULLY GRENAY on completion of relief and re-open at COUPIGNY.

10. Companies will report completion of relief both in trenches and at HERSIN.

11. The Transport Officer will send down the horses for the Field Kitchens and for one water cart on the night of the 17th inst., and Companies must make arrangements for cooking in their dixies for the 18th inst.
    Brick fire-places can be made in the SQUARE at CALONNE or in the trenches at the discretion of Company Commanders.

12. All details of Advance parties and billeting parties and approximate times of relief will be notified later.

13. PLEASE ACKNOWLEDGE.

R.C. Mayall
Capt. & Adjutant,
11th Northd. Fusiliers.

16/4/16.

S E C R E T.

BATTALION OPERATION ORDERS FOR 18TH APRIL 1916.

To be read in conjunction with Advance Orders issued 16/4/16.

1. **BILLETING PARTIES.** A Billeting party, consisting of the following Officers, N.C.O's and men will report to the Town Major, HERSIN, tomorrow morning the 18th at 11 a.m. The senior Officer will then receive a list of billets and will be responsible for the billeting of the Battalion:-
    2nd.Lt. R.Lindsay.
    2nd.Lt. E.G.Bowers.
    Transport Officer (2nd.Lt. Maclachlan.)
    Regimental Quartermaster Sergeant.
    4 N.C.O's per Company.
    1 N.C.O. each from Headquarters, Machine Gun,
    Transport & Qr.Mr's Dept.

    The N.C.O's from the trenches will report to 2nd.Lt. Lindsay at Advanced Brigade Headquarters at 8.15 a.m. and will proceed direct to HERSIN, moving in two small parties along the BULLY - HERSIN Road. The Transport and Qr.Mr's Dept. will proceed independently.

    The N.C.O's will meet their platoons and Specialists sections on arrival of the Battalion at night, at Railway Crossing Q.6.d.4.5. at 12 midnight.

2. **TRANSPORT ARRANGEMENTS.** Each Company will establish a Dump in CALONNE SQUARE, in charge of a reliable N.C.O. with small loading party. All Officers' kits, mess kits, and Company stores, will be taken to these Dumps before 8.15 p.m.; but no fatigue party must leave the front line trenches before 7.15 p.m. on any account. The Transport Officer will detail one limber wagon to each Company and Headquarters and two limber wagons to the Machine Gun Section. The Officers' baggage wagon and mess cart will also be brought down.
    The Regimental Sergeant Major will detail a reliable Sergeant to be in full charge of all Dumps and loading parties at CALONNE SQUARE.
    The loading parties will follow their wagons and be responsible for unloading at HERSIN.

3. **ADVANCE PARTIES.** Advance parties of the 2nd.South Staffs will come to the trenches during daylight on the 18th to take over all trench stores etc.

4. **TIME OF RELIEF.** The 2nd.South Staffs will commence to leave BULLY at 8 p.m.

5. **CLEANLINESS.** The Commanding Officer wishes all ranks to pay the greatest attention to leaving the trenches clean and in a sanitary condition. He wishes to draw particular attention to the necessity for cleaning up the Right and Centre Companies and all Bombing posts.
    Every endeavour should be made to leave all trenches and posts in as clean a condition as they were found when we took over.

RC Mayall
Capt. & Adjutant,
11th Northd. Fusiliers.

17/4/16.

SECRET.

BATTALION OPERATION ORDERS FOR 26TH APRIL 1916.

1. The Brigade will move into the DIVION Area for training, on Wednesday 26th April, the 11th N.F. being billeted at DIVION.

2. The Head of the Battalion will pass the Headquarter Mess at 8.40 a.m.
ORDER OF MARCH - A, B, C, D, Machine Gun, Headquarters, 1st Line Transport. There will be 100 yards interval between Companies, which will be maintained throughout the march.
ROUTE - Road Junction Q.4.b.9.9. (9 a.m.), BARLIN, RUITZ, HOUDAIN and DIVION.
The Band will play each Company in turn for one hour, commencing with "A" Company.

3. LOADING ARRANGEMENTS. Officers' kits will be stacked ready for loading either at the Headquarter Mess or at the Orderly Room by 8 a.m. The Officers' Mess Cart will be sent round to collect mess kits by 8.15 a.m. All Blankets, mens' spare kits, Company Stores etc., will be stacked at the Qr.Mr's stores by 7 a.m. Officers' Mess kit, over and above that sent with the Mess cart will be stacked there by that hour.

   Loading parties of 1 N.C.O. and 6 men per Company will report to the Orderly Officer at the Qr.Mr's stores by 7.45 a.m. The Orderly Officer will be responsible for all loading and will remain in HERSIN for three hours after the departure of the Battalion. He will make a tour of inspection round the billets and collect any claims which the owners may wish to make. The Transport Officer will provide him with a horse.

4. BILLETING PARTY. One N.C.O. from each Company (Qr.Mr.Sgts if possible), 1 from Headquarters, 1 from Lewis Detachment and 1 from Transport will parade at the Orderly Room at 8 a.m. unless otherwise ordered.
   The Signalling Corporal is responsible that seven cycles are at the Orderly Room at that hour.

5. RELIEF. The 9th Yorks will probably relieve the 11th N.F. in HERSIN. As it is impossible for the former to send Advance parties on to take over billets, the Commanding Officer trusts that Companies will take special care to leave billets clean and wholesome.

6. GUIDES. The Regimental Sergeant Major will detail three N.C.O's to report at Brigade Headquarters, COUPIGNY, at 8 a.m. to guide three motor lorries to our Qr.Mr's stores.

7. REVEILLE will be at 5.30 a.m. tomorrow. Breakfasts at 7.15 a.m.

R C Mayall

Capt. & Adjutant,
11th Northd. Fusiliers.

25/4/16.

11th Northern (?)
Army Form C. 2118.
Vol II

WAR DIARY
or
INTELLIGENCE SUMMARY.
(Erase heading not required.)

Place	Date	Hour	Summary of Events and Information	Remarks and references to Appendices
DIVION	1/5/16		Battalion carried out training in morning under company arrangements - in the afternoon rounds were practiced by each company on the trenches at 36.b.T.31.b. - H.Q. played the staff then leave at football evening (2-nil) - Operation Order to 1st Army issued. Provided 325 men for working parties - remainder of battalion paraded for route march under Capt. Walsh at 9.30am. - Billeting party under 2/Lt. Lindsay started for BEAUMETZ AIRES at 7am.	R.E. Royall
	2/5/16			R.E. Mayer
	3/5/16		Moved to BEAUMETZ (motored until 5 ½ mile - Capt. Swann alt. 100 spare men led the rest of the trenches at T.31.b. in the morning - companies carried out training in the afternoon.	Retrayall
	4/5/16		Companies did route marches and training in morning - in afternoon Capt. Swann party paraded.	Retrayall
	5/5/16		Battalion started to march for manoeuvre area at 7.40am. - arriving at BEAUMETZ-LES-AIRES about 3.20pm - 104 men fell out on the line of march (A Coy. - 19; B Coy. - 35; C Coy. - 16; D Coy. - 22; H.Q. - 5; - M.G.O) - 5 officers attended lecture on M.G. at PERNES - all men had rejoined battalion by staff parade.	Retrayall
BEAUMETZ LES AIRE	6/5/16		Battalion paraded at 9am and marched out to training area near BONY - Companies did the attack - in afternoon parade for men who fell out on line of march. - Battn. paraded 605 strong	Retrayall
	7/5/16		Battalion paraded at 8am and marched to training area round REGLINGHEM - Companies did attack and rear guard action - parade 628 strong - Companies did musketry drill near drill - parade for men who fell out in the morning.	Retrayall
	8/5/16		Battalion paraded for half battalion in attack and defence at 8am. - 610 strong - musketry & close order drill in afternoon - A Coy's Bombers in competition	Retrayall
	9/5/16		Battalion paraded for manoeuvres 698 strong - marched out but returned 11.30am owing to hurricane - no afternoon parade.	Retrayall
	10/5/16		Battalion paraded at 8am - 602 strong out training under company arrangements. - afternoon parades under company arrangements.	Retrayall
	11/5/16		Battalion paraded at 7am - 598 strong - Battn. was in reserve and carried out a flank attack went 3.30pm - Battn. was in reserve returning to billets for Brigade Day	Retrayall

WAR DIARY
or
INTELLIGENCE SUMMARY.
(Erase heading not required.)

Army Form C. 2118.

Instructions regarding War Diaries and Intelligence Summaries are contained in F. S. Regs., Part II. and the Staff Manual respectively. Title pages will be prepared in manuscript.

Place	Date	Hour	Summary of Events and Information	Remarks and references to Appendices
BEAUMETZ LEZ AIRE.	12/5/16		Battalion paraded at 7am for fatigues in the attack and digging on state trenches 600 strong – afternoon parades and training parties.	RE Reayah
	13/5/16		Brigade Fatigue cancelled owing to wet weather – Companies shot rook in morning under their own arrangements – ordinary afternoon parades	RE Reayah
	14/5/16		Battalion did arents march 566 strong in morning – Company parades in afternoon	RE Reayah
	15/5/16		Brigade Day cancelled owing to wet weather. Battalion did rute march in afternoon – 2/Lt. J. Moffatt reported for duty	RE Reayah
	16/5/16		Battalion paraded for Brigade General returning about 4 pm	RE Reayah
	17/5/16		Battalion parades 546 strong for parties in Reaygnes Section – no afternoon parades except M.I.	RE Reayah
	18/5/16		Battalion paraded and marched to rueu hts to bathe – in afternoon companies their inspected billets	RE Reayah
	19/5/16		Battalion paraded ready to move off at 7.30am and marched to PERNES – 4 men fell out, 3 to hospital – entrained at PERNES and detrained at BARLIN about 4 pm – billeted at Cité du Fosse 7.	RE Reayah
BARLIN.	20/5/16		C.O. Adjt. O.C. Coys reconnoitred the line in the morning – battalion paraded ready to move off at 5:30pm – marched to A Section of SOUTH EZ section in evening relieving 2nd Nor Fants – relief complete 9pm – Battn Hq R. 27. b. 4. 4.	RE Reayah
SOUCHEZ SECTOR Bn.	21/5/16		Were kept under intense bombardment from batteries from 3 hrs throughout the day and following night – between 6 am and 8 pm the effect of the enemy's lachrymatory shells was felt in all sectors by our men – Enemy attacked the 47th and 15th Divisions on our right – There was intermittent shelling of our battery positions behind RE BOIS DE NOULETTE thought the day – Preliminary defense scheme for A Bells horner – Lt Cot Coffin beyond from leave – all leave suspended for the present.	RE Reayah — RE Reayah
	22/5/16			RE Reayah

Army Form C. 2118.

WAR DIARY
or
INTELLIGENCE SUMMARY.
(Erase heading not required.)

Instructions regarding War Diaries and Intelligence
Summaries are contained in F. S. Regs. Part II.
and the Staff Manual respectively. Title pages
will be prepared in manuscript.

Place	Date	Hour	Summary of Events and Information	Remarks and references to Appendices
"D" Battⁿ	23rd May		Enemy shelled our heavy guns behind BOIS DE NOULETTE during early morning — There was very heavy shelling between 7.30 pm and 12 midnight on our right — Advance Infantry proceeded to trenches in evening.	R.E. Wayell
	24th May		Operation Orders for 26th issued in morning — Advance parties proceeded to trenches — working parties furnished — Rained heavily — Gas Alert received.	R.E. Wayell
"A" Battⁿ	25th May		The Battalion relieved the 10th N.F. in "A" trench SOUCHEZ — Companies eastern from BOIS DE NOULETTE at 8 pm with the intervals — Frontage from SOUCHEZ RIVER on right to S.2.C.1.8 — A Coy in front line on right with 3 pl. & 1 in support — C Coy in support at SUNKEN Road — D Coy 2 platoons at SOUCHEZ Sth S.2.C.6.4 and 2 in Headquarters reserve — Relief completed at 12 midnight — Rations and R.E. Stores carried up by 13 D.L.I. Battⁿ — C Coy went under R.E. — A. Coy & B on wire fatigue — remainder of Battⁿ.	R.E. Wayell
SOUCHEZ I S.1.b.3 & a.0 front line.	26th May		Very quiet day — enemy's snipers on VIMY Ridge very active especially against left company — one man of B Coy wounded — work on VELMA communication trench — defending front line and wiring all along.	R.E. Wayell
	27th May		Very quiet day — two small trench fights between Saskatoon & right entry. Lt Frost shot German observer — work on VELMA tunnel front line and Front 1₃ & D₁ — Rgt. Bde 1st D₁ HEADQUARTER Trench to SUNKEN Rd — S.O.S. from left Bn. of Rgt Bde 1st Dⁿ at 11.5 pm — Stood down 11.55 pm — 2 men of B Coy wounded.	R.E. Wayell
	28th May		Very quiet day — one man of "A" Coy wounded and one man of Snipers Claim to have killed a Boche — Considerable artillery activity on our left.	R.E. Wayell
"C" Battⁿ X.10.b.5.1	29th May		Battalion Operation Orders for 30th issued — Our snipers claimed 2 Boches.	R.E. Wayell
	30th May		Quiet day — the Battalion was relieved in "A" trench by 10th N.F and proceeded to Eferdun NOTRE DAME DE LORETTE — Relief complete 5.45am — A⁰ Coy in huts, B R.E. Wayell C Coy in support — D in reserve — Battⁿ in ABLAIN ST NAZAIRE.	R.E. Wayell

2353. Wt. W2544/1454 700,000 5/15 D.D.&L. A.D.S.S./Forms/C. 2118.

Army Form C. 2118.

WAR DIARY
or
INTELLIGENCE SUMMARY.

(Erase heading not required.)

Place	Date	Hour	Summary of Events and Information	Remarks and references to Appendices
"C" Position N.D. de LORETTE.	May 31st		The relief was complete at 5.45 a.m. - Companies cleaned up its day - one Platoon from reserve Company took over from Platoon of Support Company at night - D. Coy sent up wiring parties of 30 men to A - B. Coys in front line - Strength of Battalion 32 Officers + 995 O.R. (nominal)	RCMayall

June 1st 1916.

R C Mayall
Captain & Adjutant
11th Northumberland Fusiliers.

SECRET.

BATTALION OPERATION ORDERS FOR 3RD MAY 1916.

1. The Brigade will move into the Manoeuvre Area on Wednesday 3rd May, 11th N.F. being billeted at BEAUMETZ - LES AIRES.

2. The Battalion will start from the H.Q. Mess at 7.40 a.m. in the following order - C, D, A, B, Headquarters, Lewis Detachment, 1st Line Transport. 100 yards interval between Companies.

   ROUTE:- I.17.c.2.0. (8 a.m.) CAMBLAIN CHATELAIN, PERNES, SAINS LES PERNES, FIEFS LAIRES, BEAUMETZ.

   The Battalion will halt for ten minutes before each clock hour and at the 4th halt (12 noon) there will be a halt of 1½ hours for dinners. Cookers will follow immediately in rear of their Companies.

3. Instructions for billeting parties will be issued later.

4. LOADING ARRANGEMENTS. All Officers' kits will be stacked at the Qr.Mr's Stores by 6.30 a.m. All blankets, mens' spare kits, Company stores and spare Officers' mess kits will be stacked at the Qr.Mr's stores by 6 a.m.

   The Officers' mess cart will collect two Officers' mess boxes per Company by 7.15 a.m.

   O.C. Companies will detail 1 N.C.O. and six men as loading parties to report to the Regimental Sergeant Major at the Qr.Mr's Stores at an hour to be notified later.

   The Orderly Officer will superintend all loading and will remain in DIVION for three hours after the departure of the Battalion to settle any claims which may be made.

5. All ranks are to be warned that anyone who falls out on the line of march will parade before the Medical Officer as soon after arrival as possible, and if there is no adequate cause his position on the leave allotment will be put back.

R C Heayate
Capt. & Adjutant,
11th Northd. Fusiliers.

2/5/16.

Haversack rations
& Dinners on arrival

SECRET.

BATTALION OPERATION ORDERS FOR 19TH AND 20TH MAY 1916.

ORDERS FOR 19TH INST.   MOVE TO BARLIN.

1. The Battalion will parade on the Battalion Parade ground ready to move off at 7.30 a.m.

2. The Battalion will march to PERNES via FIEFS, SAINS, entraining at 1.57 p.m. and detraining at BARLIN at 2.53 p.m. March to billets allotted by the Town Major.

3. Billetting parties will proceed to BARLIN by motor bus tomorrow. Details will be issued later.

4. Haversack Rations will be carried.

5. Greatcoats will be put in the spare kit bags. Mackintosh capes or ground sheets will be carried by the men.

6. The Transport will proceed by road, starting at 7.30 a.m. unless otherwise ordered. The Transport Officer will be responsible for seeing that no vehicle carries more than the load laid down for journeys exceeding 15 miles.
The Regimental Sergeant Major will detail three guides to meet three motor lorries at the entrance of the village of BEAUMETZ at 8 a.m. on the 19th.inst. These lorries will be kept at BARLIN overnight for use on the following day. No lorry is on any account to make more than one journey in one day.

7. ROUTINE.   REVEILLE - 5.30 a.m.
                     BREAKFASTS - 6.30 a.m.
   A dump will be established at the Cross Roads by the Church, of which the Orderly Officer will be in charge. Each Company will detail 1 N.C.O. and three men (from their worst marchers) to report to the Orderly Officer at the dump at 6 a.m.
   All blankets and spare kits will be stacked at the dump by 6 a.m. Officers' Kits, Qr.Mr's Stores, Company Stores and Orderly Room Stores will be stacked at the dump by 6.30 a.m.
   The Officers' Mess cart will be sent round to collect the two Officers' mess boxes per company at 6.45 a.m.

ORDERS FOR 20th. INST.   MOVE FROM BARLIN TO BOIS DE NOULETTE.

1. The 68th. Infantry Brigade will relieve the 24th. Infantry Brigade in the SOUCHEZ Section on the 20th.Inst., the 11th.N.F. relieving the 2nd.Northants. in "D" Position, i.e. Hutments in BOIS DE NOULETTE.

2. The Transport will proceed to FOSSE 10.

3. Lewis Guns and Trench Stores will be taken over by daylight.

4. No movement of troops to and from the trenches will take place East of the Line GOUY SERVINS - FOSSE 10 before 7.45 p.m.

5. Detailed oredrs will be issued later.

17/5/16.

R C Mayn
Captain & Adjutant.
11th. Northd. Fusiliers.

To/- O.C.,

      " " Company.

                                                18th May 1916.

    Reference Battalion Operation Orders for 19th inst. para.6, the Transport will start at 8 7 a.m.

Para.7. ROUTINE. All times therein mentioned will be advanced half an hour.

                                               R.C. Mayall

                                             Capt. & Adjutant,
                                          11th Northd. Fusiliers.

SECRET.

Battalion Operation Orders for 20th May 1916.

1. The Battn. will move to Huts in BOIS DE NOULETTE, starting from the Orderly Room at ~~xxxxxxxxxxxxxxxxxxxx~~ 5.30 p.m. this afternoon.
   Order of march - C, A, B, D. 100 yards interval between Companies.
   Platoon Sergeants, acting as guides will meet their platoons at AIX NOULETTE.

2. Baggage, blanket wagons, field kitchens, watercarts and Maltese cart will follow 100 yards in rear of the last Company.
   The Officers' Mess cart will collect the boxes from the messes at 5 ~~xxx~~ p.m.
   Officers' valises will be dumped at the Transport Field by 4 ~~xxx~~ p.m.

   Remainder of the 1st line Transport and the motor lorries will move off to the Transport Lines at a time to be detailed by the Transport Officer.

   RC Magee

   Capt. & Adjutant,
   11th Northd. Fusiliers.

20/5/16.

SECRET.   BATTALION OPERATION ORDERS FOR 25TH MAY 1916.

1. The 11th N.F. will relieve the 10th N.F. in "A" position, the 11th N.F. being relieved by the 13th D.L.I. in "D" position.

2. DISPOSITION.   "A" Coy, taking over from "A" Coy 10th N.F. in front line on right.
   "B" :, taking over from "D" Coy, 10th N.F. in front line on left.
   "C" :, taking over from "C" Coy 10th N.F. in support in SUNKEN ROAD.
   "D" :, taking over from "B" Coy 10th N.F. - 2 platoons at SOUCHEZ Station and 2 platoons in HEADQUARTER TRENCH.

3. ROUTE & START.   ROUTE for A, B, and D Coys - Tramline, ARRAS ROAD Trench, COMPANY ROAD TRENCH or RATION TRENCH.
   "C" Company - Most direct route.

   Companies will start at the following times:-
      "A" Coy at 8 p.m.
      "B" : at 8.20 p.m.
      "D" : at 8.40 p.m.
      "C" : at 9 p.m.

   Headquarters will follow the two Platoons of "D" Coy to HEADQUARTER TRENCH.
   O.C. Companies will have the route reconnoitred tonight.

4. ADVANCE PARTIES.   One Officer, 4 N.C.O's, 1 Bombing N.C.O. and 1 Lewis Gun N.C.O. per Company, will proceed to the trenches tonight, returning tonight when they have reconnoitred the Company Lines. One N.C.O. per Company may be left in tonight for the purpose of taking over trench stores etc. during daylight tomorrow.
   One N.C.O. of Headquarters, to be detailed by the Regtl. Sergt. Major will accompany the Advance Party of "D" Coy and will remain overnight to take over during daylight tomorrow.

5. LEWIS GUNS.   O.C. Lewis Detachment will make his own arrangements for sending up as much of his stores as possible as far as COLONEL'S HOUSE tonight. The Lewis Detachment should proceed with the first platoon of each Company so as to relieve the guns as early as possible.

6. TRANSPORT.   As carrying fatigues will be very heavy, only what is ABSOLUTELY ESSENTIAL will be taken to the trenches. All Officers' spare kits, spare mess kits, Company Orderly Room boxes, and Company Stores will be stacked near the Railway Line opposite the Orderly Room by 7.30 p.m. tonight 24th inst.
   Nothing must be left to go back to the Transport tomorrow night and all Officers must cut down their personal kit and mess kit to the lowest possible limit.

   All Officers' Kits and mess kits for the trenches will be stacked near the Railway Line opposite the Orderly Room by 7 p.m. tomorrow night. The Transport Officer will indent for the necessary trucks to convey these and the rations up to COLONEL'S HOUSE.
   The Regtl. Sergt. Major will detail all carrying parties from "C" Company.

R C Mayah

Capt. & Adjutant,
11th Northd. Fusiliers.

24/5/16.

SECRET.

BATTALION OPERATION ORDER FOR 30TH MAY 1916.

1. **RELIEF.** The 10th N.F. will relieve the 11th N.F. in "A" position, 11th N.F. relieving the 10th N.F. in "C" position as follows:-
(a) "C" and "D" Coys 10th N.F. will relieve "A" and "B" Coys 11th N.F., respectively.
(b) "A" and "B" Coys, 11th N.F. when relieved, will relieve "A" and "B" Coys 10th N.F. respectively in the front line trenches of NOTRE DAME.
(c) "A" and "B" Coys of 10th N.F. when relieved, will ~~take over the positions~~ relieve "C" & "D" Coys 11th N.F. respectively.
(d) "C" and "D" Coys, 11th N.F., when relieved, will take over the positions of "C" and "D" Coys 10th N.F. on NOTRE DAME with the following exceptions:-
   1 Platoon of "D" Coy 11th N.F. will take over from the isolated platoon of "C" Coy 10th N.F. at X.4.d.8.6. "C" Coy 11th N.F. have all four platoons together at R.34.c.5.5., "D" Coy 11th N.F. having only three platoons in the huts at R.32. central.
(e) Headquarters, 11th N.F. will take over, when relieved by H.Q., 10th N.F., the new Headquarters on NOTRE DAME at X.5.d.4.2.
(f) Lewis Guns, on relief, will proceed to the positions allotted to their respective Companies.

2. **ADVANCE PARTIES.** 1 Officer and 4 Junior N.C.O's per Coy., together with one Lewis Detachment N.C.O. and 1 Bombing N.C.O. per Coy, and One N.C.O. from Headquarters will proceed after dusk tonight via the BAJOLLE LINE to take over in the positions allotted to their Companies. They must return before daylight and must carefully reconnoitre the route as they will be responsible for guiding their Companies tomorrow night, no guides from 10th N.F. being available.
   Company Sergt. Majors of "A", "B" and "C" Coys., and the senior Sergt. of the two platoons of "D" Coy at Headquarters, will proceed to take over stores etc., in "C" position by daylight tomorrow. They will leave the trenches at 2 p.m.

3. **BAGGAGE.** All baggage, stores etc. will be man handled to the NOTRE DAME Defences via the BAJOLLE LINE. Each Company will be responsible for carrying all its baggage immediately in rear of the Company. One of the two platoons of "D" Coy in Headquarter Trench will assist with the Headquarter baggage. The N.C.O. in charge of this platoon must reconnoitre the route from Headquarters at X.5.d.4.2. to the Huts at R.32. central.

4. **TRANSPORT.** The Transport will move to GRAND SERVINS, taking over from 10th N.F., transport of 10th N.F. taking over from 11th N.F.

5. **RATION DUMP.** Ration Dump and position of water cart for "A" and "B" Coys and Headquarters ar at X.11.b.7.1.
   For "C" and "D" Coys at R.32. central.

6. **COMMAND.** Major the Earl of Lovelace will proceed with "A" and "B" Coys and will be in command until the arrival of the Commanding Officer.

7. **ROUTE.** The route will be via the BAJOLLE LINE.

R.C.Mayall

Capt. & Adjutant,
11th North'd. Fusiliers.

29/5/16.

Army Form C. 2118.

WAR DIARY or INTELLIGENCE SUMMARY.

(Erase heading not required.)

II North Fus
Vol 9
XXIII

Instructions regarding War Diaries and Intelligence Summaries are contained in F.S. Regs., Part II. and the Staff Manual respectively. Title pages will be prepared in manuscript.

June

Place	Date	Hour	Summary of Events and Information	Remarks and references to Appendices
"C" Battⁿ N.D. De LORETTE.	1.6.15		Quiet morning. In afternoon our artillery began to bombard enemy trenches on VIMY RIDGE at 4 pm – the 6th Infantry Brigade attacked at dusk. There was heavy artillery fire after midnight. Lieut. H.M.P. West reported for duty.	R.E. Marshall
	2.6.15		Quiet day. Provided 250 men for R.E. in evening for work in BATAILLE Line and Battle Line – this Fatⁿ Thinned out a much on the front line. Both Trenches were marked successes at last – our Companies were put under cover for ½ half.	Renwick
	3.6.15		Heavy artillery fire on SOUCHEZ II in morning. Quiet afternoon – about 2 pm S.O.S. SOUCHEZ II reced But Cancelled about 6.30 pm – provided 150 men for R.E. in BATAILLE line – shot time B.D. Coy moved up from R.32 central to S.I.B. Bijoux line	Renwick
	4.6.15		Quiet morning – Relieved the 11th M.F. in A Position at 2.30 am & went into Bt	Kakkonni
"A" Batt.	5.6.15.		Enemy very quiet & inclined to be friendly. Artillery very active on our Left – had no damage done to our own trenches. In the morning HMS Field shot a German Sniper who had been causing some annoyance.	Kakkonni
	6.6.15		1 Coy of 1st Anson Batt. attached to us for Instruction in trench warfare. Enemy very quiet again with exception of Artillery. Brgd. Bge Officer arrived and Enfiled our Trench.	Holden
	7.6.15		Enemy were more active on front line causing 4 casualties, in clearing 1 attached from Anson Battalion. At 10.30 Enemy [illegible] exploded a mine near [illegible] some 6 yards (Covered?) others left Rodicalm, this however got a failure since no Crater was caused.	
	8.6.15		Lieut Short endeavour to have a [illegible] and take a Prisoner to enfuture to obtain or make to do so. He examined the enemy was a slight Bombing attack took place. The Enemy answered up to However and he got hand without any Casualties	Holdein

2353 Wt. W2544/1454 700,000 5/15 D.D.&L. A.D.S.S./Forms/C. 2118.

Army Form C. 2118.

WAR DIARY
or
INTELLIGENCE SUMMARY.
(Erase heading not required.)

Instructions regarding War Diaries and Intelligence Summaries are contained in F. S. Regs. Part II. and the Staff Manual respectively. Title pages will be prepared in manuscript.

Place	Date	Hour	Summary of Events and Information	Remarks and references to Appendices
A' Baa	9:6:16		Brigadier Congratulated Lieut Goel on the Raid. Relieved by 9th Yorks and moved to trim 10. Relieved at 10:20. Arrived trim 10 at 2:30.	Kashmir
Trim 10	10:6:16		Received order to proceed to Boruin on following day. Party under Lieut Brown proceeded to Boruin to take over.	Kashmir
" "	11:6:16		Remainder of Bn. arrived at 10. am. and marched on to Boruin 1:30 arrived at Boruin 4:30 pm and marched to Rayan.	Kashmir
Boruin	12.6.16		Received new battledress. Marched to Trim leaving at 10 am and arriving Trim at 5.30 pm.	Kashmir
Verctin	13.6.16		Day spent in hour Parade and Inspection of kit.	Kashmir
"	14:6:16		Unit Parade. Battalion meeting. Received new Ensaee & Corps etc.	Kashmir
"	15:6:16		Marched to Coyeepne only 1 man fell out. marched off at 10 am arrived 12:45 am.	Kashmir
Coyeepne	16.6.16 17.6.16 18.6.16		Battalion steady drill. Quadrennial under Companies. Battalion reorder for attack scheme - returning to billets about 3.30 pm. Battalion marched out at 8:30 pm for Brigade attack returning to billets at 2 pm. - Dr. Mr. found new clothing	Rebayah. Rebayah.
	19.6.10.		Battalion Paraded at 6:45 am for Divisional attack on trenches returning about 2 pm - the battalion was in Brigade Reserve and found working and carrying parties	Rebayah
	20.6.10		Battalion did no work steady drill under Company arrangements - Cricket match Officers v Seyts in afternoon won by officers	Rebayah
	21.6.10		Battalion marched out at 8.25 am to practice in attack on trenches by battalion brigade - G.O.C. Divison presented Ribbons to 15 Bzt-	Rebayah

10 WF

Army Form C. 2118.

WAR DIARY
or
INTELLIGENCE SUMMARY.
(Erase heading not required.)

Instructions regarding War Diaries and Intelligence Summaries are contained in F. S. Regs., Part II. and the Staff Manual respectively. Title pages will be prepared in manuscript.

Place	Date	Hour	Summary of Events and Information	Remarks and references to Appendices
COYECQUES	22nd		Battalion marched out at 9.25am for practice in attack & tactical Brigade arrangements, returning to camp about 2 pm – finals in battalion bayonet competitions	Rehayall
	23rd		Battalion did one hours steady drill in morning – advance & practice orders issued – 800 shirts & pants served out.	Rehayall
	24.5		Battalion paraded ready to move off at 10am and marched to AIRE – entrained for and left station at 4.26 pm, proceeding via LILLERS, ST. POL, DOULLENS, AMIENS detraining at 12.15 am at LONGUEAU – at 1.15 pm battalion started to march via AMIENS to PICQUIGNY arriving 6am – C. Coy billeted at ST. PIERRE 21 men fell out on the line of march but all reported within an hour. Capt. P.N. Graham reported for duty at AIRE Station.	Rehayall
PICQUIGNY	25			Rehayall
	26.5		Companies made their own arrangements for close order drill, bayonet practice &c – lectures in its review – transfers of junior officers to other battalions carried out.	Rehayall
	27"		Brigade Divine Service cancelled owing to wet weather – companies had lectures in the morning and drill in the afternoon – Brigade sports cancelled. Orders for march to POULAINVILLE issued and preparations made – orders cancelled at 2/pm Brigade will remain in present billets overnight.	Rehayall
	28"		Battalion did a route march for 2½ hours in morning – parades under coy arrangements in afternoon.	Rehayall
POULAINVILLE	29"		Battalion paraded at 3.25 pm to march to billets in POULAINVILLE – 3 men fell out on line of march but all reported – arrived 7.30 pm and were billeted in POULAINVILLE.	Rehayall
	30"			

R.C. Haygall Cpt/Adjt.
1/5 Nor Ire Fus.

68th Bde.
23rd Div.

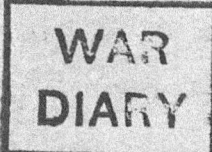

Brigade temporarily under orders
of 54th Division 16th to 20th July.

11th BATTALION

NORTHUMBERLAND FUSILIERS.

JULY 1916

Confidential.

War Diary
of
11th Service Battn Northumberland
Fusiliers

July 1916.

22.8.16.

R.E. Mayall
Capt Adjutant
for O.C. 11 North Fus

"A" Form. Army Form C. 2121.
MESSAGES AND SIGNALS. No. of Message............

23 / July
Army Form C. 2118.

WAR DIARY
INTELLIGENCE SUMMARY.
of 11th (S) Bn. Northumberland Fusiliers
Vol 10

(Erase heading not required.)

Instructions regarding War Diaries and Intelligence Summaries are contained in F. S. Regs., Part II. and the Staff Manual respectively. Title pages will be prepared in manuscript.

Place	Date	Hour	Summary of Events and Information	Remarks and references to Appendices
POULAINVILLE	1/7/16		Battalion rested in billets in POULAINVILLE all day - two communiqués received announcing success of British Hemel Advance on the Somme and to the north - the battalion paraded and moved off at an hours notice at 8.25pm and marched to FRANVILLERS on the main AMIENS-ALBERT RD -	Re Mayall
FRANVILLERS	2/7/16		Arrived at FRANVILLERS at 1am and were billeted in barns there - Battalion rested all day - Service of H.C. for C of E & C of Man. -	Re Mayall
MILLENCOURT	3/7/16		Tea - started 9.15 pm, arrived midnight. Battalion rested all day - in afternoon moved to bivouacs along the railway embankment E.9. South of ALBERT	Re Mayall
	4/7/16		Battalion rested in morning - in afternoon marched up to BÉCOURT WOOD and bivouaked there - in evening marched back to Railway Embankment and bivouaked there for the night.	Re Mayall
	5/7/16		Battalion rested in the morning and in afternoon moved to billets and bivouacs in ALBERT	Re Mayall
Front line Sydney	6/7/16		Battalion marched to BÉCOURT WOOD at 9.30am - party of fifteen proceeded during day to the trenches to reconnoitre. The Horse Shoe taken by the Yorks 10th West Riding - at 10pm the battalion left BÉCOURT Chateau to relieve the 12th D.L.I. in the line - relief was complete at 4am. - Orders issued for the battalion to attack the enemy's line along the road running East from LA BOISELLE TO CONTALMAISON between points X.16.b.1.3. and X.16.b.2.5. with a first objective along the front edge of BAILIFF WOOD (57 D S.E)	Re Mayall
	7/7/16		Artillery began heavy bombardment on objective at 7.20am - 24th Bde on our right commenced to attack CONTALMAISON at 8am. - 9th Welsh Regt. on our left attacked at 8.30am towards road to CONTALMAISON - 9th WELSH charged directly over our front and on finding that they had arrived at the Objective almost an hour before the barrage was to lift (9.30am) retired in the direction from whence - the enemy at 9am commenced a very heavy barrage on our line - at 9.15am two patrols of bombers one under Lieut E.G Bowes and the other under 2/Lt MOFFAT started bombing up the Sunken road on the right and the bn. system the left	Re Mayall

WAR DIARY or INTELLIGENCE SUMMARY

Army Form C. 2118

9th (S) Bn. N(orthumberland) Fusiliers

Place	Date	Hour	Summary of Events and Information	Remarks and references to Appendices
Bécordel	8/7/16		They were immediately followed by four patrols from C & D Companies who worked their way across the open – at 9.30 am with A and B Coys in support. The Battalion advanced on its left and D on the right with A and B Coys in support – the enemy put up a very heavy artillery barrage and tremendous bursts of machine gun fire from the right at CONTALMAISON when the 21st Bn Rsv failed to advance and from BAILIFF WOOD drove our men back – Lieut E.G. Bowen with a party of some 20 endeavoured to hang on in a shallow trench just in front of BAILIFF WOOD – the Battalion numbered about 6 officers and 160 other ranks on its return – the enemy continued to shell our trenches very heavily throughout the day. Casualties Officers Killed 2nd Lieut J.I. Pratt (A Coy)(Lewis Gun) 2nd Lieut R.W. Taylor (D Coy) – 2nd Lt J.A. Alexander (A Coy) – Lieut E.C. Stallard (C Coy) – 2nd Lieut E.W. Narren (Sigs. B. Coy) Wounded. Capt J.H. Jermain (S/C C Coy) – Capt R.A.J. Remy (OC D Coy) – Capt E.W. Narren (Boats M.B. Coy) – Capt F. Henri (OC C Coy) – Capt R.A.J. Remy (OC D Coy) – Lieut E.G. Bowen (B Coy M.) – Lieut J.B.W. Roberton (Signal Off. at duty) – Lieut C. Craig (D. Coy) – Lieut F.I. Shaw M.O. – Other Ranks Battalion went into action 682 strong and suffered about 4:30 – Killed 31 – Wounded 189 – Missing 34 – Total 252 approximately. A Coy 68; B. Coy. 42; C. Coy. 79; D Coy 48; HQ. 13. – About 10 pm the Battalion was relieved by the 13th Dl.I. and returned to bivouacs in BÉCOURT WOOD about 3am. The Battalion rested in the morning and in the afternoon paraded to find out his tunnels – in the evening two companies and HQ moved to the old British front	Remarks
	9/7/16		In the morning C & D Coys moved up to relieve the 10th S.N.F. in trenches and in the evening A & B Coys followed up and on completion relief about 11:30 pm – Shelling was heavy throughout the night and casualties were considerable.	Remarks

Army Form C. 2118.

WAR DIARY or INTELLIGENCE SUMMARY.

(Erase heading not required.)

9/11/6(S) Bn. R/gd Fusiliers

Place	Date	Hour	Summary of Events and Information	Remarks and references to Appendices
ALBERT.	10/7/16.		Enemy continued to shell our line heavily throughout the morning — in the afternoon the 69th Bgd. attacked CONTALMAISON through our lines and succeeded in taking it. The Battalion was relieved by the 1st Cameron Highlanders by 7pm and retired to billets in ALBERT by 10 p.m. Total Casualties for period in the line from July 6th to 10th:— Officers 4 killed — 8 wounded. Other Ranks — 35 killed — 213 wounded — 32 missing — 292 total Casualties.	Rehayah.
	11/7/16.		Battalion rested all day and cleaned up.	Rehayah.
	12/7/16.		Companies had full interior economy in the morning with a view to finding out free details of all deficiencies — Battalion dug trenches route march by half Companies. — Enemy shelled ALBERT frequently all day.	Rehayah.
	13/7/16.		Battalion hard use of the baths all day. — Enemy shelled ALBERT frequently all day but there were few Casualties.	Rehayah. Rehayah.
DERNACOURT	14/7/16.		Battalion commenced to move to billets at DERNACOURT at 9am — moving by companies with intervals between sections at 9am. — Rested at DERNACOURT all day.	Rehayah.
BECOURT WOOD	15/7/16.		At 8am travelled by companies to BÉCOURT WOOD in reserve to 34th Division in their attack on POZIERES — travelled there all day — attack failed — provided ration parties of 200 — one man killed.	Rehayah.
Trenches	16/7/16.		Battalion moved at 2pm by Companies to relieve the 11th Royal Warwicks and to East flank in the line X.15 d.oo. — X.21 a.4.9. — X.15.C.9.2. — X.15. b.S.8. — relief complete 4.30 pm.	Rehayah.
"	17/7/16.		Battalion moved up at 8pm in support to 12th D.L.I. in their attack on POZIERES — The Battalion was occupied — the attack having failed — in returning to its original line at 3am.	Rehayah. Rehayah.
"	18/7/16.		Battalion was shelled heavily all day — provided 250 men for digging from 8.45pm until 2.15am.	Rehayah.
ALBERT.	19/7/16.		Battalion was shelled heavily all day — evening advanced to bivouac along Railway Crossing in ALBERT — Casualties for day — relieved by the 3rd Australian Bgd. — one killed — 13 wounded — 1 missing.	Rehayah.

WAR DIARY or INTELLIGENCE SUMMARY.

Army Form C. 2118.

Of 11(S) Bn. North'd Fusiliers

(Erase heading not required.)

Place	Date	Hour	Summary of Events and Information	Remarks and references to Appendices
FRANVILLERS	20.7.14		Draft of 8 officers & 96 O.R. joined the battalion - battalion marched by entraining to FRANVILLERS - 71 men found out - 65 of draft - the following NCOs & men were awarded the Military Medal 15814 Pte V. Blore - Sergt 7185 Smith - 14056 Regt L Miller - 10940 Pte C.R. Willardson - 13358 Pte N. Robson - 7488 Pte F. Firth.	Rehayah
	21.7.16.		The Battalion paraded at 10 a.m. for speech by C.O. and by companies from 11-12 noon for inspection - Draft inspected & C.O.E. Divisional inspected and presented the six ribbons.	Rehayah
	22.7.16		Companies paraded under their own arrangements - a further draft of 150 arrived making reinforcements up to 550 approx. - battalion put on 1 hour's notice to move - companies cancelled.	Rehayah
	23.7.16.		Church of England parade in morning - hour's notice cancelled - Companies did own Route marching	Rehayah
	24.7.16.		Companies paraded under their own arrangements all day - Strength 31 officers & 1166 O.R.	Rehayah
	25.7.16.		The Brigade was inspected at 11.30 a.m. by the G.O.C. 3rd Corps General Pulteney the Bn. had added 20 officers and 876 O.R.	Rehayah
PEAKE WOOD	26.7.16		The Battalion marched from FRANVILLERS at 8.50 a.m. - bivouacked near ALBERT for 12 noon & late 4th and then marched up and relieved the 1st S.W.B. at PEAKE WOOD being support battalion, the Brigade having taken over the left of Divisional front.	Rehayah
	27.7.16.		Battalion furnished two large carrying parties to take bombs up to the front line. three men wounded and one shell shock.	Rehayah
Nr BECOURT WOOD	28.7.16		Battalion furnished large carrying fatigues - one man killed - five wounded - two shell shock - relieved at 3 p.m. by 8th Yorkshire Regt. and took over trenches in the British Support line just E. of BECOURT WOOD for 10th West Riding - Brigade in Divisional Reserve	Rehayah
	29.7.16.		Battalion rested all day - twelve wounded and one shell shock	Rehayah

961f

WAR DIARY or INTELLIGENCE SUMMARY of 11 (S) Bn. North'd Fusiliers

Army Form C. 2118.

Place	Date	Hour	Summary of Events and Information	Remarks and references to Appendices
BECOURT WOOD	30.7.16.		Battalion provided carrying party of 5 officers and 300 men to take up bombs for CONTALMAISON to forward dumps in O.G.I. - provided 4 officers and 200 men to dig jumping off trench in front of Switch Line - Casualties (unit H.M.P. West wounded - Other ranks four killed - 10 wounded - 3 shell shock - 3 missing - total 21.	R.E. Maxgall
"	31.7.16.		Battalion marched to BECOURT WOOD and rested. No Casualties.	hassau

96rf

11th N.F. July 7th 1916.

11th Northumberland Fusiliers.

Summary of Operations on July 7th

The Batt'n was ordered to attack the enemy's position from X.16.a.1.3. to X.16.b.2.5 at 9.30 a.m. A first objective given was the line X.16.C.1.9. X.16.C.5.9. on the southern edge of BAILIFF WOOD.

Bombing Attacks
At 9.15 a.m. the bombing parties of A.B.C. Coy's proceeded under Lieut E.G. Bowers down the trench leading from the second triangle at X.15.C.2.1. to the W. end of the line of trees at X.16.C.4.0. At this point bombing parties were organized and sent down the dug out line which ran in a southerly direction towards PEAKE WOOD and also along the trench which runs by the line of trees in the direction of CONTALMAISON.
The first party successfully bombed the dug-out line and captured some Germans, eight of whom were wounded by our bombs. A dug out was cleared, the prisoners put into it and a guard mounted on it until the party was re-inforced by the

13th D.L.I. the following night. (July 8th).
          The second party found the trench along the line of trees running to CONTALMAISON unoccupied.
          The remainder of the bombing parties under Lieut E.G. Bowers proceeded up a very shallow trench leading towards BAILIFF WOOD leaving the carrying parties at X.16.C.4.0 whence they soon followed up and joined Lt. BOWERS. This whole party re-inforced by men of "C" and D Coys. under Lieut. W.A. Henri and 2nd Lt. E.M. Watts worked up this trench which was very shallow and afforded practically no shelter, until held up by a strong German post and also heavy M.G. fire from CONTALMAISON. The party continued to dig in until further progress was stopped by weather conditions. After holding on to this position for over two hours under very fire, Lieut E.G. BOWERS in consultation with the other officers decided to retire to his old line.

Main Attack.
          At 9.45 a.m. "C" and "D" (each Company in four successive waves)

973.

crossed the open through a very heavy barrage of shrapnel, and made their way in spite of very heavy casualties more than half way towards the first objective, where they received the order to dig themselves in. The remnants of these two companies eventually managed to join Lt. BOWERS

the shallow trench in front of BAILIFF WOOD where they continued to dig themselves in for over two hours until the weather conditions making it impossible to dig and the M.G. fire from CONTALMAISON being very heavy the order was given to withdraw to the original line.

On receipt of the information of the position of Lt. BOWERS, his bombing parties and the remnants of "C" & "D" Companies, a message was sent from Batt⁴. H.Q. for the party to hold on until re-inforcements came up. This message did not reach Lt. BOWERS.

"A" Company moving up in support crossed over in waves and joined "C" and "D" Companies in front of the first objective. Two platoons on the left under the Company Sergt-Major together with parties of the Welsh and Wilts 9/4 Regts, after several attempts reached the final objective and crossing the road entered the trench. This party immediately began to consolidate the trench and remained there until joined later in the day by the 18th D.L.I.

"B" Company moving up in support of D Coy on the right crossed over in rear of the last wave of D Coy. Two platoons reached the trench in front of the first objective, while the last two carrying tools did not leave our own line. These two platoons subsequently made their way under Lieut HEWITT up the trench on the left of the objective to point 17 where they remained until relieved later in the day by the 10th N.F.

ALBERT
13/7/16.

P.G. Cuffin
Lieut Colonel
Commanding,
11th North'd Fus'rs

TO	O.C. 11th N.F.		9754
Sender's Number	Day of Month	In reply to Number	
B.M. 101	8		AAA

Please convey to all ranks of your unit my thanks and congratulations on your most gallant attack. aaa But for the failure of the Brigade on our right to advance on our flank you would have secured your whole objective as it was part of your battalion reached the objective and took 27 prisoners and two platoons held on in the valley. Owing to your attack the 12th DLI were able to take a German redoubt at night the enemy having had enough. You

AND SIGNALS.

Army Form C. 2121.

TO		2.		976f
Sender's Number.	Day of Month.	In reply to Number.		AAA

have	lost	some	good	Comrades
but	you	have	acted	a
have	part	in	the	British
Offensive	which	is	developing	into
a	crushing	victory	and	you
have	worthily	upheld	the	name
of	the	Fighting Fifth.		

Henry F Kroff
Brig General

July 8th 1916.

"A" Form.
MESSAGES AND SIGNALS.

Army Form C. 2121.

TO: All units 11 S N= 9718

Sender's Number: B.Q. 99
Day of Month: 8th

AAA

Brigadier congratulates all units on fine work of last three days by which the line has been advanced 750 yards aaa The enemy is very hard pressed and there is no doubt that the objective will be secured tonight aaa All ranks should realise that now is the chance to inflict a crushing defeat on enemy aaa

From: 68 th Bde
Time: 10.47 AM

To all Units 68th Brigade.

Please convey my hearty congratulations to all ranks on the fine work of the Brigade in the recent attacks.

The Brigade was allotted an ultimate objective of 500 yards. The whole of this was captured with the exception of 150 yards on the right flank, and in addition 500 yards of the objective of the Division on our left was carried and consolidated. But for the gaining of these positions the successful attack of the 69th Brigade could not have been immunk launched.

Our captures include 27 unwounded and 5 wounded prisoners, three Field Guns and many thousand shells.

Our losses have been heavy and we deplore the passing of good comrades but rarely on the Western Front has any Brigade advanced 750 yards without suffering far more severely.

In all 1650 yards of Trench were consolidated under most trying weather conditions.

The Brigade has been tried and has made good, we have an enemy in front of us who is being daily pressed and is nearing defeat and the part the Brigade has already played fills me with confidence that the 68th will take no mean share in the utter defeat of the enemies of our Country.

Signed. H. Page Croft. Brig Gen.
Commanding 68th Infntry Brigade.

July 11th 1916.

SPECIAL ORDER OF THE DAY
BY
MAJOR GENERAL J.M. BABINGTON, C.B., C.M.G.

The G.O.C. Division has very great pleasure in republishing III Corps Memo. No. C.R.3/505/A/16 dated 18.7.1916:

"The following have been awarded the Military Medal :-

13th (S) Bn. Durham Light Infantry.

No. 24775 Private W. Hutchinson.
" 15894 Sergeant F.O. Lamb.
" 18170 Sergeant T. Fitzpatrick.
" 17108 Private T. Suddes.

12th (S) Bn. Durham Light Infantry.

No. 19625 Sergeant H.T. Hitchen.
" 18397 Sergeant W. Silversides.
" 15421 Private W. Woodhead.
" 18077 Private T. Bamborough.
" 18662 L/Corpl. J.A. Speed.

68th Brigade Machine Gun Company.

No. 5466 Private G. Rich.

10th (S) Bn. Northumberland Fusiliers.

No. 10/19716 Private J. Hoyle.
" 10/16126 Private W. Jessopp.
" 10/10778 Private J. Tobbell.
" 10/7011 L/Corpl. G.W. McQueen.
" 10/19390 Private B.V. Clarke.
" 10/16076 Private A. Wilson.

11th (S) Bn. Northumberland Fusiliers.

No. 15814 Private V. Plore.
" 7135 Sergeant J.H. Smith.
" 14056 L/Corpl. L. Miller.
" 10790 Private G.R. Williamson.
" 13358 Private W. Robson.
" 7488 Private F. Firth.

11th (S) Bn. West Yorkshire Regiment.

No. 1574 L/Corpl. A. Butterworth.
" 13617 Private T.A. Wilson.

10th (S) Bn. West Riding Regiment.

No. 13050 L/Corpl. C. Leigh.
" 12257 Sergeant Brian McAvan.

8th (S) Bn. Yorkshire Regiment.

No. 14987 Sergeant H. Frobisher.
" 9113 L/Sergt. J. Whiteley.

P.T.O.

69th Brigade Trench Mortar Battery.
9th (S) Bn. Yorkshire Regiment.

No. 15815 Private F.G. Collinson.

69th Brigade Machine Gun Company.

No. 13409 Private George Daines.
" 5626 Private George Collins.

1st Sherwood Foresters.

No. 9951 Sergeant C. Thompson.

18.7.1916.
      (Signed) PERCY HAMBRO,
        Brigadier-General,
      D.A.& Q.M.G. III Corps.

19.7.1916.
      H. WILKINSON Lt-Col.,
       A.A.& Q.M.G.

68th Brigade.
23rd Division.

1/11th BATTALION

NOTTHUMBERLAND FUSILIERS

AUGUST 1 9 1 6

Army Form C. 2118.

Vol II
11 Nrd Fus

WAR DIARY or INTELLIGENCE SUMMARY.
(Erase heading not required.)

Place	Date	Hour	Summary of Events and Information	Remarks and references to Appendices
Support line O.G.1-2. Nem MAMETZ	August 1st		The Batt'n was in Brigade Reserve in trenches in front of BECOURT WOOD - Ordered to proceed for attachment of 11th N.F. and 12th K.D.L.I & 70th Bde - The Battn moved into Close Support trenches in O.G.1-2. in afternoon relieving the 6th K.O.Y.L.I - Casualties 3 killed - Six wounded - 3 shell shock - 3 missing	Relmayen
Nr BAZENTIN LE PETIT WOODS	2nd		The Batt'n provided carrying parties for rations and water to the front line - casualties 2 wounded - 2 Shell shock	Relmayen
	3rd		The Batt'n provided unloading carrying parties all day - 3 men wounded - Sgt G.H. Smedley Whittington was killed in the Brigade office at ALBERT	Relmayen
	4th		The Batt'n provided unloading carrying parties to front line - Casualties 1 Soldier wounded - 2 shell shock	Relmayen
Front Line & Intermediate Line & SWITCH	5th		The Batt'n relieved the 12th D.L.I in the front line trenches - heavily shelled during relief but quiet night - Sgt G.T. Shaw RAMC. wounded - Two killed - 7 wounded - 3 shell shock	Relmayen
	6th		Quiet day - orders received to prepare an attack - 2 killed - 2 wounded - one shell shock	Relmayen
	7th		A Coy. Carried out an attack on the SWITCH edge but at S.2.C.8.w. at 8.30a The enemy opened heavy T.M. M.G. Bombing and Rifle fire which reported our attack at once - taking wire reached from Brigade to stand fast - 2 Lt. W.M. Upton wounded - Battn was relieved in front line by 7/8 K.O.S.B. 4th Bde 15th Div - proceeded to old Battn support trenches nr BECOURT	Relmayen
BECOURT.			Heavily Shelled - 2 men wounded	
BEHENCOURT.	8th		Batt'n relieved in Reserve area by 8/10 Gordon Highlanders and marched to billets at BEHENCOURT arriving 2pm - 25men few not a batman	Relmayen

965/

=7

WAR DIARY or INTELLIGENCE SUMMARY.

Army Form C. 2118.

Place	Date	Hour	Summary of Events and Information	Remarks and references to Appendices
BEHENCOURT	9.5.		Battalion rested all day. G.O.C. Division presented D.C.M. to C.S.M. Faulkener and handed ribbons for C.S.M. Dunkiter and Sergt. Thomas (wounded) to C.O. Lieut. E.G. Bowers and Coy. Q.M.S. left as a billeting party for BAILEUL.	R. Chavayan
	10.5.		Companies did close order drill and sent out rent parties. Advance party consisting of transport and servis Gun Detachments started for POULAINVILLE at 2.30pm. Lieut. Clegg and N.C.O's started as billeting party to AILLY-LE HAUT-CLOCHER	R. Chavayan
	11.5.		Battalion entrained there at 6pm and marched to FRESHINCOURT. Thus at 2.20pm. Marched from BEHENCOURT at 6pm in tactical train — detraining at LONGPRÉ at 11pm — marched to AILLY SUR LE HAUT CLOCHER 2.15am — 2 men fell out. Battalion started at 9pm and marched to LONGPRÉ Station arriving there about 11pm.	R. Chavayan
AILLY-LE HAUT CLOCHER	12.5.			R. Chavayan
	13.5.		Battalion entrained in 3 trains at LONGPRÉ station, arriving at 1am at BAILEUL Station, arriving at 12 noon — battalion marched to billets and bivouacs in neighbourhood of FLETRE. Q. 30. d. 2. 5. Transport joined Batt. at AILLY on 11th. — Lewis Gun Detachment billeted at BOUCHON and joined battalion at LONGPRÉ S'n. on night of 12th.	R. Chavayan
FLETRE Q. 30. d. 2. 5.	14.5.		Companies did close order drill in morning. Band began to practise again. Orders received and issued for move of Brigade to STEENWERCK to relieve 122nd Brigade of 41st Division.	R. Chavayan
STEENWERCK AREA.	15.5.		Battalion started at 2pm and marched to billets and bivouacs in STEENWERCK AREA arriving about 6pm — one man fell out on line of march.	R. Chavayan
	16.5.		Companies paraded under their own arrangements for physical and close order drill — orders issued for move into the line.	
LE BIZET.	17.5.		Batt: paraded under the R.S.M. before leaving — started from STEENWERCK at 6.30pm and marched to rest billets in LE BIZET relieving 10th N.F. at 10.25pm.	966 f

WAR DIARY
or
INTELLIGENCE SUMMARY.
(Erase heading not required.)

Army Form C. 2118.

Place	Date	Hour	Summary of Events and Information	Remarks and references to Appendices
LE BIZET	18.15		Battalion was in Reserve Billets - working party of 28 officers and 180 men found for R.E. by "C" Coy.	Re Mayall
	19.15		Very wet day - Battalion billeted in this area as follows :- HQ. C.13.b.12.9 - A Coy C.7.d.2.2. - B Coy C.13.c.9.4. - C Coy. C.8.c.3.8. - D Coy C.8.c.7.9. Reference Map 36. N.W. - Battalion furnished working parties for R.E. of 2 officers & 160 men of "A" Coy - 1 officer & 30 men of "A" Coy. Evening put from sheets over "C" Coys. billets at LE PETIT RABECQUE in morning and 2 over Batln. HQ. in afternoon - Battalion provided 300 men for working party for R.E. (B.130. C.130. A.40.) - Parade Services for R.E. by N.C. Military Medal awarded to 7243 Pte L. Simpson; 5849 Pte W.W. Menders, 15495 Pte J. Nightingale, 15638 Pte E.D. Hall, 625 Sgt J.H. Scott, 823 Pte A. Goodger, 6094 Pte R. Dred, 7485 Pte E. Oldfield, 14886 Pte J. Armitage.	R. Mayall
	20.15		The Battalion found 210 men for working parties for R.E. (B. Coy 140, A. Coy 70); C. Coy - 20 HQ. Had use of Divisional Baths at PONT DE NIEPPE 2t-1 pm.	R. Mayall
	21.15		The Battalion found 250 men for working parties for R.E. (D. 90); A 100; C. 60) The Battalion had the use of the baths for 800 men - Gas Alert on.	R. Mayall
	22.15		The Battalion found 300 men for working parties for R.E. - Very quiet day - Gas Alert Cancelled. - Battalion Operation Order 2.I. issued.	R. Mayall
	23.15		B. Company moved from the Laundry in LE BIZET to STATION REDOUBT C.9.d.8.5. Relief completed by 7am. - "A" Company moved from billets in LE BIZET to MAISON 1875 V.26.c.7.5. and FUSILIER TERRACES V.27.a5.2. Relief complete 11 a.m. - Battalion provided 220 men working parties for R.E.	R. Mayall
	24.15			

9676

WAR DIARY
or
INTELLIGENCE SUMMARY.
(Erase heading not required.)

Army Form C. 2118.

Place	Date	Hour	Summary of Events and Information	Remarks and references to Appendices
Front Line Trench	25/8/16		The Battalion relieved the 10th N.F. in the left subsector of the right sector of the Divisional Front, relief complete 9.40 am. — Dispositions C. Coy right front company with Platoon in Support at RESERVE FME. — B. Coy centre front company — D. Coy left front company. — A Company in Support at LANCASHIRE SUPPORT FME with a Platoon at NABOB at PATERNOSTER ROW — Bn HQ. DESPIERRE FME — Brigade had Tea Helmet Alarm at 3 pm — Enemy Shelled LONDON SUPPORT FME C.I.b.7.5. with a hundred 5.9" Shrapnel. Quiet day.	Remayelle
	26/8/16		Very quiet day — our guns registered opposite our left company and there was slight retaliation with rifle grenades.	Remayelle
	27/8/16		One man of "B" Coy killed by M.G. fire while on sentry duty in advance bombing post at 12.30 am. — Very quiet morning — in afternoon a practice S.O.S. carried out — Lt. Cittlerton 10th N.F. wounded in our line — 1 man B Coy accidentally wounded himself by firing very light.	Remayelle
	28/8/16		Our minenwerfer mortars registered opposite left company at 11 am. — Very quiet day.	Remayelle
	29/8/16		Wet morning and quiet throughout the day — operations postponed owing to wet weather and wrong wind.	Remayelle
	30/8/16		Quiet day — wet weather — Capt C.T.H. Adamson (noted as second in command of C Coy) Capt R.B. Mitchell (noted as second in command of B Coy) joined the battalion for duty.	
	31/8/16		At 1.30 am a Gas attack was delivered from our trenches and at intervals along the Divisional front — this was followed at 3.20 am by an attempt by 2 Off. + 30 OR to raid the enemy's line, this however failed — our casualties were Killed 5", Wounded 3", Enemy Shelled battalion HQ/ & about 7 pm with heavy Shells.	Remayelle

9688

Batt'n O.O. for August 7th.   SECRET.

1. **Objective.**
The 11th N.F. will capture the corner of the Intermediate German line at about S.2.C.8.4. making blocks 30 yds E. from that point and 30 yds N. along the road. The attack will take place to-morrow at zero time.

2. **Procedure.**
Troops will be formed up in position in the following order by 8 a.m:—

(a) 1 officer + 25 men and Lewis Gun of A Coy. 11th N.F. in 1st parallel.

(b) 1 officer + 12 N.C.O's and men R.E. and 1 officer + 15 N.C.O's and men Pioneers with Lewis Gun in 2nd parallel.

(c) 1 officer + 12 men D Coy 11th N.F. carrying 3 picks, 9 shovels – 20 sandbags, 2 bombs per man in sap in rear of 2nd parallel.

(d) Lewis Gun, Signallers with line, and bomb carriers following (c)

3. **Supports.**
(a) As soon as the sap is cleared of assaulting troops 1 officer + 25 men of A Coy. will occupy 1st parallel.

(b) Reserves of R.E. and Pioneers will occupy 2nd parallel.

(c) In fire trench on the right of the sap the remainder of R.E. and Pioneers with

970F

12 men of D Coy. as support to Infantry working party will take up position.

(d) 25 N.C.Os and men will take up position on the left of the sap in the fire trench. This party will be accompanied (if needed) by Lewis Gun and team of D Coy.

4. **Reserves**
O.C. D Coy will detail 1 officer + 50 men who will remain in their own trench, to be ready to move up at a moment's notice. A guide from this party will remain with Lt. Bowers.

5. **Bombs**
All men of 11th N.Fus will carry 12 bombs and all R.E. and pioneers 4 bombs per man. Lt. Bowers. B.B.O. will remain in fire trench at sap head to organize supply of bombs.

6. **Watches**
All watches will be synchronized and zero time given at Bn. HQ. at 7am tomorrow morning.

7. **Report Centres**
Batt HQ. will remain in its present position. O.C. A Coy. will be at HQ. D Coy. in front line.

8. **Orders**
Detailed instructions have been issued to O.C. M.G. Corps, L.T.M. Battery, Bn Bombing & Signalling Officers.

10.30 pm. 6/8/16.

R.E. Mayah
Col Adjt 11th N.F.

WAR DIARY or INTELLIGENCE SUMMARY

Army Form C. 2118.

H.G.S. 11/Vol 12
11 N.F.

Place	Date	Hour	Summary of Events and Information	Remarks and references to Appendices
Front line Trenches 99 – 111.	1.9.16.		At 1.30 a.m. the enemy opened heavy artillery fire on the support and front lines of our right and centre Companies – retaliation from our field guns was quick but unsuccessful in stopping them – after 3/4 hour the barrage slackened and the enemy, we had four men wounded. – Orders were received for the batt.n to be relieved by 9/15 Y. and I. (10 "B" Coy) 15 wounded hit. Passes were cancelled at 7 p.m. – the enemy continued to shell and trench mortar our right Company lines throughout the day.	Relayed
	2.9.16.		Very quiet morning – an advance party from the 1st Seaforth Highlanders (61st Div.) came to look after our lines. – G.A.S.S.O.S for Highland Bgde on our right received at 11.30 p.m. but cancelled 12.5.	Relayed
Bailleul district.	3.9.16.		Our artillery very active in the morning – battalion was relieved by 4 Seaforth Highlanders at 5.30 p.m. and proceeded for night to 2nd Anzac Training Camp near BAILLEUL – arriving about 10.30 p.m.	Relayed
	4.9.16		Battalion marched at 10.45 a.m. to billets near METEREN arriving at 12 noon. Billets at X. 22. c. 4. 5. – 2 W's Snowdens Breen joined for duty	Relayed
	5.9.16.		The battalion marched from billets at 11.45 a.m., entrained at BAILLEUL at 1.28 p.m., detraining at ST.OMER at 3 p.m. and arriving in billets NORDASQUES at 7.30 p.m. 11 men fell out on the line of march. – Half the transport proceeded by road under Capt.n W.K. Macdonald and half by train for BAILLEUL WEST, detraining at WIZERNES and marching to billets about midnight.	98 OSB T.S.B V.B.B. Relayed
NORDASQUES	6.9.16.		Weather standard at dress Rev.n at 9.30 a.m. – Companies inspected & Battn. Regt. S. Mjr. inspected all men of the Battalion.	Relayed
	7.9.16.		The Battalion was inspected by G.O.C. Brigade in morning. – Conferences Carried out training. – Conference by officers. – Billetting party proceeded South. from ST OMER	Relayed

Army Form C. 2118.

WAR DIARY
or
INTELLIGENCE SUMMARY.
(Erase heading not required.)

Instructions regarding War Diaries and Intelligence Summaries are contained in F.S. Regs., Part II. and the Staff Manual respectively. Title pages will be prepared in manuscript.

Place	Date	Hour	Summary of Events and Information	Remarks and references to Appendices
NORDAUSQUES.	8.15		Companies carried out training under their own arrangements - billeting party left ST OMER for the South at 2 p.m. - Divisional Disinfecting Machine came.	R. Baugh
	9.15		Companies had short morning parades - Transit left at 11-30 p.m. for station	Remarque
MOLLIENS AU BOIS	10.15		Battalion marched from billets 1.40 a.m. and entrained at AUDRICQUE at 4.30 a.m. - detrained at LONGEAU at 12.30 p.m. - marched to MOLLIENS - AU-BOIS - arriving at 6 p.m. - Buses ferried.	Remarque
	11.15		Battalion rested all day. Lieut Haynes R.A.M.C. rejoined.	Remarque
	12.15		Battalion started at 8.15 a.m. and marched to MILLENCOURT arriving at 1 p.m. - no one fell out.	Remarque
MILLENCOURT	13.15		Church Parades cancelled owing to rain - Brigade staff in Army Reserve.	Remarque
	14.15		All officers - 20 O.R. per Coy. practised under R.E. for Lectures on Consolidation - had the use of its Divisional Disinfector in the morning.	Remarque
	15.15		Battalion on two minutes notice to move owing to continual attack by British and French. Tanks went for front-line. Leave MILLENCOURT at 11-45 a.m. for BECOURT WOOD. Battalion bivouaced near CHATEAU.	Lyf Bowser
	16.15		Battalion resting in BECOURT WOOD	Lyf Bowser
	17.15		Battalion resting + Church Parade scenes held in open near CHATEAU. Three officers sent to recommend limits near D.G.2.	Lyf Bowser
	18.31		Battalion leave BECOURT WOOD at 11-30 a.m. for support line behind MARTINPUICH. Taken over from 6/4th R.S.F. CAPT. MAYALL goes to hospital. Reinforcement officers go to RUE du BRAY. ALBERT	Lyf Bowser

2353 Wt. W2544/1454 700,000 5/15 D.D.&L. A.D.S.S./Forms/C. 2118.

Army Form C. 2118.

WAR DIARY
or
INTELLIGENCE SUMMARY.
(Erase heading not required.)

Instructions regarding War Diaries and Intelligence Summaries are contained in F. S. Regs. Part II. and the Staff Manual respectively. Title pages will be prepared in manuscript.

Place	Date	Hour	Summary of Events and Information	Remarks and references to Appendices
SUPPORT TRENCHES MARTINPUICH	Sept 19th		Companies in LANE'S TRENCH + 6th AVENUE. Very little shelling. Casualties Nil.	Ey Bower
"	20th		Capt Lane + Capt Adamson reconnoitre the front line. Crews containing 'B' + 'D' moved to CONTALMAISON. Lewis Cowley + Bell gun for duty, but are kept at reinforcement camp in Albert. Casualties 2 wounded	Ey Bower
CONTALMAISON	21st		Battalion notes to suggest improving trenches. Casualties 6 wounded.	Ey Bower
"	22nd		Capt Hume carries back from trace + letter at transport camp. Battalion relieves two companies of the 8th Yorks + two companies of the 9th Yorks in the front line. A Coy in Support STARFISH TRENCH, MARTIN ALLEY & MARTIN TRENCH, B Coy to PRUE TRENCH, C Coy in PUSH ALLEY + D Coy in PUSH ALLEY. Relief complete about 9·30 a.m. Casualties 2 wounded. Patrols out along EAUCOURT L'ABBAYE road at 21.E–Z.A.G.Cent.	Ey Bower
FRONT LINE	23rd		At 4 P.M. after preliminary bombardment with Stokes mortar a small attack was launched against three points held by the bosses about M.26 b. Patrols were ground if the bombers captured by bombardment + Lewis Gunmanship every to heavy M.G. fire were not established this dark. Patrols out along EAUCOURT L'ABBAYE road reached a point about 1.M.29.a.3.6 when they were held up by artillery fire, supported for by the bomb positions the time about this point. Casualties 1 killed 15 wounded. Lieut K had Smith unmounted.	Ey Bower
FRONT LINE	24th		Bombing of position continued at strong point. ALLEY + neighbourhood with 4·2" + 5·9" shewing the morning. Commenced heavy the enemy front occupied by 10 Officers + 50 other Ranks out along EAUCOURT L'ABBAYE road. Did not encounter any enemy but crossed the enemy place occupied it were breezed about M.29. a.3.6. Casualties 8 killed 29 wounded + 2 missing	Ey Bower

WAR DIARY or INTELLIGENCE SUMMARY.

Army Form C. 2118.

(Erase heading not required.)

Instructions regarding War Diaries and Intelligence Summaries are contained in F. S. Regs., Part II and the Staff Manual respectively. Title pages will be prepared in manuscript.

Place	Date	Hour	Summary of Events and Information	Remarks and references to Appendices
FRONT LINE TRENCHES BAZENTIN	25th		Battalion co-operated with 10th N.F. in attack on 26th AVENUE, but owing to heavy barrage + machine gun fire 16th M.F. had to abort its attempts + our advance by turning of no avail. Bombing continued all day at our strong points during which B/Serjt TEALE was wounded. Casualties:- Killed 14 wounded Gorman M/G. brought in from 216.2.a.G. Fired. Tank attack on front 53 fails.	
"	26th		Battalion relieved by 13th D.L.I. Relief complete by 6 a.m. Moved into left support location with H.Q. in O.G.1. Quiet day but long trip in from right. We are relieved in this location by the 9th York + Lancs. 9th Bde Relief complete about 6 o.p.m. Battalion marches into hats + bivouac at near FRICOURT near THE DINGLE. Casualties:- 3 wounded	
CAMP near FRICOURT	27th		Battalion spent the day cleaning up + inspection of man returns etc. Man clothing inspect. Casualties Nil	
"	28th		Working party of 4 officers + 250 men + Battalion of N.C.O.s for road making near CONTALMAISON. Battalion bath during the afternoon + evening at BECOURT WOOD. 2/Lieut Moffatt + 13 men goes to hospital Casualties. Nil	
"	29th		Working party supplied of 2 officers + 100 men. 25 men from each Coy. Remainder of Battalion parades under Coy. arrangements. Casualties 1 wounded Lt.Col Eaton goes to hospital. Reinforcements Co. X.20.C. Working parties supplied as follows 4 officers + 200 men; 50 men from each company during 26th AVENUE. 10 officer + 50 men sent to CONTALMAISON VILLA to work in Chew relief work party of 12th D.L.I. carrying grenades. This party arrive at CONTALMAISON	
"	30th		1 officer + 3 Gunners with 150 men digging near the near DESTREMONT FARM. Casualties 2/Lt Pauling wounded. O.R. 13 wounded.	

WAR DIARY or INTELLIGENCE SUMMARY

Army Form C. 2118

Vol 13

Place	Date	Hour	Summary of Events and Information	Remarks and references to Appendices
LOZENGE WOOD.	Oct 1st 1916.		Working party of 4 Officers & 150 other ranks under Capt Adamson supplied to dig jumping off trench behind DESTREMONT FARM for the attack made by 70th Brigade on the LE SARS line. 2nd Lt Cowling was wounded. +12 O.R.	E.M. Mackett
CONTALMAISON	Oct 2nd 1916		Battalion moved into the Cutting at CONTALMAISON. Rain fell without ceasing all day. Casualties Nil.	E.M. Mackett
LE. SARS.	Oct 3rd 1916.		Battalion took over from 4th N.F. 50th Div. in O.G.1. & O.G.2. A & B Companies in O.G.2. C & D in O.G.1. Casualties 2 killed 2 wounded.	E.M. Mackett
	Oct 4th 1916.		Very faint quiet but owing to a small bombing attack on our left, our trenches here were heavily shelled at night. Casualties 3 killed, 11 wounded.	E.M. Mackett
	Oct 5th 1916.		Quiet day. At night A Coy formed a bombing block near the TANGLE, 200 yards from our front line. 26th Avenue was deepened & cleared.	E.M. Mackett
	Oct 6th 1916.		Quiet day. At 10 PM A Coy attacked & seized the TANGLE, but had to withdraw later owing to heavy shell fire & number of casualties. L.S.A.Bn had 150 yards of C Coy line. Casualties. 10 killed +17 wounded. Battn relieved by N.S.L.I. & went into C position	E.M. Mackett
	Oct 7th 1916.		at 1.45 PM. 12 R. Yorks. D.L.I. attacked L.E.SARS in conjunction with 69th Brigade & objectives gained. Division took 560 prisoners. 2 M.G. batts. with D Coy were attached to 13 D.L.I. for carrying. B & C Coys took up their old positions in O.G.1 & O.G.2 as D.L.I. went over. A Coy went back to STAR FISH LINE. Our bombardment was intense for three hours after ZERO. Casualties 1 killed 14 wounded	E.M. Mackett

WAR DIARY or **INTELLIGENCE SUMMARY.**
(Erase heading not required.)

Army Form C. 2118.

9831

Place	Date	Hour	Summary of Events and Information	Remarks and references to Appendices
	9 Oct 5/16.		Batln. HQ which were in SPENCE TRENCH were heavily shelled. Lt BOWERS was wounded, three men killed & the dug-out blown in. HQ moved to CRESCENT ALLEY. Batln. was relieved by 7. Camerons. Moved to BECOURT WOOD. Relief very slow, the rest of Batln. arrives BECOURT at 4.30 AM on 9th. Casualties 3 killed 4 wounded.	B.Macleitt
BECOURT WOOD.	Oct 9th. 16.		Day was spent at the baths in BECOURT WOOD. Every man had clean change of clothing. Casualties. Nil.	B.Macleitt
	Oct 10th.16		Companies had General Kit inspection & refitting. Casualties. Nil.	B.Macleitt
	Oct 11th.16		Batln. entrained at ALBERT at. 7.30 PM. arrives at destination 12 hours late.	B.Macleitt
ALLY LE HAUT CLOCHER.	Oct 12th.16		Arrives LONGPRE 12 midday. Marched to AILLY LE HAUT CLOCHER. Had same billets as before	B.Macleitt
St RICQUIER	Oct 13th.		Marched to St RICQUIER. Arrives at 4.30 P.M.	B.Macleitt
	Oct 14th.16		Day spent at St RICQUIER. Companies paraded for 2 hours in morning	B.Macleitt
	Oct 15th.16		Entrained at ST RICQUIER at 3.30 AM arrived PROVEN 11.30 AM. Marched through POPERINGHE to ERIE Camp. arrives 3.30 PM. very little room, one station B Coy went into TORONTO Camp with B.n. S.L.I	B.Macleitt
ERIE CAMP? SHEET: 28. BELGIUM FRANCE G.II.C.6.2.				

WAR DIARY
INTELLIGENCE SUMMARY

Army Form C. 2118.

Place	Date	Hour	Summary of Events and Information	Remarks and references to Appendices
	Oct.17.16		Rain fell on & off most of the day. 25% allowed into POPERINGE in pass	S.W.Hackett
	Oct.18.16		Companies paraded for two hours in morning. Rope boxing in afternoon. Wet night. G.O.C. Division presented Medal Ribbons at 4 P.M.	G.W.Hackett
YPRES	Oct.18.16		Batn. moved to the HOSPICE YPRES. Moved by train. Relieves the Australians	S.W.Hackett
	Oct.19.16		Wet day. Working parties of 100 men & 2 Officers at night. No casualties	S.W.Hackett
FRONT LINE	Oct.20.16		Moved into front line. Relieved 10th N.F. in Right Batt. of Left Brigade. H.Q. at TOURELLES. One Casualty during relief. Major S.Mills Pratt D.S.O. assumed command of Btn.	B.W.Hackett
	Oct.21.16		Very quiet day. Trenches very wet. Work carried out on drainage. Parapets very low. Can be seen almost everywhere in our S.P.B. Casualties nil	S.W.Hackett
	Oct.22.16		Very Quiet. Casualties nil	S.W.Hackett
	Oct.23.16		Relieved by 8th Yorks. Relief complete 1.30 A.M. 24th/10/16. Trains to POPERINGHE	S.W.Hackett
POPERINGHE	Oct.24.16		Rifle & General Kit Inspection during afternoon.	B.W.Hackett
	Oct.25.16		Batt. have fitted with new Box Respirators which were tested with keeping Gas. Two Companies had baths.	B.W.Hackett
	Oct.26.16		Whole Battalion went to baths. Change of clothing.	S.W.Hackett

Army Form C. 2118.

WAR DIARY
or
INTELLIGENCE SUMMARY
(Erase heading not required.)

Instructions regarding War Diaries and Intelligence Summaries are contained in F.S. Regs., Part II and the Staff Manual respectively. Title Pages will be prepared in manuscript.

Place	Date	Hour	Summary of Events and Information	Remarks and references to Appendices
POPERINGHE	27 Oct		Brigade was inspected by Gen. Plumer, G.O.C. 2nd Army.	S.W.Slackett
	28 Oct.		Battn. Parade on football ground at station. Proceeded working party at night to trenches. N.1 Casualties.	S.W.Slackett
The BUND ZILLEBEKE	29 Oct		Relieved 11th Sherwood Foresters in ZILLEBEKE BUND. Trained from POPERINGHE to YPRES. N.1 Casualties.	S.W.Slackett
	30 Oct		Spent day on our front. Heavy shelling by our artillery afternoon on our right. Working parties of 2 Officers & 175 men. Casualties N.1	S.W.Slackett
	31 Oct.		Spent day. Look done on dugouts in the BUND. Clearing old gun pits to make dugouts. Working parties at night of 2 Officers & 200 men.	S.W.Slackett

984
EB

L.P. Slackett. 2 Lt. & Adjutant
for O.C. 11th Northumberland Fusiliers

THE ATTACHED IS THE WAR DIARY OF THE 11TH (SERVICE) BATTALION NORTHUMBERLAND FUSILIERS FOR THE MONTH OF NOVEMBER 1916.

4/12/16.

E.M. Watts
Lieut.
A/Adjutant,
for O.C. 11th Northumberland Fusiliers.

Army Form C. 2118.

WAR DIARY
or
INTELLIGENCE SUMMARY

(Erase heading not required.)

Instructions regarding War Diaries and Intelligence Summaries are contained in F. S. Regs., Part II. and the Staff Manual respectively. Title Pages will be prepared in manuscript.

Nov/14

Place	Date	Hour	Summary of Events and Information	Remarks and references to Appendices
BUND. ZUEBEKE	Nov.1.16		Quiet day. Large working parties at night. Casualties 1 killed 6 wounded	SWMachell
TRENCHES A Bathn Reft. Bde.	Nov.2		Relieved 10th NF in "A" portion. Right Brigade. Quiet Relief. Casualties Nil.	SWMachell
	Nov.3		Quiet day. Casualties Nil.	SWMachell
	Nov.4		Enemy bombarded from 2.30 – 5 P.m. with Trench Mortars. Shrapnel. Front line has been hit in several places. Also DAVISON ST & CANADA TR. Casualties Killed 1. Wounded 2.	SWMachell
	Nov.5		Quiet day. Casualties Nil.	SWMachell
	Nov.6		Enemy bombarded left Coy front with "Minnies". Relieved in evening by 10th NF. Relief Complete by 8 Pm. Casualties Nil.	SWMachell
HOSPICE YPRES	Nov.7th		1st inspection. Working parties of 4 Officers & 300 men.	SWMachell
	Nov.8th		Two Coys has baths at Infantry Barracks. Working parties 4 Off. 300 men	SWMachell
	Nov.9		Two Coys has baths at Infantry Barracks. Working parties 4 Off. 300 men Nov.10th.	SWMachell

WAR DIARY
or
INTELLIGENCE SUMMARY

(Erase heading not required.)

Army Form C. 2118.

Place	Date	Hour	Summary of Events and Information	Remarks and references to Appendices
A.R.Coys H.Q TORONTO Camp	Nov. 10th		Working party of 50 men during day. Returned by 9th Yorks in the evening. Trains from YPRES to BRANDOEK at 7.30 PM. Marches to TORONTO & ERIE Camps. Arrived 8.30 PM.	E.W. Mackett
TORONTO Camp	Nov. 11th		Day of Rest. Lewis Gun Classes Started.	E.W. Mackett
Coys B. ERIE Camp	Nov. 12th		Church Parade in Y.M.C.A. hut in ERIE Camp. General Rabuyter inspector Holding Camps & all Trenches, also toured Military detail	E.W. Mackett
ERIE Camp	Nov. 13th		A. & B. Coys inspected by C.O.	By Mackett E.W. Mackett
	Nov. 14th		C.O. & Coy. inspected by C.O. Corps Commander. Winter Camp	E.W. Mackett
	Nov. 15th		Baths at Poperinghe. Wire practice carried out.	E.W. Mackett
A Bath Left Subs	Nov. 16th		Returned. 9th York Lancs in A section. Left Brigade Sector. Entrained at 4.30 PM. Relief Complete at 6.10 PM. Carruthers Hit.	E.W. Mackett
J.Q at WM. ERIES.	Nov. 17th		Quiet day. No Casualties. Bosch Trench raided on our left. 28 Prisoners taken.	E.W. Mackett
	Nov. 18th		Quiet morning Enemy Trench Mortars. Communication Trenches in the afternoon. No Casualties	E.W. Mackett
	Nov. 19th		Quiet day. No Casualties	E.W. Mackett
	Nov. 20th		Relieved by 10th H.L.I. Relief Complete at 8 P.M. Marched back to Infantry Barracks YPRES. No Casualties.	E.W. Mackett

WAR DIARY or INTELLIGENCE SUMMARY

Army Form C. 2118.

Place	Date	Hour	Summary of Events and Information	Remarks and references to Appendices
INFANTRY BARRACKS YPRES.	1916 Nov. 21		300 men on working parties during day + night. No casualties	S.W.Machell
	Nov. 22	300 men	working parties. No casualties	S.W.Machell
	Nov. 23	300 men	on working parties. YPRES. Relief during afternoon. No casualties	S.W.Machell
	Nov. 24		Reliefs 10th R.F. in A. Section left sector. One casualty (not dying rept)	S.W.Machell
A. Battn Nov 25th Left Kein Nov 26th L.A.Q. at 10.1.V. Ples	Nov 25th		Quiet day. No casualties. A few heavy trench mortar bombs were put on to the extreme right of the Battn sector, little damage was done, & no casualties. An officer's patrol had a thunderflash or bomb thrown at him	E.M.Satto
	Nov 26th		At 2.30 several heavy shells were put in vicinity of Batt Hd Quarters. Otherwise a quiet day.	E.M.Satto
	Nov 27th		A Raid was attempted on enemy dep. J.9.a.1.5 (ZILLEBEKE 28 NW H4 NE 3. parts of.) The party consisted of 3 Officers + 35 O.R. The party came under fire soon after getting over the parapet at 12.30 am, but nevertheless worked their way to within about 20 yards of the sap when they were bombed & fired at by Machine Guns & Rifles. The raid had much little chance of success	E.M.Satto

WAR DIARY
or
INTELLIGENCE SUMMARY
(Erase heading not required.)

Army Form C. 2118.

Place	Date	Hour	Summary of Events and Information	Remarks and references to Appendices
	1916 Nov. 28th continued		that it was decided to return to our trenches. No casualties.	E McSatto
	Nov. 29th		A quiet day on Battn front. Relieved by 1st Yorks Regt. Relief complete at 9.30 p.m. Entrained at YPRES arriving for BRANDHOEK — arriving & marched thence to TORONTO and ERIE Camps, arriving about 2.30 a.m.	E McSatto E McSatto E McSatto E McSatto
	Nov. 30th		Re fitting and Kit Inspection. Baths at POPERINGHE.	E McSatto
	Dec 1st		Bus & rifle practice & Baths at POPERINGHE	
	Dec 2nd		Return to training programme.	
	Dec 3rd		Church Parade. YMCA Hut in BRIGADE Officers and transport lines cancelled. Bored Grates	

1/12/16

E McSatto Lieut.
A/Adjt 11th North'd Fus.

Army Form C. 2118.

Vol 15
1/1st Northumberland Fusiliers

WAR DIARY
or
INTELLIGENCE SUMMARY
(Erase heading not required.)

Place	Date	Hour	Summary of Events and Information	Remarks and references to Appendices
TORONTO Camp	1916 Dec 1st		Drill and Wiring practice. Baths at POPERINGE	ShuSatto
	Dec 2nd		Drill and Wiring practice. "A" Coy. moved into ERIE Camp.	ShuSatto
	Dec 3rd		Church parade in Y.M.C.A. Hut in ERIE Camp. Officers and Lewis Gunners carried out Revolver practice.	ShuSatto
	Dec 4th		Drill and Wiring practice. Working party 2 Officers and 110 men on front line.	ShuSatto ShuSatto
	Dec 5th		Drill, & fatigues improving Camp.	ShuSatto
	Dec 6th		Drill and Wiring practice. Fatigues improving Camp.	ShuSatto
	Dec 7th		Treatment of feet & preparing for trenches. Left TORONTO Camp at 4 p.m. Arrived at the Hospice (YPRES "D" position) 6.30 p.m.	ShuSatto
HOSPICE YPRES	Dec 8th		Quiro day. Working parties of over 200 men at night.	Ratchell Ratchell
	Dec 9th		A few shells fell in YPRES. Casualties Nil. Working parties strafing at night.	Ratchell Ratchell
	Dec 10th		The Square at YPRES has shelled about 1.30 p.m. Same working parties at night. No casualties	Ratchell

Army Form C. 2118.

WAR DIARY
or
INTELLIGENCE SUMMARY

(Erase heading not required.)

Instructions regarding War Diaries and Intelligence Summaries are contained in F. S. Regs., Part II. and the Staff Manual respectively. Title Pages will be prepared in manuscript.

Place	Date	Hour	Summary of Events and Information	Remarks and references to Appendices
"A" Batty Right Bah.	Dec 11.16		Enemy shelling YPRES from 10-10.30 AM, One shell fell in the Courtyard of the HOSPICE wounding two men. Retired 10h.30F in A position Rept Rele Sector. Relief Completed at 5PM.	G W Maclell
	Dec 12.16		A quiet morning. Slight Trench Mortar activity about 3.30PM. Canadies Nil.	G W Maclell
	Dec 13.16		Our trenches here Trench Mortars in the afternoon, and of day fight too Spot. Canadies. 1. killed & 3 wounded.	G W Maclell
	Dec 14.		Artillery activity on Communication & Support trenches. Casualties 2 wounded.	
	Dec 15.		There was an intense bombardment all along Batln front from 8 7AM-10 AM. The front trench, living TRENCH, CANADA ST, MEAGH ST, WIGAN ST 1ST PETERS ST were all very badly knocked about, also wire infront of centre right Coy lines which was badly cut. All was Quiet until 4.15PM when two "minnies" fell in our abot our front. At 4.18 PM the S.O.S. was sent up to start again 40 men tried to man our trench. They bombed are Sap heading at about traversing 2. Then retired leaving three dead in our trench. The bombardment which was of intense volume continued until 5 PM. Our trenches were practically obliterated ; large working parties were sent up at night Got a busy Trench 'Relief' was postponed 24 hours Casualties 2 killed & 7 wounded	G W Maclell

WAR DIARY
or
INTELLIGENCE SUMMARY

(Erase heading not required.)

Army Form C. 2118.

Instructions regarding War Diaries and Intelligence Summaries are contained in F. S. Regs., Part II. and the Staff Manual respectively. Title Pages will be prepared in manuscript.

Place	Date	Hour	Summary of Events and Information	Remarks and references to Appendices
ZILLEBEKE Dun II	Decr. 16		Trenches Quiet. A fair amount of work was done in cleaning trenches. Relieved at night by 10th N.F. Casualties nil	S.M. Mackell
	17.		Very quiet day. 220 men & 5 officers here on working parties at night	S.M. Mackell
	18.		Quiet day. 3 Officers & 220 men on working parties. Casualties nil.	S.M. Mackell
	19.		do do	S.M. Mackell
A Position Right Bde Sector Trenches I. 30. 1 to I. 30. 9.	20.		A good deal of shelling towards ZILLEBEKE a few trench shells fell by the Bom.P. Relieved 10th N.F. in "A" Position. Casualties nil	S.M. Mackell
	21.		A good deal of shelling during the day. Quiet night.	S.M. Mackell
	22.		Very heavy trench mortaring at 6 p.m. Trenches badly damaged. 4 wounded.	S.M. Mackell
	23.		Quiet day. Relieved by 10th Bde & battalion moves back to TORONTO Camp, arrived at Camp about 2 o'clock.	S.M. Mackell
TORONTO CAMP	24		Day of rest & cleaning up.	S.M. Mackell

Army Form C. 2118.

WAR DIARY
or
INTELLIGENCE SUMMARY

(Erase heading not required.)

Instructions regarding War Diaries and Intelligence Summaries are contained in F. S. Regs., Part II. and the Staff Manual respectively. Title Pages will be prepared in manuscript.

Place	Date	Hour	Summary of Events and Information	Remarks and references to Appendices
TORONTO CAMP.P.	25/12/16.		Church Parade in Morning. Men's Christmas dinners at 1 oclock. & Concert in evening at Y.M.C.A. ERIS Camp.	E.W. Mackell
	26/12/16.		Working Parties of 150 men. Company Training. Parade for Divisional Montagina decorations by Corps Commander.	E.W. Mackell
	27/12/16.		Working Parties of 100 men. Company Training.	E.W. Mackell
	28/12/16.		Working Parties of 100 men. Company Training.	E.W. Mackell
	29/12/16.		Baths at Poperinghe. New draft of 156 men joined Battalion.	E.W. Mackell
	30/12/16.		Company Training.	E.W. Mackell
	31/12/16.		Relieved 9th York Tenes in Infantry Barracks at YPRES.	E.W. Mackell

E.W. Mackell Capt.
for O.C. 9th Yorks Regt

2/1/17.

The attached is the War
Diary of the 11th (Service) Battalion
Northumberland Fusiliers, for the
month of January 1917.

A.E.Lyne Major
~~Capt. & A/Adjutant~~
for O.C. 11th Northumberland Fusiliers

2/2/17.

Army Form C. 2118.

WAR DIARY
or
INTELLIGENCE SUMMARY

XI NF   Vol 16

(Erase heading not required.)

Instructions regarding War Diaries and Intelligence Summaries are contained in F. S. Regs., Part II and the Staff Manual respectively. Title Pages will be prepared in manuscript.

Place	Date	Hour	Summary of Events and Information	Remarks and references to Appendices
INFANTRY BARRACKS YPRES.	JAN. 1. 1917		Very Quiet day. Two hundred men out at rifle or bombing park. The duckboards between STAFFORD ST & HALIFAX ST here shelled. Casualties 1 killed & 2 wounded	B.M.Maclot
	JAN. 2		YPRES was shelled slightly about 1 P.M. Offensive Raids Birch Wood bombing parties. Casualties Nil	B.M.Maclot B.M.Maclot
	Jan 3		Quiet day. Casualties Nil	
A. Rather Right Rdr Sector	Jan 4		Returns to N.F. in A. pointer Right Rdr sector. Casualties. Nil	B.M.Maclot
	Jan 5.		Morning Quiet. Some little artillery activity during the afternoon.	
	Jan. 6.		Rather more activity than during the last few days. YPRES was heavily shelled. Casualties. Nil	B.M.Maclot B.M.Maclot
	Jan 7.		Quiet day in line. A little shelling behind. Casualties 2 wounded	B.M.Maclot
	Jan 8.		Very heavy shelling behind. Shelled all day. The BUND & YPRES & the duckboards were also the duckboard & railway in many places. The bridle over the moat received a direct hit here retired by 10 N.F. Ypres back to the Barracks. Casualties Nil	B.M.Maclot

WAR DIARY
or
INTELLIGENCE SUMMARY
(Erase heading not required.)

Army Form C. 2118.

Place	Date	Hour	Summary of Events and Information	Remarks and references to Appendices
Barracks, YPRES	Jan 9 (10?)		A few shells fell in Ypres during the day. No attacks but working parties. One officer sent up to the line for wiring. Casualties Nil.	J.W. Machell
	Jan 10 (11?)		Quiet day. Wired working parties. 250 O. Ranks. Two new Officers joined. Casualties Nil.	J.W. Machell B.W. Machell
	Jan 11		A few shells fell in the Brave. Working parties at night. Casualties Nil.	
A. Rath K.W. Ridge	Jan 12		Relieved 10th N.F. in A Section. Very quiet day. About 9 pm. M.G. fire sent up till our left. All batteries opened fire. At 9.30 pm all had quiet. Casualties Nil.	J.W. Machell
	Jan 13		Very quiet day & night. Casualties Nil.	J.W. Machell
	Jan 14		Lovers both shelled about 2 pm. Very little damage done. Casualties 1 wounded.	J.W. Machell
	Jan 15		Very quiet. Casualties Nil.	J.W. Machell
	Jan 16		Relieved by 11th West Yorks. Neighbourhood here shelled during relief, also YPRES. Shell hit on railway line. Steer & Gosser. Yrs. Dismantys & Road. Marched to Camp. Arrives about 3 AM. Casualties Nil.	J.W. Machell

Army Form C. 2118.

WAR DIARY
or
INTELLIGENCE SUMMARY
(Erase heading not required.)

Instructions regarding War Diaries and Intelligence Summaries are contained in F.S. Regs., Part II. and the Staff Manual respectively. Title Pages will be prepared in manuscript.

Place	Date	Hour	Summary of Events and Information	Remarks and references to Appendices
TORONTO CAMP.	17/1/17.		Day of Rest, chewing up.	J.M.Machell
	18/1/17.		Baths at Poperinghe all day. Company training. Chesses lots for leave summer Squadron. NCO's s.C. New YMCA hut opened by General Babington.	J.M.Machell
	19/1/17.		Minus Parade. Company Parade. Working parties of 2 Offrs 150 men.	J.M.Machell
	20/1/17.		Company Parades etc. Working party of 1 Off. & 150 OR.	J.M.Machell
	21/1/17.		Church Parade. Night working party of 1 Off & 150 OR.	J.M.Machell
	22/1/17.		Scheme for starting communication between Infantry & Aeroplanes by means of flares, lamps & ground sheets. Corps Commander present. Baths at Poperinghe. Route marched in afternoon.	J.M.Machell
	23/1/17.			J.M.Machell
	24/1/17.		Relieved 8th Yorks Lancs in Rt position Potijde Sector. Entrenched Braddock. E.Pm. A Coy in Infantry Barracks. B Coy Moffices. C.Cy Cavalry Barracks. D Cy HQ The RUND.	J.M.Machell
	25/1/17.		Our heavy artillery bombarded Shrewsbury works. Very little retaliation behind lines. No casualties. Working Parties of 2 Offs & 150 OR.	J.M.Machell
	26/1/17.		Very quiet day. Great amount of aircraft activity, mostly British. 2 Officers & 240 OR on working parties.	J.M.Machell

2449 Wt. W14957/Mg0 750,000 1/16 J.B.C. & A. Forms/C.2118/12.

Army Form C. 2118.

WAR DIARY
or
INTELLIGENCE SUMMARY

(Erase heading not required.)

Instructions regarding War Diaries and Intelligence Summaries are contained in F. S. Regs., Part II. and the Staff Manual respectively. Title Pages will be prepared in manuscript.

Place	Date	Hour	Summary of Events and Information	Remarks and references to Appendices
BnHQ.	Jan 27.17		Kaiser's birthday. Day bright. Passed out quietly. 2 Offrs & 240 men out on working parties. Casualties Nil	E.M.Mackesy
	Jan 28.17		Relieved 10th N.F. in "B" Section. Very quiet relief. Casualties Nil	E.M.Mackesy
B. Sec. Fm.	Jan 29.17		Very Quiet. Casualties Nil	E.M.Mackesy
Right Section	Jan 30.17		Very quiet. More movement than usual noticed behind the German lines. Our own troops in trenches. Casualties Nil	E.M.Mackesy
	Jan 31.17		Very Quiet. Observation day. Enemy aircraft active over left. Sect. at night. Casualties Nil	E.M.Mackesy
	Feby 1.17		Fine day. Enemy raided Left Bde of Division on our left. Sect. at night. Casualties Nil	

E.M.Mackesy
Capt. & Adjt.
for O.C. 14th Bn Royal Irish Rif.

THE ATTACHED IS THE WAR DIARY OF THE 11TH (SERVICE) BATTALION NORTHUMBERLAND FUSILIERS, FOR THE MONTH OF FEBRUARY 1917.

[signature]

Capt. & A/Adjutant,
for O.C. 11th Northumberland Fusiliers.

WAR DIARY or INTELLIGENCE SUMMARY

Army Form C. 2118.

XI NF Vol 17

Place	Date	Hour	Summary of Events and Information	Remarks and references to Appendices
"C" Position	Feb 1. 1917		Quiet day. Relieved by 10th NF & moved to C. position. Casualties Nil.	SWMachett
	Feb 2. 1917		Had to move another Company into trenches. Disposition Bns HQ 12 Coys The BUND, 1½ Coys STAFFORD ST, 2 Platoons WINNEPEG ST. Casualties Nil. 2 Officers & 75 men on working parties.	SWMachett
	Feb 3		Great aircraft activity. 5 Officers & 240 men on working parties. Casualties Nil.	SWMachett
	Feb 4		Quiet day. 5 O/s & 225 men on working parties. Casualties Nil.	SWMachett
	Feb 5		Relieved 10 NF in B. position.	SWMachett
"B" Position	Feb 6		JHQ move to Valley Cottages. Quiet relief. Enemy put a few shrapnel over VANCOUVER ST. About 3 AM. At 6 pm Enemy bombarded CRAB CRAWL, VANCOUVER ST, VIGO ST, WINNIPEG ST with Trench Mortars. Very little damage was done. Casualties 6 men wounded.	SWMachett
	Feb 7		Quiet day in the line YPRES the back areas shelled intermittently all day.	SWMachett
	Feb 8		Quiet day. a few shells fell near CRAB ORCHARD during the afternoon.	SWMachett SWMachett
	Feb 9		Quiet day. About 8 pm the Enemy started a heavy bombardment on our right, our guns opened heavy firing immediately. The bombardment went along to the left finishing about 9 pm ZILLEBEKE was heavily shelled during the "Strafe". Relieved by 10 West Riding at 11 pm. moved to TORONTO CAMP. Every thing Quiet	SWMachett

2449 Wt. W14957/M90 750,000 1/16 J.B.C. & A. Forms/C.2118/12.

WAR DIARY
or
INTELLIGENCE SUMMARY
(Erase heading not required.)

Army Form C. 2118.

Place	Date	Hour	Summary of Events and Information	Remarks and references to Appendices
TORONTO CAMP.	Feb.10.17		Day of rest & cleaning up.	S.M.Maskell
	Feb.11.17		Special Platoons formed in each Company according to new Regulations.	M.Maskell
	Feb.12.17		Ladies Park of 1 officer & 40 men. One hundred men inoculated by M.O. Rest of Battalion at Company Training.	M.Maskell
	Feb.13.17		Same working party. Baths at Poperinghe all day.	M.Maskell
	Feb.14.17		Battalion parade for C.O.'s inspection. Company training in the afternoon.	M.Maskell
	Feb.15		G.O.C. Brigade inspected the Battalion by Companies. Rest of the day training under Company arrangements.	M.Maskell
	Feb.16		Company training. Special Platoons here practised in bomb attack.	M.Maskell
INFANTRY BARRACKS YPRES.	Feb.17		Relieved 11th Sussex & Forester in D Section. Very quiet night. Casualties Nil	M.Maskell
	Feb.18		Quiet day. Very little shelling on either side. 2 Officers & 200 men on working parties at night. Casualties Nil	M.Maskell
	Feb.19.		Very quiet. Same working parties as on 18th. Casualties Nil	M.Maskell

Army Form C. 2118.

WAR DIARY
or
INTELLIGENCE SUMMARY
(Erase heading not required.)

Instructions regarding War Diaries and Intelligence Summaries are contained in F. S. Regs., Part II. and the Staff Manual respectively. Title Pages will be prepared in manuscript.

Place	Date	Hour	Summary of Events and Information	Remarks and references to Appendices
Feb 20	Feb 21		Quiet day a few gas shells fell toward YPRES station. Casualties Nil.	E.M.Wackett
	Feb 22		Quiet day. very misty. A little shelling at night. Casualties Nil	E.M.Wackett
	Feb 22		Relieved 10th N.F. in B. section 10p.m. sector. Relief complete at 7.30 p.m. No casualties	E.M.Wackett
	Feb 23		Very misty. No shelling.	E.M.Wackett
	Feb 24		A small mine was exploded on our left about RAILWAY WOOD. A good deal of artillery activity followed. The CRATER was shelled with this bomb. No casualties	E.M.Wackett
	Feb 25		Very misty morning. Cleared later. GORDON HOUSE & INFANTRY POST were shelled in the afternoon. No casualties	E.M.Wackett
	Feb 26		Clear day. RAILWAY COTTAGE was shelled with 5.9's about 9.30 p.m. Relieved by 16th Sherwood Foresters. Relief complete at 12 midnight. Entrained at YPRES, detrained BRANDHOEK & marched to E camp arriving at 3 A.m. 27th. Casualties Nil	E.M.Wackett
E. Camp. A.30.a.5.5 Belgium 28 N.W.	Feb 27		Cleaning up & refitting	E.M.Wackett
	Feb 28		Marched to Z camp about 7 miles 10a.m. E camp at 9.15 arrived Z camp 1p.m.	E.M.Wackett Capt. M.N.Wackett for O.C. 11th North'd Fusrs

THE ATTACHED IS THE WAR DIARY OF THE 11TH (SERVICE) BATTALION NORTHUMBERLAND FUSILIERS FOR THE MONTH OF MARCH 1917.

P.C. Mayall

Capt. & Adjutant,
1/4/17.   for O.C. 11th Northumberland Fusiliers.

Army Form C. 2118.

WAR DIARY
or
INTELLIGENCE SUMMARY
(Erase heading not required.)

Vol 18

Place	Date	Hour	Summary of Events and Information	Remarks and references to Appendices
Watten	March 1 1919		Marched from Z Camp to BOLLEZEELE. Starts at 9.15 a.m. arrived 4.30 p.m. Marching good.	Whitelett
BOLLEZEELE	March 2		Day of cleaning up & refitting. Inspection of billets by C.O.	Whitelett
	March 3.		Platoon Training Commenced. Three training fields and a range allotted to Battn.	Whitelett
	March 4.		Platoon Training. Officers instructed in the Lewis Gun.	Whitelett
	March 5.		Firing on Range. Platoon training	Whitelett
	March 6.		do	Whitelett
	March 7.		Baths for A & C Coys. HQ Training	Whitelett
	March 8.		Baths for B & D Coys. & Tpt. Platoon Training	Whitelett
	March 9.		Platoon Training. Accident in C Coy billet. Cpl. Smart killed & 2 men wounded.	Whitelett
	March 10.		Battn visited by Soc. Stanton. Funeral of Cpl. Smart held in BOLLEZEELE CEMETERY.	Whitelett
	March 11.		Church Parade. Tactical scheme for all Officers in morning.	Whitelett
	March 12		Company Training on 39A St Training Area	Whitelett
	" 13.		Platoon & Company Training. Firing on Range	Whitelett
	" 14.		Platoon " " " " " "	Whitelett
	" 15.		Baths & Training. Firing on Range	Whitelett
	" 16.		Baths & Company Training. Trn. Area	Whitelett
	" 17.		Battalion Route March from 9 a.m. to 1 p.m.	Whitelett
	" 18.		Church Parade & Preparing for move.	Whitelett
	19		Battalion paraded at 9 a.m. & marched to HOUTKERQUE arriving at 12.30 p.m.	Whitelett

WAR DIARY
or
INTELLIGENCE SUMMARY

(Erase heading not required.)

Army Form C. 2118.

Place	Date	Hour	Summary of Events and Information	Remarks and references to Appendices
HOUTKERQUE	20/3/17		Battalion paraded ready to move off at 10 am from HOUTKERQUE and marched to P Camp.	Relinaques
P. Camp.	21/3/17		Arriving 12.45 pm. Capt. R.C. Kingate rejoined from England and 2nd Lt. E.W. Abbott reported for duty and was posted to "C" Company. Battalion moved to X Camp in afternoon. Major Fair took over command of Battalion on C.O. proceeding on leave.	Relinaques
X. Camp.	22/3/17		Battalion paraded under company arrangements. 2/Lts E.P. Bell and R.F. Bolton posted to "B" and "A" Companies respectively. Football match started for duty and were posted to "B" and "A" Companies respectively. Football match in afternoon.	Relinaques
	23/3/17		Battalion provided working parties of 250 men to work under R.E. Signals. Played football match v 38th Div D.A.C. won (1-0). Officers match postponed.	Relinaques
	24/3/17		Provided working parties of about 250 men. had use of bathes in afternoon. Company Commanders Conference in morning. Football match H.Q. v Transport. H.Q. won (2-0).	Relinaques
	25/3/17		Provided working parties of about 250 men. Cup x Ranges in Quest Army Hd. Football Match 11th N.F. v 10th N.F. Lost (1.8).	Relinaques
	26/3/17		Battalion provided 266 men for working parties – Scit H.M.P. West rejoined and took over command from 2/Lt Clegg of "B" Coy – 2/Lt E.G. Bowers M.C. rejoined and assumed duties of Bn "Bombing officer".	Relinaques
	27/3/17		Battalion provided 266 men for working parties – Range practice for "C" Coy's Lewis Gunners and "B" Coy in Gas Masks.	Relinaques
	28/3/17		Battalion provided 466 men for working parties – Classes of Signallers started. Bearers – Football match. V. Q.4 Hussars Lost (1-2).	Relinaques
	29/3/17		Battalion provided 367 men for working parties – G.O.C. Brigade Inspector of Camp cancelled. Gen. Hunter-weston commanding VIIIth Corps inspected Camp.	Relinaques
	30/3/17		Battalion found 439 men for working parties – G.O.C. Division inspected 1 platoon of "C" Company (No.10) – Army 38 Div inspected Camp.	Relinaques

Army Form C. 2118.

WAR DIARY
or
INTELLIGENCE SUMMARY

(Erase heading not required.)

Instructions regarding War Diaries and Intelligence Summaries are contained in F. S. Regs., Part II. and the Staff Manual respectively. Title Pages will be prepared in manuscript.

Place	Date	Hour	Summary of Events and Information	Remarks and references to Appendices
X Camp	31/3/17		Provided 339 men for working parties – Signalling, Lewis Gun and Grenadier Training under specialist officers – officers forming football match v 9th (Warwicks?) (S—o) transport wagon to fresh standings. Strength 42 officers – 805 O.R. (fighting) Trench strength 35 officers – 616 O.R.	R.C.Magall.

March 31st 1917.

R.C. Magall
Captain Adjutant
for O.C. 11th Northumberland Fusiliers

2449 Wt. W14957/M90 750,000 1/16 J.B.C. & A. Forms/C.2118/12.

SECRET.

11TH NORTHUMBERLAND FUSILIERS - ORDER NO. 1.

1. The 68th Brigade will move tomorrow to the HOUTKERQUE Area.

2. REVEILLE - 5.30 a.m.

   The 11th N.F. will parade on the road, with the head of the column at the cross roads at A.19.b.2.0. ready to move off at 8.55 a.m. Order of march - C, D, A, B, H.Q., 1st Line Transport. Lewis Detachments will march in rear of their respective Companies.

   ROUTE - ZEGGERS CAPPEL, ESQUELBECQ, WORMHOUDT, HERZEEELE. There will be a halt at 12.50 p.m. for dinner, the march being resumed at 2p.m.

3. TRANSPORT ARRANGEMENTS. 1 lorry will report at each Company Headquarters at 6.30 a.m. tomorrow. This will carry the Officers' valises, Company blankets, packs, stores.

   The Officers' valises of Headquarters, mens' packs and blankets will be stacked outside Headquarter billet by 6.30 a.m. The Qr.Mr. will send 2 G.S. wagons to collect them at that hour. The blankets of the Transport personnel will also be carried on these wagons.

   The Mess cart will be sent round to collect the two Mess boxes per Company at 7.45 a.m.

4. DRESS. The Haversack will be worn on the back in place of the valise, with Steel helmet and Mess tin fastened in the manner demonstrated to Company Sergt. Majors tonight.

                                                  Capt. & A/Adjutant,
                                                  11th Northd. Fusiliers.

18/3/17.

SECRET.

COPY No. 10

11th NORTHUMBERLAND FUSILIERS - ORDER No. 2.

1. The 11th N.F. will move tomorrow to "P" Camp, A.15.d., Sheet 28 N.W., via WATOU, ST.JAN - ler - BIEZON, Switch Road and A.21.

    The Battalion will parade on the road, with head of the column at Headquarter Mess, ready to move off at 9.45 a.m. Order of march - D, A, B, C, H.Q., 1st Line Transport.

2. ADVANCE PARTY. A lorry will start from the Square, HERZEELE, at 8 a.m. tomorrow to convey advance parties to their camps. It will stop at HOUTKERQUE to pick up parties billeted there. The same party that came in advance yesterday will proceed by this lorry.

3. TRANSPORT. 1 lorry will report to each Company, and the G.S. wagons to Headquarters, at 7 a.m. When loaded they will proceed to the camp via E.13.c. - DROGLANDT - WATOU. The Qr.Mr. will point out this route to the N.C.O. in charge of the lorries.
    All lorries to be clear of WATOU by 10.30 a.m.

    The mess cart will commence to collect the two mess boxes per Company at 8 a.m.

19/3/17.

Capt. & A/Adjutant,
11th Northd. Fusiliers.

SECRET.   Copy No. 10

11th NORTHUMBERLAND FUSILIERS – ORDER NO. 3.

1. The 11th N.F. will move into X Camp this evening, relieving the 10th S.W.B.

   The two baggage wagons will be available for moving Officers' kits and blankets, commencing with "A" Coy at 11 a.m.

2. The N.C.O's who are proceeding to take over the new camp will return to "P" Camp as soon as the S.W.B. have vacated "X" Camp, and guide their Companies to the new position.

3. Companies will proceed independently as soon as their N.C.O. reports.

   Capt. & A/Adjutant,
   11th Northd. Fusiliers.

21/3/17.

Copy No. 1 – C.O.
" No. 2 – 2nd in Command.
" No. 3 – 6 – Companies.
" No. 7 – T.O.

Copy No. 8 – Qr.Mr.
" No. 9 – Sergt. Major.
" No. 10 – File.

WAR DIARY
or
INTELLIGENCE SUMMARY

Army Form C. 2118.

XI N F

Place	Date	Hour	Summary of Events and Information	Remarks and references to Appendices
X Camp. A.16.c.11.6 Belgium 28.N.W.	1/4/17		Provided 339 men for working parties - Hut Orderly Officer - Football Match HQ v Transpt (2-0)	Renayall
	2/4/17		Received warning order to prepare for move to BOEZEELE area at 9am - Provided 339 men for working parties on G5 & G6 - D Coy had the use of Lorries in own own Camp - Major J.G. Owen from the R.S.K.a.Y.L.I. joined and assumed duties as Second in Command and in absence of CO took over command of the Battalion from Major A.J.T Nelson. — CO. inspected the Camp working parties on G5 and G6 to ascertain progress - Orders received at 4.30am for working parties to continue at 3.30pm. — C.O inspected A. Coy's billet at ROUSSEL FARM — Drew fur parades mire to BOEZEELE AREA received and moved at 11 pm —	Renayall
	3/4/17		Battalion moved to BOEZEELE — Transpt & Lewis Gun Section moved by road at 9am and arrived about 6pm — The Battn paraded at 10.30am. marched to BRANDHOEK station and entrained there at 11pm - Battn detrained at ESQUELBECQ at 3.30pm and marched to BOEZEELE and was billetted there. — 2 Lt Watson rejoined. ₹ B Coy attached to 1st Australian Coy in YPRES. 2 Lt E.P. Bell & 2 Sn men attached to R.E in YPRES.	Re Royall
BOEZEELE	4/4/17		Company Commander re-disposed of Companies for inturn economy — had use of Brigade Baths all day — G.O.C's warm until the Battalion —	Renayall
	5/4/17		Companies paraded under their own arrangements for elementary training. Funeral of the late Battalion at Brigade Baths — CO inspected billets and training — Capt W.K. MacLachlan proceeded on Special Leave.	Renayall
	6/4/17		Companies paraded under their own programmes — CO inspected Companies in morning — G.O.C. Brigade inspector C.O's Companies in close order drill in afternoon. Football Match officers 105 M.F v 115 N.F lost (1-5)	Re Royall
	7/4/17		Church parade under Capt Adamson at 11am — Companies dis 1 Physical Drill buffet in afternoon - no work in afternoon —	Renayall
Easter Sunday	8/4/17		Draft of T.O.R. (all old 11 N.F.) arrived — no work in afternoon.	
	9/4/17		Battalion Drill in Area C.3 Sub-area 4 — Close Order Drill inspection of platoons by Coy - Cross Country Race for Brigade in afternoon — we only secured a place 1C 6 15 - 2 Lt Edgar When rejoined from leave.	Renayall

WAR DIARY or INTELLIGENCE SUMMARY

Army Form C. 2118.

Instructions regarding War Diaries and Intelligence Summaries are contained in F. S. Regs., Part II. and the Staff Manual respectively. Title Pages will be prepared in manuscript.

(Erase heading not required.)

Place	Date	Hour	Summary of Events and Information	Remarks and references to Appendices
BOEZEELE.	10.4.17		Battalion paraded on "C" Area — close order drill and artillery formations — Section 1 to all Battalion Officers at 2.30pm by Major J. S. Owen. — 1st Round of Rugby Competition 11th N.F. v. 10th N.F. won 12/15 to nil (4 tries)	Re: Mayall.
	11.4.17		Conference in close order drill from 10am—11am at B.I.Q. & HOFFLAND — Battalion paraded on Area C 3 at 11.30am for practice in attack — Sir Brigadier Inspected Competition the Battalion received three 1st's (Heavy draught — pair of mules — Single mule) — one second (one seat) — one third (riding officers horse)	Re: Mayall.
	12.4.17		Battalion had March of Brigade Battn all day and every man had a hurt — Many men drawn for Conference — Conference meeting for close order work and further in artillery or attack formations — Warning order for move to BRAND HOEK reserve — Rain at 5pm —	Re: Mayall.
G.12.C.4.0	12.4.17		Battalion marched abt 8am and marched to ESQUELBECQ Station entraining at 10am and detraining at POPERINGHE at 12 noon — Took over the camp at G. 12. C. & D from the 17/5 K.R.R. (17"Bn) arriving at 1.15pm — Transport moved by road arriving about 4.30pm and took over Stabling at G.16. d. 6.6. — Lt Col St Hill rejoined from leave.	Remayall.
	14.4.17		Conference at dugout of O.C. Coys all day. — Orders received for Batt'n to march to relieve 116" Bde 16 Hussars — Advance party of 10 Officers & 4 N.C.O's per Coy proceeded by train at 9pm to YPRES to take over.	Remayall.
HOOGE SECTOR	15.4.17		Battalion paraded at 8pm in the camp and marched to BRANDHOEK siding entraining at 563 O.R. at 8.40pm detraining and marched near enemy YPRES — Guides from 12 Royal Suffolk guided entrance in — D Coy: Front line — C Coy dugouts — B Coy Support — A Coy Reserve = H.Q. TUILLERIES. Relief completed 1.20am. — Very Quiet night — Major Owen proceeded on leave — Major Lane, Capt Bebaick & S.O. Officer proceeded to & — Transport lines.	Remayall.
	16.4.17		Enemy shelled VINCE S'r' WELLINGTON Crescent in morning but no casualties otherwise quiet day.	Remayall.

Army Form C. 2118.

WAR DIARY
or
INTELLIGENCE SUMMARY

(Erase heading not required.)

Place	Date	Hour	Summary of Events and Information	Remarks and references to Appendices
Centre Sub Sect HOOGE	17/4/17		Very quiet morning - Change of dispositions - Battalion became Support battalion by 10th W.F. left Maple and 13-B7.1. right bales cleared in - D platoon no. :- A Coy RITZ STREET; B Coy WELLINGTON CRESCENT. (left of Support Bn) - C Coy 2 platoons in WELLINGTON CRESCENT and two platoons in MAPLE TRENCH :- D Coy Inf in INFANTRY BARRACKS YPRES — H.Q. remained in TUILLERIES — Relief complete 11.20pm. - Rations arr. at around 12.12am	R.E. Mayor
Support Battalion	18/4/17		Very quiet day - Battalion furnished working parties for R.E. on VINCE ST, WELLINGTON CRESCENT, MAPLE STREET and RITZ ST. - Capt Blackett assumed command of Support filers over proceeded to England to fetch filers - no casualties	R.E. Mayor
	19/4/17		Enemy shelled intermittently during morning over a very extensive front - Major A.G. Lane proceeded to 31st Inf. Base Depot on leave famed more infet - Capt WK Malcolm returned from leave	R.E. Mayor
	20/4/17		Considerable artillery activity by own guns throughout the day - very severe reconnoissance over a very extensive front - 2nd St Cowling rejoined from Lewis Gun School at LE TOUQUET. Three officers proceeded over HILL 60 Sector.	R.E. Mayor
	21/4/17		Considerable aerial activity in the evening — quiet day on our sector of the line - Trench strength 27 officers + 523 O.R.	R.E. Mayor
	22/4/17		Enemy artillery active during the morning especially in back areas - a few shells round the TUILLERIES — great aerial activity all day — another party of officers proceeded over HILL 60 Sector.	R.E. Mayor
left Battalion (front line) Map ZILLEBEKE 28 N.W. N.E.	23/4/17	5.0 P.M. 1.45pm	Enemy artillery more active during the morning - the TUILLERIES were shelled with 5.9 Shells. - Advance parties proceeded up to trenches in running to take over. - Stationary Battalion HQ Half-way-house - C Coy Right front Coy WARRINGTON AV. S.29.c.6.3 - S.24.b.15.4 x ROYERS WALK S.24.b.2.3; B Coy Right front Coy Belvoir S.18.a.2.7.; A Coy and S.24.c 9.16.c.5.5.; LEINSTER ST S.17.c.2.2.; ROSSLYN ST S.17d.S.w.; D Coy Left front Coy Belvoir S.18.a.2.7.d S.u.6 Railway Cutting S.16 a.3.8; - Relief complete 11.15pm. - Own artillery commenced a 2 days forthwith on enemy front on Durward front. - no casualties.	R.E. Mayor
	24/4/17	1/10 am	Fur bombardment continued all day on enemy front from HILL 60 - enemy retaliated on right Brigade in the morning. The Left Battn. Ext. over WARRINGTON AV from our C coy who proceeded to MAPLE & WELLINGTON CRES. Relief Complete 2.30am (Br.) - The D Was on our left carried out artillery strafe at 10pm. - had no casualties in C Coy by enemy counter.	R.E. Mayor

WAR DIARY or INTELLIGENCE SUMMARY

Army Form C. 2118.

Place	Date	Hour	Summary of Events and Information	Remarks and references to Appendices
Left Sect. (Front Line) Z.11.B.6 & 6 2SN.W.M.E. 1/10,000	25/4/17		Artillery bombardment continued on our right on enemy's positions on Hill 60 (3rd day) – very quiet day in our sector – News of 'C' Coy wounded.	Remayall
	26/4/17		Enemy's light artillery activity on Hill 60 late evening (4th day) – Our Brigade artillery had a Practice Barrage at 4pm and answered tactically on Hill 60 – Seft - one man of 'D' Coy wounded by M.G. Bullets.	Remayall
	27/4/17		Remained artillery but one in front of Hill of Coy in rest – enemy shelled our left support trench greatly (left Front Coy) and B. Coy separately during the day – A. Coy relieved B. Coy in the front support line. J.17.c.5.7. no casualties.	Remayall
	28/4/17		Artillery active on our right but very little activity in our sector – warning order received that the Brigade is to be relieved in the next two days – Pte Allen of "A" Coy accidentally wounded by the grenade – Pte Bean of "A" Coy slightly wounded – two other casualties – out of 19 guns available on evening of 19th Brigade of 19th Division will relieve our Brigade. It's likely to be preceded by 2nd Lt Kenton – advance party of 9/10(S) Bn Royal Welsh Fusiliers front of NAPLE ST. – one aeroplane shot down to hover of 11pm.	Remayall
	29/4/17		Advance party under 2/Lt Exley reported at Bn HQ at 8am to proceed to STEENVORDE - Second Advance party under 3/Lts Shackleton & Shaw reported to Company Normal at 10 am - F at 10am. May 1st - Strength 24 Officers 507 OR	Remayall
	30/4/17		30/4/17 Strength 42 Officers - 765 OR	Remayall

R. Mayall
Captain & Adjutant
11th(S) Bn. North'd Fusiliers

SECRET. COPY NO. 10

11TH NORTHUMBERLAND FUSILIERS ORDER NO. 4.

1. The Battalion will probably entrain at BRANDHOEK Station at 11.30 a.m. tomorrow, moving off from "X" Camp about 9.30 a.m. Orders will be issued later.

2. ROUTINE.   Reveille - 5.30 a.m.
                  Breakfasts - 7 a.m.
   Haversack rations and filled waterbottles will be carried. Dinners on arrival of transport.

3. LEWIS GUNNERS. The Lewis Guns and spare parts will be carried by Nos. 1 & 2 of the Teams, on the train.
   The six handcarts will proceed by road with the Transport, drawn by:—

   14 men of "A" Coy.
   14 men of "D" "
   7 men of "B" "
   7 men of "C" "

   under L/Sgt. Smith of "C" Coy.
   Parade ready to move off on Battalion Parade Ground at 7.45 a.m. "A" Company to be at "X" Camp by 7.30 a.m.
   The packs and magazine boxes will be handed in to the Qr.Mr. to be conveyed by lorry.

4. MESS CART. The Mess Cart will call for "A" Coy's Mess boxes at 7 a.m. and at "X" Camp for the remainder at 7.45 a.m. Nothing but the two Mess boxes per Company will be carried on the cart.

5. TRANSPORT. Watercarts, field kitchens, Maltese cart, Officers' Mess cart, Tool cart and G.S. wagons, will be loaded up and ready to leave "X" Camp at 8 a.m.

6. ENTRAINMENT. Capt. G.H. Blackett is appointed Battalion Entraining Officer. He will be at the Station three quarters of an hour before the train is due to start.

   On receipt of orders "A" Company will proceed direct to the Station by the shortest route.

7. The men will carry their packs.

Capt. & Adjutant,
11th Northd. Fusiliers.

3/4/17.

Copy No. 1 - C.O.   Copy No. 6 - "D" Coy.
"   No. 2 - 2nd in Command.   "   No. 7 - T.O.
"   No. 3 - "A" Coy.   "   No. 8 - Qr.Mr.
"   No. 4 - "B" "   "   No. 9 - Sergt. Major.
"   No. 5 - "C" "   "   No. 10 - File.

SECRET. COPY NO. 10.

11th Northumberland Fusiliers Advance Order No. 4.

1. The 11th N.F. will probably move from X Camp to BOLLEZEELE East on April 4th.

2. An Advance Party, under 2nd. Lt. E. G. Simons, consisting of Company Qr.Mr. Sergts., 1 N.C.O. each from H.Q., Transport and Qr.Mr's Staff, will assemble at Brigade Headquarters, "D" Camp, A.30.b.3.3., at 8 a.m. tomorrow morning.

   2nd. Lt. Simons and the C.Q.M.S. of "A" Coy will proceed direct to Brigade H.Q.

   The remainder of the party will parade under the senior N.C.O. at "X" Camp, ready to move off at 7 a.m.

3. TRANSPORT ARRANGEMENTS. Blankets will be stacked in bundles of ten ready for loading at 7 a.m., at the placed arranged by the Qr.Mr. with Company Qr.Mr.Sgts.

   Officers' valises & Company Stores will be stacked at the same place by 7.30 a.m.

   "A" Company's blankets and kits will be stacked at their own billet and a lorry will collect them.

R C Mayall.

Capt. & Adjutant,
11th Northd. Fusiliers.

3/4/18.

Copy No. 1 – C.O.
" No. 2 – 2nd in Command.
" No. 3 – "A" Coy.
" No. 4 – "B" "
" No. 5 – "C" "

Copy No. 6 – "D" Coy.
" No. 7 – T.O.
" No. 8 – Qr.Mr.
" No. 9 – Sergt. Major.
" No. 10 – File.

SECRET. COPY NO. 10

11th NORTHUMBERLAND FUSILIERS - ORDER NO. 5.

1. Reference Sheet 27 and 28. 1/40,000.

    The Brigade will relieve the 117th Brigade in the BRANDHOEK Area on the 13th and 14th inst.

    The 11th N.F. will encamp at G.12.c.4.0.

2. **ROUTINE.**   Reveille — 5 a.m.
    Breakfasts — 6.30 a.m.
    The unexpired portion of the day's ration will be carried on the man, and waterbottles will be filled before starting.

3. **PARADE.**   The Battalion will parade ready to move off at 8 a.m.
    Order of march — H.Q. Signallers and Runners, "D", "A", "C", "B", H.Q. Coy., 1st Line Transport, Lewis Gun Handcarts.
    Head of column at "D" Coy's Billet in B.19.
    Packs, with the exception of those of the seven men detailed to draw each Lewis Handcart, will be carried on the men.

4. **ADVANCE PARTY.** 2nd. Lt. E.G. Simons, Company Qr.Mr.Sgts., and one N.C.O. from H.Q., are detailed as Advance party. They will proceed by train with the Battalion.

    REAR PARTY.   The Orderly Officer and one N.C.O. per Company (with the day's ration), will remain behind to hand over billets and stores.

5. **ENTRAINING OFFICER.**   Lieut. E.G. Bowers, M.C., is appointed Battalion Entraining Officer and will report to the Staff Captain at ESQUELBECQ Station at 9.15 a.m. He will be provided with a cycle and entraining state.

6. **TRANSPORT ARRANGEMENTS.**   Baggage arrangements will be in accordance with the instructions issued earlier this evening.
    The Qr.Mr. will arrange for the loading of H.Q. baggage, which will be ready, stacked outside H.Q. Billet, by 7.15 a.m.

    LEWIS HANDCARTS.   The Lewis Handcarts will be taken empty by road, drawn by seven men per cart, will under L/Sgt. Smith of "C" Company.

7. **PLEASE ACKNOWLEDGE.**

8. **BILLETS.** One Officer per Company will inspect the billets, after the Company has paraded ready to move off.

R.C. Mayall
Capt. & Adjutant,
11th Northumberland Fusiliers.

12/4/17.

Copy No. 1 — CO.
2 — A
3 — B
4 — C
5 — D
6 — T.O.
7 — Qr M?
8 — Sergt. Major
9 — 2nd Command

10 File

SECRET.   COPY NO. 10.

11TH NORTHUMBERLAND FUSILIERS - ORDER NO. 6.

1. Reference Sheet 28. 1/40,000.

   The Brigade will relieve the 116th Brigade in the HOOGE Sector on the night 15/16th April, the 11th N.F. relieving the 12th Royal Sussex Regiment in the Centre Sub-Sector.

2. The following will be taken over:- Trench and R.E. Stores, Defence Schemes, Log Books, Maps, air photos and statement of work in progress and proposed.

3. All movement East of VLAMERTINGHE by daylight, will be in parties not greater than four men at 50 yards interval.

4. PARADE. The Battalion will parade ready to move off at 8 p.m. in the camp. Order of march - D, C, B, A, H.Q.
   Entrain at BRANDHOEK at 8.45 p.m.

   Guides will meet the Battalion at the level crossing, I.7.c.4.7., at 9.15 p.m.
   ROUTE - VINCE STREET.
   Movement East of YPRES will be by parties not larger than a platoon at 100 yards interval.

5. DISPOSITION. Front Line - "D" Company - 4 Platoons in WARRINGTON AVENUE.
   Close support - "C" Company - 1 Platoon FORT STREET,
                                 1   "   LOVERS WALK.
                                 2   "   MAPLE TRENCH.
   Support - "B" Company - 4 Platoons WELLINGTON CRESCENT.
   Reserve - "A" Company - 4 Platoons - RITZ STREET.

   Headquarters - TUILERIES, I.22.b.4.8.

   Brigade Headquarters will be at the RAMPARTS, YPRES.

6. O.C. "C" Company will arrange to take over the stores in MAPLE COPSE.

7. Completion of relief will be reported to Bn. H.Q., by runner, as early as possible.

8. Acknowledge.

9. Transport arrangements will be notified later.

                                               R.C. Mayall
                                               Capt. & Adjutant,
                                               11th Northd. Fusiliers.
14/4/17.

         Copy No.1 - C.O.   No.6 - "D" Coy.
           " No.2 - 2nd in Command.   No.7 - T.O.
           " No.3 - "A" Coy.   No.8 - Qr.Mr.
           " No.4 - "B" "   No.9 - Sergt. Major.
           " No.5 - "C" "   No.10 - File.

SECRET.   COPY NO. 10
           11TH NORTHUMBERLAND FUSILIERS - ORDER NO. 7.
           ----

1.   The 11th N.F. will relieve the 10th N.F. in the Left Sector of
   the Brigade Front on the night of April 23rd.

2. DISPOSITION.   Right front Coy - "C" Coy 11th N.F. will relieve
                                      "D" Coy 10th N.F.
                    Left front   " - "B" Coy 11th N.F. plus 1 Platoon
                                      of "D" Coy will relieve "B" Coy
                                      10th N.F.
                    Support Coy   - "A" Coy 11th N.F. will relieve
                                      "A" Coy 10th N..F.
                    Reserve Coy   - 3 Platoons of "D" Coy 11th N.F.
                                      will relieve "C" Coy 10th N.F.

3. ADVANCE PARTIES.   1 Officer and 4 N.C.O's per Company and 1 N.C.O.
   from H.Q. will proceed in the morning to take over usual stores,
   maps, log books, etc.   The N.C.O's will return to their respective Companies and will guide their Platoons to their positions at
   night.

      The Signal Officer will arrange for the relief of the Signals.

4.   Companies will move independently to their positions by the
   most direct route.   No ~~movement~~ movement before 8.45 p.m.

5. RATIONS.   With the exception of the Left Front Company, all
   Companies will furnish their own ration parties.   Ration party
   for the Left Front Company will be found by the Support Company.

6.   Disposition reports, in accordance with specimen issued a
   few days ago, will be rendered to H.Q. immediately relief is
   complete.

      Lists of stores, maps, log books, etc., taken over will be
   sent in to H.Q. by 12 noon on 24th inst.

7.   Relief complete will be reported to H.Q. as early as possible.

8.   ACKNOWLEDGE.

                                              R.C. Mayall

                                              Capt. & Adjutant,
22/4/17.   11th North'd Fusiliers.

        Copy No.1 - C.O.   Copy No.6 - Signal Officer.
         "   No.2 - "A" Coy.   "   No.7 - T.O.
         "   Nos.3 - "B" "   "   No.8 - Qr.Mr.
         "   No.4 - "C" "   "   No.9 - R.S.M.
         "   No.5 - "D" "   "   No.10 - File.

SECRET.   COPY NO. 7

11TH NORTHUMBERLAND FUSILIERS ORDER NO. 8.

1. The 68th Brigade will be relieved by the 58th Brigade on the night of 30th April/1st May, the 11th N.F. being relieved by the 9th Royal Welsh Fusiliers, in the Left Sub-Sector.

2. No Company will move until relieved by a Company of the incoming Battalion.

3. All Trench Maps, Photos, Defence Schemes, Trench Stores and documents will be handed over to relieving Companies and receipts taken. These will be forwarded to Battalion H.Q., together with handing over lists by 12 noon on the day after relief.

4. Gum Boots in the line will be handed over. They must be collected at each Company H.Q. and handed over in bulk.

5. **GUIDES.** One guide per platoon and one from H.Q., under an Officer to be detailed by O.C. "B" Coy will report at Orderly Room at 7 p.m. They will be at the YPRES Siding about H.12. central at 9 p.m. to meet the incoming Units, and will guide them up by the most direct route.

6. The Battalion, when relieved, will entrain at YPRES at 2 a.m., detraining at GODEWAERSWELDE, and march to STEENVOORDE Area.

7. TRANSPORT. All Lewis Guns and equipment, and stores to be taken back by transport, will be sent to the Company Ration Dumps.
   Each Company will leave one man at the Dump in charge of the Stores until arrival of the Transport.

8. Completion of relief will be reported over the 'phone by sending the Christian name of the Company Commander.

R C Mayall

Capt. & Adjutant,
11th Northumberland Fusiliers.

30/4/17.

```
Copy No. 1  -  C.O.          Copy No. 6  -  R.S.M.
  "  No. 2  -  "A" Coy.        "  No. 7  -  File.
  "  No. 3  -  "B"  "
  "  No. 4  -  "C"  "
  "  No. 5  -  "D"  "
```

Issued at 10 a.m.

WAR DIARY or INTELLIGENCE SUMMARY

Army Form C. 2118.

XI NF 9.F.20

Place	Date	Hour	Summary of Events and Information	Remarks and references to Appendices
STEENVOORDE AREA	1/5/17		Relieved at 1 a.m. in left bath front line of Div. Sector by 9th R.W.F. - entrained at YPRES Siding at 2.30 a.m. and detrained at GODEWAERSVELDE at 3.30 a.m. So waited at station in town and then marched to billets in area arriving at 5.30 a.m.	Rewayall
	2/5/17		Battalion rested and cleaned up all day for G.O.C. Division's inspection.	Rewayall
	3/5/17		Battalion cleaned up for inspection during the morning - the Battalion was inspected by G.O.C. Division at 5 p.m. - Paraded 31 officers & 576 men (609 total strength) - battalion dismissed. Companies carried on training under their own arrangements according to programme laid down - Signal class re-assembled - Recreation HQ v Tr. at Cricket - HQ won by runs.	Rewayall
	4/5/17		Companies carried out platoon training in Area "A" in the morning - Major Owen struck off the strength of the battalion owing to ill health.	Rewayah
	5/5/17		Companies carried out company training in Area "B" - Cricket match HQ v E'Coy won by HQ. 87 to 49.	Rewayah
	6/5/17		Church parades in the morning - officers staff rode to MONTE de CAT in the afternoon.	Rewayah
	7/5/17		Brigade Signal (Lewis) schemes were arranged in the morning carried out - Brigade Sports continued - 11th N.F. were finalists of the Rugby Competition beating the 13th R.W. by 20 pts to nil.	Rewayah
	8/5/17		Battalion parades cancelled owing to inclement weather - Companies remained in their billets all day - Brigade Sports finished - 11th N.F. won 2 events in Boxing.	Rewayah
TORONTO CAMP	9/5/17		Battalion marched out of STEENVOORDE at 9 a.m. and marched into TORONTO CAMP at 1.10 p.m. taking over from 1st Royal Irish Lancs Regt - 22 men fell out en route - Orders received for Battn to relieve 10th WORCESTERS in BUND at 10/11 inst.	Rewayah
	10/5/17		Advance party proceeded at 1 p.m. to RAILWAY DUGOUTS and Camms Bridge. Battalion paraded ready to move off at 10.15 p.m. - entrained at 2.35 p.m. - 1st Battalion arrived at 11 p.m. and detrained at YPRES SIDING - Relief complete 1.20 a.m. Very quiet relief.	Rewayall

WAR DIARY or INTELLIGENCE SUMMARY

Army Form C. 2118.

(Erase heading not required.)

Instructions regarding War Diaries and Intelligence Summaries are contained in F. S. Regs., Part II. and the Staff Manual respectively. Title Pages will be prepared in manuscript.

Place	Date	Hour	Summary of Events and Information	Remarks and references to Appendices
Reserve Batt. of Right Brigade	11/3/17		Battn. in position by 1.20 a.m. — H.Q. in dugouts at S.W. end of BUND 7.20.c.1.1.14 and all four Companies in RAILWAY DUGOUTS — enemy commenced shelling our area with heavies at 6.30 p.m. and ceased at 11 p.m. — Casualties four wounded — provided 380 O. Ranks for working parties. — Trench Strength 26 officers and 499 Other Ranks. — Draft of 250 Other Ranks arrived at Transport from MAPLE and who posted to "D" Company.	R. Mayall
	12/3/17		Effective strength of battalion 40 officers 1773 other ranks. — Deficiency on establishment of 3 officers and 196 Other Ranks inclusive of attached. — Enemy's artillery very active during the morning on our near positions — draft of 25 Other Ranks up with transport. — no casualties — 360 O.R. W.P.	R. Mayall
	13/3/17		Artillery and aerial activity throughout the day but no casualties — provided 360 O.R. for working parties — 13th D.L.I. left front Battalion raided by enemy about 4 a.m. — enemy faction and was easily driven off. — orders received for this battalion to relieve 13th K.R.I. on night of 14". and wounded to Companies at 9.15 p.m.	R. Mayall
Left Front Battn. of Divisional Front	14/3/17		Advance parties proceeded up to the trenches in the morning and battalion commenced leaving its Bund at 6 p.m. and relieved the 13th K.R.I. in the left sub-sector of the Brigade front — relief completed 12.30 a.m. Battalion HQ at RUDKIN HOUSE — A. Company in reserve in MAPLE STREET — B. Coy right front company CANADA STREET — C. Coy. left front company WINNIPEG STREET — D. Company REDAN and OBSERVATORY TRENCH — Capt Puckey proceeded on leave.	R. Mayall
	15/3/17		Enemy moderately active with artillery and minenwerfer on our front and close support line — draft of 78 men arrived and were sent up divided equally between the four Companies — 11th Naked Fire Order No 12 issued at 6.30 p.m. At 3.26 a.m. enemy started a violent bombardment of our front, shortly on its left — casualties damage done to trenches on the left — very quiet day — at 11 p.m. after one minute preliminary bombardment two parties set out from our trench under 2/Lt Hunter and Sergt Harvey of B. Company — they worked the enemy parapet but after having a fierce bomb fight were forced to return without entering enemy trenches — Casualties 1 killed & 2 wounded. — Orders Report attached.	R. Mayall
	16/3/17			R. Mayall
	17/3/17		Orders received and issued for relief of the Brigade by the 69th Bde on night 17/18th but cancelled on receiving travelled weakness on left company front. — S.O.S. went up from next line on our right at about 9.15 p.m. but few rounds fell within sub Section	R. Mayall

2449 Wt. W14957/Mgo 750,000 1/16, J.B.C. & A. Forms/C.2118/12.

WAR DIARY
or
INTELLIGENCE SUMMARY

(Erase heading not required.)

Army Form C. 2118.

Place	Date	Hour	Summary of Events and Information	Remarks and references to Appendices
Left Front Sub Sec 2nd Div Front	18/5/17		Gas S.O.S. received from Right Company about 8am. but cancelled by 8.15am - alarm spread owing to misinformed officer of fresh draft - quiet day - Battalion was relieved in the line by 9th Yorks - relief complete 3am. - Proceeded to SCOTTISH LINES and all present in camp at 8am 19th(inst)	Rewayah
SCOTTISH LINES	19/5/17		Battalion rested all day - orders received to detach two companies to be attached for duty with the Corps Heavy Artillery - A.Coy proceeded to H.23.C.6.0 and D.Coy to N.2.L.&.2 Major R.H. Gill from the 10th West Riding Regt. joined for duty as 2 in Command on 19.3 - Church Parade Service in the morning - Commanding Officer inspected his drafts at 2 pm of 25/16 D Coy (10th inst.) - 78 to all Coys. (14th) - 25/16 B Coy (19th) all inspected by Medical Officer.	Rewayah
	20/5/17			Rewayah
	21/5/17		G.O.C. Brigade inspected all new drafts at 10am in drill order - found 5 officers + 200 men for working parties from B&C Coys - Companies paraded under their own arrangements 68th Brigade Instruction No 1 & 2 received - Capt. Hayne R.A.M.C. and 2Lt Watson rejoined from leave - draft of 67 received (13/16 A, 20/16 B-C, 14/5 D).	Rewayah
	22/5/17		Commanding Officer inspected new drafts at 10am. - 2nd Lt. Moffat I.O. proceeded up to H.Q. RAILWAY DUGOUTS to choose site for Battn Dump for Emergency Rations - selected at the BUND in rear of dug outs 46-47 - Conference of C.O. Company Commanders at Brigade School to select parties of carrying loads - furnished 200 men for working parties	Rewayah
	23/5/17		Company paraded - furnished 200 men for working parties - orders received to A&D Coys to return from attachment to X Corps Heavy Artillery - Major Gill President of Court of Enquiry beyond STEENWORDE - 150 men went to Div Gas Officer for Helmet Refitting	Rewayah
	24/5/17		Battalion furnished 250 men for working parties - 2 casualties wounded by M.G. fire had the use of the baths at WINNIPEG CAMP for 300 men - 200 men went to Div Gas Officer to have helmets refitted	Rewayah
	25/5/17		125 men went to Div Gas Officer to have helmets refitted - provided 10th + 50 O.R. for A.Coy for working party - Conference of all officers to discuss plans for Ensuing Operations working party cancelled - Trench strength 683	Rewayah

W4957/Mpo 750,000 1/16 J.B.C. & A. Forms/C.2118/12.
2449 9^m.

WAR DIARY
or
INTELLIGENCE SUMMARY

(Erase heading not required.)

Army Form C. 2118.

Place	Date	Hour	Summary of Events and Information	Remarks and references to Appendices
SCOTTISH LINES.	26/5/17		Companies sent the remainder of their men to the Div. Gas Officer in the morning and company paraders – provided 105 Pioneers and 500 O.R. for working parties under Lieut. C.S. Bowman for carrying Ammunition – two casualties in A. Company (1 killed + 1 wounded)	R.E. Khayall
	27/5/17		Church parades in the morning – battalion rested all day and found no working parties – draft of 27 men arrived and posted to B & D Companies – Gas Alarm during Colonel St. Hill, Capt. Maclellan & Mitchell proceeded to STEENVOORDE to interview meeting on minature HILL 60 Tueler – Adjutant & Capt. Mitchell attended service on River Lizzer at X Corps Nucleus School BOESCHEPE – B and C Companies found 200 men for working parties and relieved two companies of 10th N.F. in the BUND for working parties under C.R.E.	Re Khayall
	28/5/17			Re Khayall
	29/5/17		The half battalion left in camp furnished 150 men for working parties during the day & night – had the use of the baths	Re Khayall
	30/5/17		Found 190 men for working parties – C.O. issued in Command proceeded up to Trenches in the afternoon.	Re Khayall
	31/5/17		Advance parties proceeded up the line in the morning – the battalion relieved the 8th KOYLI in the centre – Subsects of the Divisional front in the evening. Battalion HQ in LARCH WOOD SUBWAY – A Company in neighbourhood of MARSHALL WALK, SWITCH ST. etc B Company right front company in neighbourhood of BATTERSEA FARM S29 C Company left front company in Company Trench, ZILLIBEKE SWITCH ST – D Coy in Support in LARCH WOOD SUBWAY – Relief complete – Trench Strength 28 Off/ 169 O.R. Relief complete 12.5 a.m.	Re Khayall

June 1917.

Re Khayall
Lt Col Adjutant
1/1 S) Bn Northumb. Fusiliers

SECRET.   COPY NO. 10.

11TH NORTHUMBERLAND FUSILIERS ORDER NO.9.

1. The 68th Brigade Group will relieve the 56th Brigade Group in the OUDERDOM Area on the 9th inst., the 11th N.F. relieving the Loyal NORTH LANCS. Regt., in TORONTO CAMP.

    On the night of 10/11th the Brigade will relieve the 57th Brigade in the Right Sector of the 19th Divisional Front, 11th N.F. probably being in reserve.

2. ADVANCE PARTY. 1 N.C.O. from "A" and "D" Coys and 1 from Transport will report to the Regtl. Sergt. Major at 7.45 a.m. and will proceed to the Headquarters, 13th D.L.I., where they will be picked up by motor lorry and conveyed to the new area.

    The N.C.O. of "A" Coy will be responsible for the accommodation of Headquarters and Right Half Battalion, and the N.C.O. of "D" Coy will be responsible for the Left Half Battalion.

3. MARCH. The Battalion will parade, ready to move off, in column of route, at 9.15 a.m. Order of march - H.Q. Signallers and Runners, D, A, B, C, H.Q., 1st Line Transport.
    Head of column at road junction K.32.d.4.0.
    1st Line Transport will be collected under arrangements made by the Transport Officer.

    ROUTE:- ABEELE, Southern SWITCH ROAD.

4. SANITATION. The Orderly Officer - 2nd.Lt. E.G.Simons - will remain at Battalion H.Q., until 11 a.m. Each Company will leave a Sanitary Squad to ensure that their billets are left clean and latrines filled in. They will report to the Orderly Officer at H.Q. at 10.45 a.m. and the Transport Officer will detail one G.S. Limbered wagon to bring on their brushes and tools.

5. DUTIES TO BE FOUND IN NEW AREA. O.C. "A" Coy will detail 1 man for Y.M.C.A. Hut in TORONTO CAMP. Report at 12 noon on 10th inst.
    O.C. "B" Coy will detail 1 N.C.O. and 6 men to report to the Divisional Bomb Officer at Bomb Store, Den GROEBEN CABARET, at 12 noon on 10th inst.
    O.C. "C" Coy will detail 1 N.C.O. and 3 men to report to the Divisional Bomb Officer at Dump "A", at TRANSPORT FARM, by noon on 11th inst.

6. TRANSPORT ARRANGEMENTS. O.C. Companies will arrange to stack all their Officers' Valises, Mess kit, and mens' blankets, Company Stores, etc., at their Coy. H.Q. as near the road as possible, by 8.15 a.m. 1 L/Cpl. & 2 men per Company will be left to load.
    2 motor lorries will report to the Qr.Mr. at H.Q. at 8.30 a.m. and he will be responsible for collecting the Stores from the Company Dumps.

R.C. Mayall
Capt. & Adjutant,
11th Northd. Fusiliers.

10.30 pm.

8/5/17.

Copy No.1 - C.O.   Copy No.6 - T.O.
  " No.2 - "A" Coy.   " No.7 - Q.M.
  " No.3 - "B" "   " No.8 - Signal Officer.
  " No.4 - "C" "   " No.9 - R.S.M.
  " No.5 - "D" "   " No.10 - File.

SECRET.   COPY NO. 10

11TH NORTHUMBERLAND FUSILIERS ORDER NO. 10.

1. The 68th Brigade will relieve the 57th Brigade on the night of 10/11th inst., in the Right Sector of 19th Divisional Front, 11th N.F. relieving 10th Worcesters in RAILWAY DUGOUTS.

   Battalion Headquarters will be at the S.W. corner of the BUND.

2. The Battalion will parade, ready to move off at 10.15 p.m. on the road in the camp. Order of march "A", "B", "C", "D", H.Q.

   Entrain at BRANDHOEK at 11 p.m. Guides meet Battalion at Railway Crossing I.14.c.8.8. at 11.15 p.m.

3. Defence Schemes, Trench stores, aeroplane photos, maps and documents will be taken over.

4. The Signalling Officer, 1 Officer per Coy., 1 N.C.O. from H.Q., and 1 per Platoon, will proceed into the line by daylight tomorrow. They will report at Battalion H.Q. at 1 p.m. and will proceed to RAILWAY DUGOUTS to meet guides at 3.30 p.m. there.

5. TRANSPORT ARRANGEMENTS. Companies will stack all Stores in dumps near the Guard Room as arranged by the Regimental Sergeant Major. Stores to be taken to trenches will be kept separate from those to be taken back to Transport Lines. Officers' valises and blankets will be taken up.

   All Stores will be stacked by 9.30 p.m.

6. Companies will take over from corresponding Companies of 10th Worcesters.

                                                R C Mayall.
                                                Capt. & Adjutant,
                                                11th Northd. Fusiliers.

9/5/17.

Copy No.1 — C.O.   Copy No.6 — T.O.
Copy No.2 — "A" Coy.   Copy No.7 — Q.M.
Copy No.3 — "B" "   Copy No.8 — Signal Officer.
Copy No.4 — "C" "   Copy No.9 — R.S.M.
Copy No.5 — "D" "   Copy No.10 — File.

SECRET.   COPY NO. 1

11TH NORTHUMBERLAND FUSILIERS – ORDER NO.11.

1. **RELIEF.** The 11th N.F. will relieve the 13th D.L.I. in the Left Sector of the Brigade Front on the night May 14/15th, 13th D.L.I. on relief taking over from 11th N.F. in the BUND and RAILWAY DUGOUTS.

2. **DISPOSITION.**
   Right Front Coy – "B" Coy 11th N.F. relieves "A" Coy 13th D.L.I.
   Left   "   " – "C" Coy 11th N.F. relieves "B" Coy 13th D.L.I.
   Support Company – "D" Coy 11th N.F. relieves "D" Coy 13th D.L.I.
   Reserve Company – "A" Coy 11th N.F. relieves "C" Coy 13th D.L.I.
   Headquarters will be at RUDKIN HOUSE.

3. **ORDER OF RELIEF.** Companies will pass the S.W. corner of the BUND at the following times:-
   2 Platoons "D" Coy – 9 p.m. (These proceed to GLASGOW POST and GAP TRENCH).
   "B" Company ——— 9.5 p.m.
   "C"   "   ——— 9.15 p.m.
   2 Platoons "D" Coy – 9.25 p.m.
   "A" Company ——— 9.30 p.m.
   Headquarters ——— 9.40 p.m.

   Companies will proceed via trench running on S. side of ZILLEBEKE LAKE, and ZILLEBEKE STREET.
   Platoon guides from 13th D.L.I. will be at junction of ZILLEBEKE STREET and VINCE STREET at 9.30 p.m.

4. **ADVANCE PARTIES.** Advance parties consisting of 1 Officer per Coy., 6 N.C.O's per Coy (including 1 Lewis Gun N.C.O. & 1 Signalling N.C.O.) and 1 N.C.O. from H.Q. will proceed to take over in the morning.
   All Trench Stores, documents, etc., will be taken over and lists sent in to Orderly Room by 10 a.m. 15th inst.

5. **HANDING OVER.** Advance parties from 13th D.L.I. will arrive in the afternoon to take over dugouts from 11th N.F.
   All Stores, and maps issued in this position, will be handed over.

6. **TRANSPORT ARRANGEMENTS.** All Blankets, Officers' valises, and stores to be taken back to Transport Lines will be stacked at TRANSPORT FARM by 9 p.m. under arrangements to be made by the Regtl. Sergt. Major.
   Stores to be taken to trenches will be stacked, at the same time and place, in separate heaps.
   Each Company will leave a loading party of 1 N.C.O. & 3 men in charge of the stores.
   The Transport Officer will arrange for the collection of the stores and for conveying them to their respective destinations.

   Lewis Guns will be man handled to the trenches.

7. **RATIONS AND WATER.** Rations for H.Q. and "A" Coy are dumped at VALLEY COTTAGES, I.23.c.8.6, and thence man handled to STAFFORD STREET and RUDKIN HOUSE.

SHEET NO.2.   13th May 1917.

7. CONTINUED.

Rations for the remaining three Companies are dumped where the Tramline crosses the road at I.22.b.75.40, thence they are pushed to tramhead from where they are man handled to the trenches. "A" Company carry the rations for all Companies, Headquarters carry their own.

The Regtl. Sergt. Major will detail the necessary parties and give them instructions.

Drinking water is brought up nightly in water carts to ZILLEBEKE DUMP, and distributed by "A" Coy in petrol tins to all four Companies.
Cooking water is drawn for all Companies from the stream in ZILLEBEKE STREET by a permanent party from "A" Coy. The Regtl. Sergt. Major will issue the necessary instructions for this detail.

8. REPORTS.   All reports, including the Situation Reports, will be sent in the to the Intelligence Officer by runner, at the same hours as in the last Sector.

The Disposition report will be rendered to H.Q. by 9 a.m. 15th inst.

9. DETACHED.   Detached duties furnished by the Battalion in this position will be relieved by 13th D.L.I. tomorrow, and details on relief will rejoin their Companies in the line.

10. COMPLETION OF RELIEF.   Completion of relief will be reported, by runner, as early as possible.

R C Mayall.
Capt. & Adjutant,
11th Northd. Fusiliers.

Issued at 9.15 p.m.
13/5/17.

Copy No.1	–	C.O.	Copy No.6	– "D" Coy.
" No.2	–	O.C., 13th D.L.I.	" No.7	– T.O.
" No.3	–	"A" Coy.	" No.8	– Qr.Mr.
" No.4	–	"B" "	" No.9	– R.S.M.
" No.5	–	"C" "	" No.10	– File.

SECRET.

Headquarters, 23rd Division.
Right Group R.A.   For information.
O.C. 10th N.F.   do
O.C. 11th N.F.   do
O.C. 12 D.L.I.   do
O.C. 13 D.L.I.   do
O.C. M.G.Co.   do
O.C. T.M.B.   do

Re your S.G.421/1 dated 13th May.

1. I do not consider that time permits of anything like adequate preparations being made for a raid on any scale tomorrow night. I therefore propose to send out two fighting patrols of 11th N.F. each consisting of 1 officer and 12 to 15 men, with the object of obtaining identifications and doing as much damage as possible.

2. (a) No. I (Right) Patrol will proceed from CRATER POST about I.30.a.6.¼ straight into the enemy front line opposite that post and form a block North and South.

   (b) No. II (Left) patrol will proceed from "F" SAP about I.30.b.0.3½. straight into the enemy front line at the S.E. end of the Sap, and bomb South.

3. PROGRAMME.

   ZERO.   Right Group will barrage 100 yards beyond enemy front line on immediate front of attack. Also standing barrage on flanks of attack and C.T's leading to rear.
            Hows. blocking C.T's.
            No. II patrol advances.

   ZERO + ½.   No. I patrol advances.

   ZERO + 1.   Barrage on front line lifts to support line forming with standing barrage a box barrage round trench attacked and remaining until R.A. Liaison Officer with Battalion Commander orders it to cease.

4. Parties will not remain in enemy line later than ZERO + 15.

5. STOKES MORTARS in LIVING TRENCH and Lewis Guns in STEWART STREET and Sap "G" will co-operate.

C. J. Wallace Major
for
_____ Brig General.

14/5/17.   Commanding 68th Infantry Brigade.

SECRET. RIGHT GROUP. Copy No.9.
23rd DIVISIONAL ARTILLERY.
OPERATION ORDER No.1.

Reference Sheet
ZILLEBEKE 1/10,000. Ed.5a.   15th May 1917.

1.   On the night of the 16/17th May 1917 two fighting patrols of the Left Battalion 11th N.F. each consisting of 1 Officer and 12 to 15 men will enter the enemy front line trench with the object of obtaining identifications and doing as much damage as possible.

2.   No.1 (Right) patrol will proceed from CRATER POST about I.30.a.6002 at ZERO plus ½ minute straight into the enemy front line opposite that post and form a block North and South.

3.   No.2 (Left) Patrol will proceed at ZERO from "F" Gap about I.30.b.0035 straight into the enemy front line at the S.E. end of the Sap and bomb South.

4.   Patrols will not remain in the enemy line later than ZERO plus 15 minutes.

5.   D.T.M.O. will arrange for the Medium Trench Mortars to fire well over front line from I.30.c.5385 to I.30.b.3530 from ZERO to ZERO plus 1 minute.

6.   The Right Group will co-operate as shown in attached Table "A".

7.   Watches will be synchronised at the Right Group Headquarters at 5-0 p.m. on 16th May. One Officer per Battery will attend with two watches for this purpose.

8.   The orders to cease firing will be given by the Liaison Officer (to be detailed by O.C. Right Sub-Group) at 11th N.F. Headquarters immediately on information from Battalion Commander that the patrols have returned.
        The order will be passed by him direct to Batteries of 103rd Brigade and through 103rd Brigade Headquarters to Right Group Headquarters to batteries of 102nd Brigade.

9.   ZERO hour will be communicated later.

10.   ACKNOWLEDGE.

                                        (Sd) ....

                                        Lieut. & Adjt.,
15.5.17.   RIGHT GROUP.

Copies to:-
        No.1 to A/102.
        No.2 to D/102.
        Nos.3 to 7 to Right Sub-Group.
        No.8 to D.T.M.O.
        No.9 to H.Q. 68th Inf.Bde. (for information).
        No.10 and 11 filed.

TABLE "A"

TIME	UNIT	TASK	RATES OF FIRE.
ZERO until order to cease fire.	A/102 (3 guns)	Barrage front trench I.30.c. 3070 to I.30.c.5075	**18-Pdrs.** ZERO to 1 — 4 rounds/per gun per minute.
	(3 guns)	Barrage COMMUNICATION TRENCH I.30.c.5075 to I.30.c.5060 I.30.c.6858.	1 to 2 do. do. 16
	A/103 (4 guns)	Barrage front trench I.30.b.3530 to I.30.b.6545	16 onwards — 1 do. do.
	(1 gun)	Search COMMUNICATION TRENCH I.30.b.4232 to I.30.b.6010	
	D/102 (1 section)	Bombard TRENCH JUNCTIONS I.30.c.5060 and I.30.c.6858	**4.5" How:** Half above rates.
	D/103	Bombard TRENCH JUNCTIONS I.30.d.2055 I.30.d.2578 I.30.d.6595 I.30.b.6010 DUGOUTS I.30.c.3.0. COMPANY H.Q. J.25.a.00.00	
ZERO to ZERO 1	C/103	Barrage 100 yards over front line I.30.c.5585 to I.30.a.9010.	
	B/103	Barrage 100 yards over front line I.30.a.9010 to I.30.b.3530.	
ZERO 1 until order to cease fire.	C/103	Barrage from I.30.c.6858 to I.30.d.1085.	
	B/103.	Barrage from I.30.d.1085 to I.30.a.6010.	

Ammunition 18-Pdrs: ZERO to 1 Shrapnel.

ZERO 1 onwards. Half Shrapnel Half H.E.

Code to be used on night of May 16th.
— " " " " —

No. I. Party.   P.
No. II Party.   Q.

SECRET

Has left our trenches   A.
Has entered enemy's trenches. V.
Held up by wire   C.
Held up by M.G. fire   D.
Hostile barrage on No Man's Land E.
Prisoners captured   F.
Our casualties, wounded.   G.
Our casualties, killed   H.
Has returned to our trenches. K.
More Bombs required   B.
Our casualties, missing   O.

Numerals   Z = 1.
            Y = 2.
            X = 3
            W = 4
            L = 5
            M = 6
To/68th Brigade   R = 7
Capt Adamson.   S = 8
Lt. West   T = 9
Adjutant.
Bn. Signalling Officer.   U = 10.

15/5/17

R. Hoyle
Capt & Adjt
17 N.F.

SECRET.   COPY NO.

11TH NORTHUMBERLAND FUSILIERS ORDER NO.12.

Reference Map Sheet
ZILLEBEKE 1/10,000. Ed.5a.   15th May 1917.

1. There are several gaps in the enemy's wire in front of our trenches
between I.30.a.6.¼. (CRATER POST) and I.30.b.0.3½. (Sap "F").
    At I.30.a.6.¼. there are two small gaps about 8 yards wide and at
I.30.b.0.3½. a large gap about 30 yards wide. There is also another
gap reported at I.30 a.7.½.
    From observation the enemy does not appear to be holding his front
line very strongly.

2. In retaliation for the enemy's raid on the morning of the 13th and
in order to procure prisoners for the purpose of obtaining identifications of the unit on our immediate front, it is proposed on the night
of May 16th to enter the enemy's trenches.

    No.1 Right Patrol, consisting of 10 men under an N.C.O. of "B" Com-
pany, will proceed from a point 40 yards S.W. of the junction of the
right end of CANADA STREET with the front line, and will enter the
enemy's trenches by the two small gaps at I.30.a.6.¼. and form a
block North and South.

    No.2 Left Patrol, consisting of 15 N.C.O's and men selected by, and
under the charge of, 2nd.Lt. J.W. Hunter, will proceed from "F" Sap,
about I.30.b.0.3½. straight into the enemy's front line at the S.E. end
of the sap and bomb south.

    Between this date and ZERO hour tomorrow the Officer and N.C.O. i/c
Patrols will make careful reconnaissance, both by daylight and at night,
of the front to be raided.

    The right party will be under the supervision of Lieut. H.M.P. West,
and the left party under Capt. C.J.H. Adamson. These Officers will
establish posts at the jumping-off places, and the Signalling Officer
will arrange for them to be in direct communication with Battalion
Headquarters.

    On return to our lines, both parties will assemble at "B" Company's
Headquarters, CANADA STREET, where an issue of rum and a hot meal will
be provided.

    The Officer and N.C.O. i/c Raiding Parties will draw from Battalion
Headquarters, Body Shields, Wire Cutters and Knob-kerries, and arrange
for the wearing of Masks and Gloves or the blacking of the hands and
faces of their men.

4. Lewis Guns will be mounted at the Bombing Post in Sap "G" on the
Left, and at I.30.a.5½.0. on the right. These guns will cover the
Raiding parties and engage any of the enemy's machine guns that open
fire. The right gun will be found by "B" and the left gun by "C"
Company. A third Lewis Gun will be found by "B" Company and mounted
in Trench I.30.4. to sweep the enemy's front line till ZERO plus 1,
when it will cease fire and be withdrawn under cover.

SECRET.   COPY NO. 2

11TH NORTHUMBERLAND FUSILIERS ORDER NO. 12.

Reference Map Sheet
ZILLEBEKE 1/10,000. Ed.5a.   15th May 1917.

1. There are several gaps in the enemy's wire in front of our trenches between I.30.a.6.¼. (CRATER POST) and I.30.b.0.3½. (Sap "F").
   At I.30.a.6.¼. there are two small gaps about 8 yards wide and at I.30.b.0.3½. a large gap about 30 yards wide. There is also another gap reported at I.30.a.7.½.
   From observation the enemy does not appear to be holding his front line very strongly.

2. In retaliation for the enemy's raid on the morning of the 13th and in order to procure prisoners for the purpose of obtaining identifications of the Unit on our immediate front, it is proposed on the night of May 16th to enter the enemy's trenches.

3. No.1 Right Patrol, consisting of 10 men under an N.C.O. of "B" Company, will proceed from a point 40 yards S.W. of the junction of the right end of CANADA STREET with the front line, and will enter the enemy's trenches by the two small gaps at I.30.a.6.¼. and form a block North and South.

   No.2 Left Patrol, consisting of 15 N.C.O's and men selected by, and under charge of, 2nd.Lt. Hunter, will proceed from "F" Sap, about I.30.b.0.3½. straight into the enemy's front line at the S.E. end of the sap and bomb South.

   Between this date and ZERO hour tomorrow the Officer and N.C.O. i/c patrols will make careful reconnaissance, both by daylight and at night, of the front to be raided.

   The Right party will be under the supervision of Lieut. H.M.P. West, and the Left Party under Capt. C.J.H. Adamson. These Officers will establish posts at the jumping-off places, and the Signalling Officer will arrange for them to be in direct communication with Battalion Headquarters.

   On return to our lines, both parties will assemble at "B" Company's Headquarters, CANADA STREET, where an issue of rum and a hot meal will be provided.

   The Officer and N.C.O. i/c Raiding Parties will draw from Battalion Headquarters, Body Shields, Wire Cutters, and Knob-kerries, and arrange for the wearing of masks and gloves or for the blacking of the hands and faces of all their men.

4. Lewis Guns will be mounted at the Bombing Post in Sap "G" on the left, and at I.30.a.5½.0. on the right. These guns will cover the Raiding parties and engage any of the enemy's machine guns that open fire. The Right Gun will be found by "B" Company and the Left Gun by "C" Company. A third Lewis Gun will be found by "B" Company and mounted in Trench I.30.4. to sweep the enemy's front line till ZERO plus 1, when it will cease fire and be withdrawn under cover.

11TH N.F. ORDER NO. 12.   Sheet 2.   15th May 1917.

5.   ZERO hour will be at 10 p.m. at which hour the Artillery will barrage 100 yards behind the enemy's front line on the immediate front of attack and also place a standing barrage on the flanks of the attack and on the Communication trenches leading to the rear.

No. 2 Patrol will advance at ZERO hour.

No. 1 Patrol will advance at ZERO plus ½.

At ZERO plus 1 front barrage lifts on to the enemy's support line, and with the standing barrage on flanks forms a box barrage round the raided area.

Patrols will not remain in the enemy's lines later than ZERO plus 15.

6.   STOKES Mortars in LIVING Trench will co-operate.

7.   The Medical Officer will arrange for first aid to be rendered at "B" Company's Headquarters if required.

8.   During the raid front line Companies will remain in readiness, under cover, with sentry posts on the ALERT.

9.   Watches will be synchronised at Battalion Headquarters at 8 p.m. on the 16th May 1917.
     1 Officer per Company will attend with two watches for this purpose.

10. Reports to RUDKIN HOUSE.

11. ACKNOWLEDGE.

R.C. Mayall.

Capt. & Adjutant,
11th Northd. Fusiliers.

Issued at 6.30 p.m. 15/4/17, by runner.

Copy No. 1 - H.Q. 68th Inf. Bde.   Copy No. 6 - "D" Coy.
  " No. 2 - C.O.   " No. 7 - 2nd. Lt. Hunter.
  " No. 3 - "A" Coy.   " No. 8 - N.C.O. i/c Patrol
  " No. 4 - "B" "   No. 1.
  " No. 5 - "C" "   " No. 9 - Signal Officer.
                                       " No.10 - File.

11TH N.F. ORDER NO.12.   Sheet 2.   15th May 1917.

5. ZERO hour will be at 10 p.m. at which hour the Artillery will barrage 100 yards behind the enemy's front line on the immediate front of attack and also place a ~~barrage~~ standing barrage on the flanks of the attack and on the Communication trenches leading to the rear.

No.2 Patrol will advance at ZERO.

No.1 Patrol will advance at ZERO plus ½.

At ZERO plus 1, front barrage lifts on to the enemy's support line and with standing barrage on flanks forms a box barrage round the raided area.

Parties will not remain in the enemy's lines later than ZERO plus 15.

6. STOKES Mortars in LIVING TRENCH will co-operate.

7. The Medical Officer will arrange for first aid to be rendered at "B" Company's Headquarters if required.

8. During the raid front line Companies will remain in readiness, under cover, with sentry posts on the ALERT.

9. Watches will be synchronised at Battalion Headquarters at 8 p.m. on 16th May 1917.
   1 Officer per Company will attend with two watches for this purpose.

10. Reports to RUDKIN HOUSE.

11. ACKNOWLEDGE.

RC Mayall

Capt. & Adjutant,
11th Northd. Fusiliers.

Issued at 6.30 p.m. 15/5/17, by runner.

```
Copy No.1 - H.Q. 68th Inf.Bde.      Copy No.6  - "D" Coy.
"    No.2 - C.O.                    "    No.7  - 2nd.Lt. Hunter.
"    No.3 - "A" Coy.                "    No.8  - N.C.O. i/c Patrol
"    No.4 - "B"  "                                 No.1.
"    No.5 - "C"  "                  "    No.9  - Signal Officer.
"    HX.                            "    No.10 - File.
```

SECRET.　　　　　　　　　　　　　　　　　　　　　　　　　　　COPY No. 2

ADDITIONAL INSTRUCTIONS TO 11TH N.F. ORDER NO.12.

1. Lieut. H.M.P.WEST and Capt. C.J.H.ADAMSON will ensure that all men of the Right and Left Patrols respectively have had all marks of identification removed before they leave our trenches.

2. It is possible that the 24th Division on our left will carry out a hurricane bombardment at ZERO – 2. Great care must be taken that this is not confused with our own guns at ZERO.

3. O.C. Patrols will see that every man of their parties has been given his specific job before setting out, i.e. Blockers, Moppers-up, Men in charge of prisoners, Stretcher Bearers, etc.

4. Reference para.5 of 11TH N.F. ORDER NO.12, ZERO hour will be at 11 p.m. instead of 10 p.m.

5. ACKNOWLEDGE.

R.C.Mayall

Capt. & Adjutant,
11th Northd. Fusiliers.

16th May 1917.

Issued at 1.30 p.m. 16/5/17, by runner.

　　　　Copy No.1 – H.Q., 68th Inf.Bde.　　Copy No.6 – "D" Coy.
　　　　 "   No.2 – C.O.　　　　　　　　　 "   No.7 – 2nd.Lt. Hunter.
　　　　 "   No.3 – "A" Coy.　　　　　　　　"   No.8 – N.C.O. i/c
　　　　 "   No.4 – "B" "　　　　　　　　　　　　　　　Patrol No.1.
　　　　 "   No.5 – "C" "　　　　　　　　 "   No.9 – Signal Officer.
　　　　 "　　　　　　　　　　　　　　　　　 "   No.10 – File.

60

SECRET.   COPY No. 10

ADDITIONAL INSTRUCTIONS TO 11TH N.F. ORDER NO.12.

1. Lieut. H.H.P.WEST and Capt. C.J.H.ADAMSON will ensure that all men of the Right and Left Patrols respectively have had all marks of identification removed before they leave our trenches.

2. It is possible that the 24th Division on our left will carry out a hurricane bombardment at ZERO – 2. Great care must be taken that this is not confused with our own guns at ZERO.

3. O.C. Patrols will see that every man of their parties has been given his specific job before setting out, i.e. Blockers, Moppers-up, Men in charge of prisoners, Stretcher Bearers, etc.

4. Reference para.5 of 11TH N.F. ORDER NO.12, ZERO hour will be at 11 p.m. instead of 10 p.m.

5. ACKNOWLEDGE.

                                                    R.C.Mayall
                                                    Capt. & Adjutant,
                                                    11th Northd. Fusiliers.

16th May 1917.

Issued at 1.30 p.m. 16/5/17, by runner.

            Copy No.1 – H.Q.,68th Inf.Bde.   Copy No.6 – "D" Coy.
             "   No.2 – C.O.   "   No.7 – 2nd.Lt. Hunter.
             "   No.3 – "A" Coy.   "   No.8 – N.C.O. i/c
             "   No.4 – "B" "   Patrol No.1.
             "   No.5 – "C" "   "   No.9 – Signal Officer.
             "   "   No.10 – File.

D4.

SECRET

O.C. 11th N.F.

NOTES ON YOUR RAID ORDERS.

1. All identification marks must be removed from your men.

2. Should the 24th Division join in with a hurricane bombardment at ZERO - 2, great care must be taken that this is not confused with our own guns bombardment at ZERO.

3. As the task allotted to the Right N.C.O. party seems only to block the German Trenches and bring in Prisoners is it not a little too big?

4. I conclude every man has been given his job, i.e. Blockers, Moppers up, men in charge of Prisoners, Stretcher Bearers, etc.

5. Some Signal must be arranged from our front line to show when the party have been in Trench say 10 minutes.

6. ZERO hour will be 11 p.m.

Brig General.
Commanding 68th Infantry Brigade.

16/5/17.

SECRET.   G.124/1/8.

Reference Trench Map ZILLEBEKE 28 N.W.4 and N.E.3 (parts of).

1. In retaliation for hostile raid on May 13th. and to procure identifications and damage the enemy two fighting patrols of the 11th N.F. will enter the enemy trenches at MOUNT SORREL on the night 16/17th May.

2. (a) No. I (Right) Patrol consisting of 15 N.C.O's and men will proceed from a point in our front line trench about I.30.a.6.¾ straight into the enemy front line opposite that point and will form blocks North and South.

   (b) No. II (Left Patrol) consisting of 1 Officer and 15 O.R. will proceed from "F" Sap about I.30.b.0.3½. straight into the enemys front line at the S.E. end of the Sap and bomb South.

3. PROGRAMME.

   ZERO.   No. II Patrol advances.
   Right Group will barrage 100 yards beyond enemy front line on immediate front of attack; also standing barrage on flanks of attack and C.T's leading to the rear (detail attached). 2 Light Trench Mortars commence hurricane bombardment of enemy trenches about I.30.d.0.9.

   ZERO + ½.   No. I Patrol advances.

   ZERO + 1.   Barrage on front line lifts to support line forming with standing barrage a box barrage round trench attacked and remaining until R.A. Liaison Officer with Battalion Commander orders it to cease (see R.A.Programme).

4. Parties will leave enemy line not later than ZERO + 15.

5. Lewis and Vickers Guns will co-operate from our front line.

6. 24th Division R.A. have been asked to create a diversion at ZERO - 2 on their front.

7. Brigade Signal Officer will synchronise watches at 6 p.m.

8. ZERO hour will be 11 p.m.

                                                      Major.

                              Brigade Major, 68th Infantry Brigade.

16/5/17.

TABLE "A".

TIME.	UNIT.	TASK.	RATES OF FIRE.
			18 Pdrs.
ZERO until order to cease fire.	A/102 (3 Guns).	Barrage front Trench I.30.c.30.70 to I.30.c.50.75	ZERO to +1. 4 rounds per gun per minute.
	(5 Guns).	Barrage COMMUNICATION TRENCH I.30.c.50.75 to I.30.c.50.60 I.30.c.68.58.	+1 to +16 2 do
	A/103. (4 guns)	Barrage front trench I.30.b.35.30 to I.30.b.65.45.	+16 onwards. 1 do
	(1 gun).	Search COMMUNICATION TRENCH I.30.b.42.32 to I.30.b.60.10.	
			4.5" How.
	D/102. (1 section).	Bombard TRENCH JUNCTIONS I.30.c.50.60. and I.30.c.68.58.	Half above rates.
	D/103.	Bombard Trench Junctions I.30.d.20.55 I.30.d.25.78 I.30.d.65.95 I.30.b.60.10 DUGOUTS I.30.c.5.0. COMPANY H.Q. J.25.a.00.00.	
ZERO to ZERO+1.	C/103.	Barrage 100 yards over front line I.30.c.55.85 to I.30.a.90.10.	
	B/103.	Barrage 100 yards over front line I.30.a.90.10 to I.30.b.35.30.	
ZERO+1 until order to cease fire.	C/103.	Barrage from I.30.c.68.58 to I.30.d.10.85.	
	B/103.	Barrage from I.30.d.10.85 to I.30.a.60.10.	

AMMUNITION 18 Pdrs.   ZERO to +1 Shrapnel.

ZERO+1 onwards. Half shrapnel half H.E.

To/ 2nd Lt. Hunter. O.C. No. 2. Patrol.
N.C.O. B Coy. O.C. No. 1. Patrol.
Capt. Adamson.
Lieut. West.

Following has been received from Brigade:- "Some signal must be arranged from our front line to show when the party has been in the Trench Say 10 minutes"

For this purpose Lt. West and Capt. Adamson will each arrange to fire three white parachute lights in succession from our front line. The patrols will take this as a signal to return if any are still out. These will be fired at Zero + 10.

I am sending herewith 3 parachute lights to O.C. B & C. Coys (companies have some in case these are duds).

I am also sending tape for parties to take out with them to find their way back by.

16.5.17

R C Mayall
Captain Adjt
11 (S) Bn Northd Fus

To/O.C. B. Coy   SECRET.

    Please detail 2 stretcher bearers of your company to wait at the entrance of the dugout 10 yards South of F Sap for any casualties in No 2 Patrol. They should be there from Zero time till the return of No 2 Patrol.

    Repeated to M.O.

16.5.17

R.C. Mayall
Actg Adjutant
11/S/Bn. North Fus.

To/O.C. C. 'Coy   SECRET.

With reference to para 4 of 11th N.F. Order No 12 please note that your gun to be mounted in Sap G. will not be required as this position will be occupied by a Vickers Gun from the M.G. Company.

16.5.17

R.C. Mayall
Capt Adjt
11th (S) Bn North'd Fus.

To Adjutant
11th N.F.

No. I Raiding party.

The party was in position at 10.43 P.M. Between 10.48 and 10.58 P.M. an enemy M.G. fired three bursts from a position about ½ left, across our front. Our artillery opened about ½ minute too early. At zero + ½ the party, led by Sgt. Hand, climbed over the parapet and went straight for the enemy trench. As Sgt. Hand reached the top of the parapet the Bosche put up a very light and after that, generally speaking, kept the place lit up. The party, putting out the tape as they went, went straight ahead and disappeared into the smoke and dust caused by our barrage. A few seconds later bombs began to burst on the spot at which I expected the party to enter

the enemy trench, I concluded that
they had got into the trench.
Our artillery appeared to lift soon
after I lost sight of the party.
The bombing grew more intense and
at about 11.5 P.m. seemed to draw
nearer to our trench. At about 11.6 P.m.
the men began to return. They all
came in within about 15-20 yds. of the
trench just where they went out and all were in by 11.9 P.m.
I was not sure of one man at 11.10 P.m.
So fired a white parachute light. It
was no dud. I then discovered that
all had returned. One was wounded
and seemed in great pain and several
were scratched with wire.

The accounts I have heard from the
Sgt. and the men are consistent.
The party got close to the barrow
ditch and found a gap through both
rows of wire: the barrage was still
on the front line however so they all

lay down. The Sgt. states that all his men were up with him.

In about 20 seconds the artillery lifted, and the party thinking they had a "walk over" were about to rush the trench when the Boche threw a number of hand grenades simultaneously and then continued to throw them. Our men bombed the trench but did not get in. I don't know exactly how many bombs our men threw but I should think quite twelve; probably more. They then returned, the Boche flinging bombs after them.

The machine gun never fired a round. It must I think have been knocked out by our artillery as I can not imagine why it did not fire.

The enemy sent up a light which split into two green ones at about 11.10 P.M. and another at about 11.15 P.M. Then

was no apparent result.
Since our artillery ceased, everything
has been quiet.

H M P West
Lt.

17/5/17

To Adjutant.
11th R. Fus.

From In[telligence] Officer
11th R. Fus.

No 11.
Party laid out in No Man's Land about 20x from parapet & at zero time approached enemy's line. Mr Hunter Sgt Evans & Bolton reached enemy's parapet throwing bombs. The enemy was in the trench & threw bombs back & fired their rifles. Mr Hunter they had disappeared instead of following close behind. After firing two shots & throwing bombs the officer's party of three returned.

A further report will follow

J Moffat.

11.38 pm.

From Capt. Adamson.

To Adjt

Got to my post at 10.45 & found that Mr Hunter already had his men out over the Parapet. I saw them start from the fire step but apparently they did not all start & Mr Hunter found himself on the Boche Parapet with a Sergt only. I did not see any one enter the trenches. All party No 2 is in, two men came in before 10 minutes was up & I sent the lights up to turn & Mr Hunter & 3 others returned very soon after

SECRET.   COPY NO. 1

11th NORTHUMBERLAND FUSILIERS – ORDER NO.13.

Ref. Map Sheet 28 N.W., 1/20,000.   16th May 1917.

1.   The Brigade will be relieved by 69th Brigade on the night of 16/17th May, 11th N.F. being relieved by 9th Yorks., in the Left Sub-Sector, and proceeding on relief to SCOTTISH LINES.

2.   The Quartermaster, with the Coy.Qr.Mr.Sgts., will take over the huts at SCOTTISH LINES. The Coy.Qr.Mr.Sgts. will meet the Companies and guide them into their huts.

   The Battalion may arrive any time after 3 a.m., and guides must be there at that hour.

   The Officers' Riding horses will be in KRUISSTRAAT by midnight and wait for their respective Officers.

3.   Companies on relief will <u>march</u> independently to the Reserve Area, via I.13.b.0.7. – KRUISSTRAAT.

4.   Platoon guides and one guide from H.Q., will be at the CONTROL POST, ZILLEBEKE, at 10.15 p.m. O.C. "D" Company will detail one guide for Lewis Gun at GLASGOW POST to report at Battalion H.Q. at 6.45 p.m.

5.   Companies will send all stores, kit, etc., to their respective Ration Dumps as early as possible after dusk and leave loading parties. The Transport Officer will arrange to collect the stores.

   The Transport Officer will arrange to send the Lewis Gun Limbers to the respective Ration Dumps of the Companies by midnight. On relief the Lewis Gun Teams will carry their guns to the ration dumps, load them on the limbers, and accompany the limbers to the Reserve Area. All Lewis Gun Ammunition, parts, etc., will be carried on the limbers and the latter will remain at the dumps until each team has arrived.

6.   Relief complete will be reported by sending the Company Commander's SURNAME over the 'phone.

7.   ACKNOWLEDGE.

                                                       R C Mayall
                                                       Capt. & Adjutant,
                                                       11th Northd. Fusiliers.

Issued at 12.45 a.m. 17/5/17, by runner.

    Copy No.1 – C.O.   Copy No.6 – T.O.
    "   No.2 – "A" Coy.   "   No.7 – Qr.Mr.
    "   No.3 – "B" "   "   No.8 – Signal Officer.
    "   No.4 – "C" "   "   No.9 – R.S.M.
    "   No.5 – "D" "   "   No.10 – War Diary.

To:- Headquarters,

68th Infantry Brigade.

17th May 1917.

I beg to report that in accordance with instructions contained in your G.124/1/8 dated 16th inst., two patrols left the trenches at ZERO hour and ZERO plus ½.

(i) The Right Patrol proceeded direct to the German trench and found the narrow Gap strongly held by the enemy, who were in readiness for them. A bombing fight took place in which one of the patrol was wounded, and the patrol was forced to return to our trenches, arriving there at ZERO plus 15.

(ii) The Left patrol advanced at ZERO hour, but owing to the darkness and the roughness of the ground, this party lost touch with one another and 2nd.Lt. Hunter, the Officer in charge, arrived at the enemy's parapet with only two men with him. The enemy immediately opened fire on them. Having thrown all their bombs and one of the men being wounded, the rest of the party not having come up, 2nd.Lt. Hunter was forced to retire back to our trenches, where he arrived at ZERO plus 20, and found that the remainder of the party had returned on the recall signal. This consisted of three Parachute Lights fired from two places in our trench at ZERO plus 10.

Before the preliminary bombardment opened, the enemy's trench was very quiet, with occasional Very Lights fired at intervals. One machine gun, about the centre of the portion to be raided, was very active, but on the opening of the bombardment, ceased fire altogether. As soon as the bombardment opened, two lots of single green rockets, splitting into

Sheet 2.   17th May 1917.

two, were sent up from the enemy's trenches, and a red rockets fired from his trench to the right.   No apparent action followed.   The enemy's artillery was silent throughout the raid and beyond a few Trench Mortars on our front line trenches no retaliation was attempted.

                                        Lt. Colonel,
                    Commanding
                    11th(S)Bn. Northumberland Fusiliers.

SECRET.   COPY NO. 1

11TH NORTHUMBERLAND FUSILIERS – ORDER NO. 14.

Ref. Map Sheet 28 N.W.1/20,000.   27th May 1917.

1. "B" and "C" Companies, 11th N.F., will relieve "C" and "D" Companies 10th N.F. respectively in the BUND, after dark, on the night of 28/29th May.

2. These Companies will work under the orders of the C.R.E. and will take over all working parties, etc., from the Companies of 10th N.F., commencing work on the night of 29/30th.

3. Captain C.J.H. Adamson will be in command of the two Companies.

4. Advance parties, consisting of 1 Officer and 4 N.C.O's per Company, will proceed to take over dugouts during the morning of the 28th inst.

5. Companies will parade, ready to move off at 9 p.m. in Fighting Order, with greatcoats rolled in the manner demonstrated by the R.S.M. to Company Sergeant Majors this afternoon.

6. The Transport Officer will make arrangements for collecting Officers' valises and mess kit, and conveying them to the BUND after dark.

    The Qr.Mr. will arrange for the collection of mens' packs and for removing them to the Transport Field.

    The Transport Officer will send a limber to the Camp at 1.30 p.m. tomorrow to take Officers' spare kit to the Store in POPERINGHE.

7. Each Company will draw a cycle from Headquarters for use of their orderly whilst at the BUND.

8. Relief complete will be reported over the 'phone by sending the word "HOUSE".

8. Acknowledge.

R.C. Mayall
Capt. & Adjutant,
11th Northd. Fusiliers.

Issued at 2 p.m. 27/5/17, by runner.

Copy No.1 – C.O.   Copy No.4 – "C" Coy.
"   No.2 – O.C., 10th N.F.   "   No.5 – T.O. and Qr.Mr.
"   No.3 – "B" Coy.   "   No.6 – File.

SECRET.   COPY NO. 10

11TH NORTHUMBERLAND FUSILIERS - ORDER NO.15.

Ref. Map Sheet 28 N.W. 1/20,000.   30th May 1917.

1. The 11th N.F. will relieve the 8th K.O.Y.L.I. in the Centre Sub-Sector of the Divisional Front on the night May 31/1st June.

2. The following will be the disposition:-

   Battalion H.Q. — LARCH WOOD SUBWAY.
   Left ~~Right~~ Front Coy — "C" Coy, 11th N.F. relieve "D" Coy., K.O.Y.L.I.
   Right ~~Left~~ "   " — "B" Coy 11th N.F. relieves "B" Coy., K.O.Y.L.I.
   Support Company — "D" Coy 11th N.F. relieces "A" Coy., K.O.Y.L.I.
   Reserve Company — "A" Coy 11th N.F. relieves "C" Coy., K.O.Y.L.I.

   Companies will take over the same dispositions as those of the unit they relieve with the exception that for the night 31st May/1st June, and until relieved, "C" Coy will find the garrison for LONE TREE POST and FOSSE WOOD POST in addition to their own Posts at BERRY POST and ALLEN CRATER.

   "C" Company will also find a platoon to garrison WANGARATTA TRENCH by night.

3. One Officer & 6 N.C.O's per Coy., (including 1 Signalling and 1 Lewis Gun N.C.O.) & 1 N.C.O. from H.Q., will proceed to the trenches during the morning to take over all Defence Schemes, Trench Stores, Aeroplane photos and secret maps.
   Lists of all stores etc taken over will be rendered to Battn. H.Q. by 10 a.m. 1st June.

4. "B" and "C" Companies will move up into the line under orders to be issued by O.C. Detachment, 11th N.F.   Platoon guides for these Coys will report at the BUND by 9 p.m.
   The Lewis Guns of "B" and "C" Coys will relieve by daylight.   Guides will report at the BUND by 5.30 p.m.   The guns will be man handled.

   Other Units will move off from the camp as follows:-
       "D" Coy — 7.15 p.m.
       H.Q. " — 7.20 p.m.
       "A"   " — 7.25 p.m.

   ROUTE — Cross roads G.24.c.5.5. - H.24.a.95.95. - S.E. by path and corduroy road to TROIS ROIS — by country track to SUBWAY under Railway Dugouts.

   Platoon guides will meet these Companies and Headquarters at the SUBWAY underneath the Railway at 10 p.m.

   The Platoon of "C" Coy to garrison the detached posts will report at RAILWAY DUGOUTS for guides at dusk.

Sheet 2. 30th May 1917.

The Lewis Guns of "A" and "D" Coys will be carried on Pack Mules in rear of their respective Coys.

All movement East of the VLAMERTINGHE - OUDERDOM Road will be by platoons at 50 yards interval. Troops cannot pass the Control Post at H.16.d.1.1. before 9 p.m.

5. All kits and stores of "B" and "C" Coys for the trenches will be man handled.

All Officers' valises, etc. of these two Companies to be taken to Transport will be stacked under a guard at TRANSPORT FARM and the Transport Officer will arrange to collect them on his return.

All kits, stores, of H.Q. "A" and "D" Coys will be stacked in dumps under arrangements made by the Regtl. Sergt. Major by 6 p.m. The Transport Officer will arrange for the collection and conveyance to respective destinations.

6. The following are the arrangements for rations, water and cooking in this sector:-
Rations for Right front Company, Support Company and Battn. H.Q., come to JACKSON'S DUMP.
Rations for Left Front Company and Reserve Company come to MANOR FARM.

Water for Right front Company, Support Company and Battn. H.Q., comes to JACKSON'S DUMP in water carts and is there put into petrol tins.
Water for Left front Company and Reserve Company is obtained from spring at STREAM CORNER.

Ration and water parties for the Right front Company are found from the Support Company and the Left front Company from the Reserve Company.
The Regimental Sergt.Major will issue the necessary detail for these parties.

Cooking for Battn. H.Q., Right front Company and Support Company is done in the tunnels.
Cooking for the left front Company is done in ZILLEBEKE SWITCH.
Cooking for Reserve Company is done at STREAM CORNER.

7. Relief complete will be reported by sending the Company Commander's Christian name.

8. ACKNOWLEDGE.

R.C. Mayall
Capt. & Adjutant,
11th Northd. Fusiliers.

Issued at 11 p.m. by runner.

Copy No.1 - C.O.
" No.2 - "A" Coy.
" No.3 - "B" "
" No.4 - "C" "
" No.5 - "D" "

Copy No.6 - T.O.
" No.7 - Qr.Mr.
" No.8 - Signal Officer.
" No.9 - R.S.M.
" No.10 - File.

SECRET.   COPY NO. 1

11TH NORTHUMBERLAND FUSILIERS — ORDER NO.15.

Ref. Map Sheet 28 N.W. 1/20,000.   30th May 1917.

1.   The 11th N.F. will relieve the 8th K.O.Y.L.I. in the Centre Sub-sector of the Divisional Front on the night May 31/1st June.

2.   The following will be the disposition:-
            Battalion H.Q.   —   LARCH WOOD SUBWAY.
        Left Front Coy   —   "C" Coy 11th N.F. relieve "D" Coy 8th K.O.Y.L.I.
        Right   "   "   —   "B" "   "   "   "   "B" "   "   "
        Support Company   "D" "   "   "   "   "A" "   "   "
        Reserve   "   —   "A" "   "   "   "   "C" "   "   "

    Companies will take over the same dispositions as those of the units they relieve with the exception that for the night 31st May/1st June, and until relieved, "C" Coy will find the garrison for LONE TREE POST and FOSSE WOOD POST in addition to their own posts at BERRY POST and ALLEN CRATER.

    "C" Company will also find a platoon to garrison WANGARATTA TRENCH by night.

3.   One Officer & 6 N.C.O's per Coy., (including 1 Signalling N.C.O. and 1 Lewis Gun N.C.O.) & 1 N.C.O. from H.Q., will proceed to the trenches during the morning to take over all Defence Schemes, Trench Stores, Aeroplane photos and secret maps.
    Lists of all stores taken over will be rendered to Battn. H.Q. by 10 a.m. 1st June.

4.   "B" and "C" Coys will move up into the line under orders to be issued by O.C. Detachment, 11th N.F.   Platoon guides for these Companies will report at the BUND by 9 p.m.
    The Lewis Guns of "B" and "C" Coys will relieve by daylight. Guides will report at the BUND by 5.30 p.m.   The guns will be man handled.

    Other units will move off from camp as follows:-
            "D" Coy — 7.15 p.m.
            "H.Q." — 7.20 p.m.
            "A" Coy — 7.25 p.m.

    ROUTE — Cross roads G.24.c.5.5. — H.24.a.95.95 — S.E. by path and corduroy road to TROIS ROIS — by country track to SUBWAY under RAILWAY DUGOUTS.

    Platoon guides will meet these Companies and Headquarters at the SUBWAY underneath the Railway at 10 p.m.

    The Platoon of "C" Coy to garrison the detached posts will report at RAILWAY DUGOUTS for guides at dusk.

    The Lewis Guns of "A" and "D" Coys will be carried on Pack Mules in rear of their respective Companies.

    All movement East of the VLAMERTINGHE — OUDERDOM Road will be by platoons at 50 yards interval.   Troops cannot pass the Control Post at H.16.d.1.1. before 9 p.m.

SECRET.   COPY NO. 1

11TH NORTHUMBERLAND FUSILIERS - ORDER NO.15.

Ref. Map Sheet 28 N.W. 1/20,000.   30th May 1917.

1. The 11th N.F. will relieve the 8th K.O.Y.L.I. in the Centre Sub-sector of the Divisional Front on the night May 31/1st June.

2. The following will be the disposition:-
       Battalion H.Q.   - LARCH WOOD SUBWAY.
       Left Front Coy - "C" Coy 11th N.F. relieve "D" Coy 8th K.O.Y.L.I.
       Right   "   " - "B" "   "   "   "   "B" "   "   "   "
       Support Company - "D" "   "   "   "   "A" "   "   "   "
       Reserve   "   - "A" "   "   "   "   "C" "   "   "   "

    Companies will take over the same dispositions as those of the units they relieve with the exception that for the night 31st May/1st June, and until relieved, "C" Coy will find the garrison for LONE TREE POST and FOSSE WOOD POST in addition to their own posts at BERRY POST and ALLEN CRATER.

    "C" Company will also find a platoon to garrison WANGARATTA TRENCH by night.

3. One Officer & 6 N.C.O's per Coy., (including 1 Signalling N.C.O. and 1 Lewis Gun N.C.O.) & 1 N.C.O. from H.Q., will proceed to the trenches during the morning to take over all Defence Schemes, Trench Stores, Aeroplane photos and secret maps.
    Lists of all stores taken over will be rendered to Battn. H.Q. by 10 a.m. 1st June.

4. "B" and "C" Coys will move up into the line under orders to be issued ___ N.F.   Platoon guides for these Companies will ___ p.m.
    ___ " and "C" Coys will relieve by daylight. Guides ___ by 5.30 p.m.   The guns will be man handled.

    ___ off from camp as follows:-
        ___ 7.15 p.m.
        ___ 7.20 p.m.
        ___ 7.25 p.m.

    ROUTE - Cross roads G.24.c.5.5. - H.24.a.95.95 - S.E. by path and corduroy road to TROIS ROIS - by country track to SUBWAY under RAILWAY DUGOUTS.

    Platoon guides will meet these Companies and Headquarters at the SUBWAY underneath the Railway at 10 p.m.

    The Platoon of "C" Coy to garrison the detached posts will report at RAILWAY DUGOUTS for guides at dusk.

    The Lewis Guns of "A" and "D" Coys will be carried on Pack Mules in rear of their respective Companies.

    All movement East of the VLAMERTINGHE - OUDERDOM Road will be by platoons at 50 yards interval.   Troops cannot pass the Control Post at H.16.d.1.1. before 9 p.m.

Sheet 2.   30th May 1917.

5. All kits and stores of "B" and "C" Coys for the trenches will be man handled.

All Officers' valises, etc., of these two Coys to be taken to Transport Lines will be stacked under a guard at TRANSPORT FARM and the Transport Officer will arrange to collect them on his return.

All kits, stores, etc., of H.Q., "A" and "D" Coys will be stacked in dumps under arrangements made by the Regtl. Sergt. Major, by 6 p.m. The Transport Officer will arrange for the collection and conveyance to respective destinations.

6. The following are the arrangements for rations, water and cooking in this sector:-
Rations for Right front Coy, Support Coy., and Battn. H.Q. come to JACKSON'S DUMP.
Rations for Left Front Coy and Reserve Coy come to MANOR FARM.

Water for Right Front Coy, Support Coy and Battn. H.Q. comes to JACKSON'S DUMP in water carts and is there put into petrol tins.
Water for left front Coy and Reserve Coy is obtained from spring at STREAM CORNER.

Ration and water parties for the Right front Coy are found from the Support Company and for the Left front Company from the Reserve Company.

The Regtl. Sergt. Major will issue the necessary detail for these parties.

Cooking for Battn. H.Q., Right front Company and Support Company is done in the Tunnels.
Cooking for the Left front Company is done in ZILLEBEKE SWITCH.
Cooking for Reserve Company is done at STREAM CORNER.

7. Relief complete will be reported by sending the Company Commander's Christian name.

8. ACKNOWLEDGE.

R.C. Mayall.
Capt. & Adjutant,
11th Northd. Fusiliers.

Issued at 11 p.m. 30/5/17, by runner.

```
Copy No.1  -  C.O.           Copy No.6  -  T.O.
  "  No.2  -  "A" Coy.         "  No.7  -  Qr.Mr.
  "  No.3  -  "B"  "           "  No.8  -  Signal Officer.
  "  No.4  -  "C"  "           "  No.9  -  R.S.M.
  "  No.5  -  "D"  "           "  No.10 -  File.
```

TABLE "B".

ITEM	To be found by	Strength. Off. O.R.		PLACE	Remarks.
1.	"D" Coy.	1	6	"B" DUMP, ZILLEBEKE.	These details will parade at H.Q. at 12.30 p.m. tomorrow 31st inst., under the Officer, and will report at 70th Brigade H.Q., RAILWAY DUGOUTS, at 3.30 p.m.
2.	"D" "		1 N.C.O. 3 men.	CONTROL POST, I.21.d.4.4.	Names of all ranks detailed for these duties will be reported to this office by 8.30 a.m. tomorrow, and separate instructions will be written out for each party.
3.	"A" "		2	GUMBOOT STORE, TRANSPORT FARM.	
4.	"A" "		1 N.C.O. 3 men.	WATER TANKS, I.21.b.1.2.	Rations for 1st June must be taken by each man. Rations for subsequent days will be sent to Battalion H.Q., LARCH WOOD, and party No.5 must send a man there daily to draw them.
5.	"A" "		1 N.C.O. 3 men.	WATER TANKS, FOSSE WOOD.	Items 1, 2, 3, and 4 will be relieved by 12 D.L.I. by 3 p.m. 1st June.

R. Mayall

Capt. & Adjutant,
11th Northd. Fusiliers.

30/5/17.

SECRET.

To/- O.C., " " Coy.

30th May 1917.

1.   The instructions contained in S.S.135, Sect.XXX ("Instructions for the Training of Divisions for Offensive Action"), and Appendix II, page 7, "Organisation of an Infantry Battalion and the Normal Formation for the Attack", regarding the number of Officers etc. to take part in the attack will be adhered to in the forthcoming operations.

2.   The following Officers and other ranks will not accompany the Battalion in the attack, and will proceed to the Brigade Reinforcement Camp on Y/Z night:-

Headquarters. Officers.   Major R.H.Gill   -   Second-in-Command.
                          Capt.G.H.Blackett - Assistant Adjutant.
                          2nd.Lt. H.E.Cowling - Lewis Gun Officer.
                          2nd.Lt. A.M.Lyone - Brigade Bombing Officer.

              Other ranks.   Orderly Room Staff 2
                             Signallers 4
                             Runners 4

"A" Company. Officers.   Capt. R.Lindsay.
                         2nd.Lt. H.H.Allison - Attached R.E.
                         1 Other Subaltern.

              Other Ranks.   Bombing Instructor 1
                             Sergeant 1
                             Corporal 1
                             Lance Corporal 1
                             Runner 1
                             Rifle Bombers 4
                             Scouts or snipers 4
                             Lewis Gunners 8

"B" Company. Officers.   Lieut. H.M.P. West.
                         2nd.Lt. E.L.G.Clegg - Hospital.
                         2nd.Lt. C.A.Hewitt - Attached Brigade.
                         2nd.Lt. A.T.Exley   - Leave.
                         2nd.Lt. J.H.Dunn-Yarker - Course.
                         1 Other subaltern.

              Other Ranks.   Coy Sergt. Major 1
                             Lewis Gun Instructor 1
                             Sergeant 1
                             Corporal 1
                             Lance Corporal 1
                             Rifle Bombers 4
                             Scouts or snipers 4
                             Lewis Gunners 8
                             Runner 1

"C" Company. Officers.   Lieut. J.R.Lunn   ----- Hospital.
                          1 other Subaltern.

    Other ranks.   Coy Sergt. Major 1
                          Lewis Gun Instructor 1
                          Sergeant 1
                          Corporal 1
                          Lance Corporal 1
                          Rifle Bombers 4
                          Scouts or snipers 4
                          Lewis Gunners 8
                          Runner 1

"D" Company. Officers. * Capt. W.K.Maclachlan - Temporarily attached to
                                                    Battn. H.Q.
                          2nd.Lt. C.B.Longbotham - Wireless Course.
                          2nd.Lt. W.G.Edgar   ----- Clearing battlefield.
                          1 other Subaltern.

    Other ranks.   Gas Instructor 1
                          Sergeant 1
                          Corporal 1
                          Lance Corporal 1
                          Rifle Bombers 4
                          Scouts or snipers 4
                          Lewis Gunners 8
                          Runner 1

3.   To provide the number of Signallers which may be required for Command Posts, Relay Posts, etc., no Company will take more than two Signallers with it in the Attack.

    The remainder will either be left behind at the Brigade Reinforcement Camp or temporarily attached to Battalion H.Q. according to instructions which will be issued later by the Signal Officer.

4.   In each unit down to and including platoons and sections, it must be clearly understood who is to take command in the event of the Commander becoming a casualty.

    * Goes up with Battn. H.Q. on Y/Z Night.

                                                                 R.C. Mayall.
                                                            Capt. & Adjutant,
30th May 1917.   11th Nortbd. Fusiliers.

WAR DIARY or INTELLIGENCE SUMMARY

Army Form C. 2118.

Place	Date	Hour	Summary of Events and Information	Remarks and references to Appendices
CENTRE SUB SECTOR	1/6/17	6.30am to 7pm	The Battalion was in positions by 1am – our artillery cut wire strong went on day from 6.30am to 7pm – our heavy 6" howitzers fired on enemy's front and Support line from 8am to 2pm – our artillery carried out practice barrage at 3.30pm – enemy artillery was active throughout the day – METROPOLITAN LEFT was blown in the morning and there was general activity in our lines.	Rehayah.
	2/6/17		Our artillery was cut all day and carried out bombardment of enemy's trenches. Enemy opened an intense bombardment on our sector at 9.30pm which lasted until 11.30pm – our artillery retaliated effectively – no infantry action followed. – 2/Lt. West was slightly wounded.	Rehayah
	3/6/17	3.30am	B. Company had 3 men killed and 2 men wounded in ARIEN CRATER. Its early morning was quiet – enemy's artillery was very active throughout the night and constantly retaliated to be called for up to 2am. Our artillery continued its bombardment during the morning and afternoon but enemy was quiet all the day. – D. Coy relieved B. Coy on the night off the line and A Coy relieved C. Coy on the left company front.	Rehayah
	4/6/17		Heavy shelling during the morning especially in neighbourhood of LARCH WOOD. Murnilo – the Battalion was relieved by the 6th Yorks at night and proceeded to the BUND – Relief complete 3.30am.	Rehayah
	5/6/17		Battalion remained in the BUND all day – Reinforcements proceeding back to the Reinforcement Camp during the night including Major Gill, Capt. Blackett, Capt. Lindsay, Capt. West, 2/Lt ER Bell & 2/Lt Simmons, 2/Lt. Hunter and 70 Other ranks.	Rehayah
	6/6/17		Orders were issued for Battn. to take part in the 2nd Army offensive moving in Brigade Reserve to the 69th Brigade.	Rehayah

WAR DIARY or INTELLIGENCE SUMMARY

Army Form C. 2118.

Place	Date	Hour	Summary of Events and Information	Remarks and references to Appendices
Hill 60 Sector. ZILLEBEKE 28.N.W.	7/6/17		The Battalion left the BUND at 12.30am and was in positions of assembly at 2.30am as follows :- Batt. HQ. LARCH WOOD DUGOUTS. J.29.C.2.9. – A Company in BATTERSEA FARM J.23.C.9.3. – B Coy. in NYE Trench J.29.C.8.6. (2 platoons under orders of 2/Lt. Penney attached to 11th West Yorks) – C Coy in BATTERSEA FARM J.23.C.9.3 – D Coy in PANAMA CANAL J.28.d.6.2. – Strength of Battalion going into action 21 Officers + 601 O.R. - At Zero Hour 3.10am according to programme the mine in Hill 60 – CATERPILLAR went off and barrage opened. – 2 Platoons of B Coy under 2/Lt. Penney (No. 7 & 8) moved over after the last wave of 11th W. Yorks into the enemy's front line. – D Coy moved up through the enemy's barrage to LEEK TRENCH – C Company moved up through the barrage to LARCH WOOD TUNNELS and A Company to ZILLEBEKE SWITCH. – Enemy's retaliation was very heavy especially round LARCH WOOD and S.P.9 where A Coy suffered heavily going through the barrage. Orders received at 10am for D Coy to reinforce the 8th Yorks on the right and this relieved for 2 hours after being delayed owing to heavy casualties to St. G. P. Stirling was carried out by Capt. E.G. Bowers M.C. – Subsequently 2 Platoons under extreme right edge of BATTLE WOOD. – 2 Platoons of B Company under Capt. Mitchell were ordered to reinforce the 12 "D.L.I." who had taken the final objective on the left and after considerable delay this order was executed – subsequently these Platoons became attached to the 8th Yorkshire Regt. – C Company found carrying parties and every man made three journeys up to BATTLE WOOD with S.A.A. bombs, ammunition A Company furnished rations for the two companies up in the line. During the day the G.O.C. Brigade reconnoitred his Brigade Reserve and D Coy and 2 Platoons of B Coy under 2/Lt. Penney were withdrawn to LARCH WOOD TUNNEL. C Company A Coy furnished Carrying parties – About 12 midnight rations were received for the Battalion less 2 platoons of B Coy under Capt. Mitchell. Battalion returning to the BUND and the orders expected. by 3.30am 9/7/17	Rehayan

Rehayan |
| | 8/6/17 | | | |

WAR DIARY or INTELLIGENCE SUMMARY

Army Form C. 2118.

Place	Date	Hour	Summary of Events and Information	Remarks and references to Appendices
Attack on Hill 60.	9/6/17		Battn. remained in the BUND all day. Casualties during the operations were: 2nd Lt. R.F. Bolton wounded (since died of wounds) — 2nd Lt. G.T. Weir — 16 O.R. killed — 98 wounded (1 remained at duty) — 11 missing. Total 20ff. + 125.	Rehuyzal.
Camp O.	10/6/17		2 Retns of B. Coy. rejoined the Battn in the BUND at 7:15 am — Orders received for 2 Coys & Battn HQ. (B & D) to return to Camp O. G. 24. d. 77. and A & C. Coys under Major R.H. Gill to come under G.O.C. 69 Bde at 6 pm — B & D Coys arrived in Camp about 8:30 pm. — A. Coy attached to 8/5 Yorks and C. Coy to 11 Yorks.	Rehuyzal.
	11/6/17		B & D Coys had baths at POPERINGHE. — A. & C. Coys in the line attached 16 & 69 Bde	Rehuyzal.
	12/6/17		B. Bn. rested all day. A. & C. Coys relieved, proceeded to the BUND	Rehuyzal.
THIESTOUCK B	13/6/17		Battn. (B. D Coys & HQ) paraded at 4 am and marched to billets in THIESTOUCK arriving at 6:30 am. — A & C. Coys proceeding from YPRES by train arrived about 9 am.	Rehuyzal.
Q. 25. G. 3. 3.	14/6/17		Battn. rested all day — 3 Coys (A.B.C. in tents) — D. Coy in huts.	Rehuyzal.
Hay 27 SE	15/6/17		Cleaning, refitting. — Issue of Clothes. G.O.C. Division inspected the Battalion in the morning and made a complimentary speech on recent action — Signal & Lewis Gun Classes started	Rehuyzal.
	16/6/17		Companies paraded under their own arrangements. Courts hunted on Ptes Stephen and Treron and the latter acquitted — Court of Inquiry assembled by order of Capt R.B. Mitchel O.C. "B" Coy	Rehuyzal.
	17/6/17		Lt Col A. St. Hill to enquire with the conduct of the fighting on June 7/8/17.	Rehuyzal.
	18/6/17		Church parade. — Court of Inquiry reassembled at proceedings forwarded to Brigade — Lewis Gun & Lg Gun & Lg Mortar — Clars continued. Casualties Killed Hitler been paraded.	Rehuyzal.

WAR DIARY
INTELLIGENCE SUMMARY

Army Form C. 2118.

Place	Date	Hour	Summary of Events and Information	Remarks and references to Appendices
TAKESTAR Q.35.C. B.3.	19/6/17		Parades under Company arrangements – Range allotted 15 C. Coy in the morning and A Company in the afternoon.	Renayah
B.3.	20/6/17		Parades under Company arrangements – 1X Corps Range in R.33.a. allotted to the Battn and given to B & C Companies.	Rehnayah
	21/6/17		Parades under Company arrangements – Lt Col St Hill proceeded on leave – Capt Adams and 2 Lt Swann	Rehuayah
	22/6/17		Parades under Company arrangements – Bath in the afternoon.	Rehuayah
	23/6/17		The Brigade Horse Show took place - we took first and two seconds at it, of seven events – Company training in the morning – Cricket Match Officers v Sergeants won by Officers 57 to 45 – Divisional Service – Regimental Match Y.2 of Army Stage Parade won by 9/15 mins 15:14	Rehnayah Rehuayne
	24/6/17		Company parades.	Rehuayne
	25/6/17		Company parades – Divisional Horse Show – The Battalion won two third Prizes (T.T.) i.e. NCO's Turn-out and Pair of light Draft) – and several minor races.	Rehuayne
	26/6/17		Company parades. Batt: Officers Cricket Match V Officers 10th N.F.	Rehuayne
	27/6/17		G.O.C. Division presented Medals to the Brigade at 11.30 a.m. the following were of the Battalion received Military Medals 15182 Cpl R.N. Myers: 14672 Sgt E. Rhodes : 15.954 L.Cpl W. Prothero. 38752 Pte C. Storer. 10416 Pte D. McGurn Pte Riddle : 34471 Sgt H. Turner. 38752 Pte C. Storer. 10416 Pte D. McGurn wounded : 11014 Pte A. Dunton (A. Leave) : 19817 Pte J.D. Downie (dis : fumes) The Reserve Bn was followed by a demonstration of Rifle Grenades and Smoke Screen the area 23 Officers + 440 OR was inspected by Gen. Sir Herbert Plumer. The Battalion together with 10th N.F. Commanding 2 1/2 Army – 22 Officers + 544 OR on Parade – 1 1/2 hours route march.	Rehuayah Rehuayah
	28/6/17			Rehuayah

Army Form C. 2118.

WAR DIARY
or
INTELLIGENCE SUMMARY
(Erase heading not required.)

Place	Date	Hour	Summary of Events and Information	Remarks and references to Appendices
THIESHOUK	29.6.17		Company Parades in the morning - Preparations for move.	R.Meayall
MICMAC CAMP H.B.I.G.	30.6.17		The Battalion paraded at 5.30 a.m. and marched to MICMAC CAMP H.B.I.G. near OUDERDOM - on way fell out on the line of march - The Battalion marched in two half battalions with 200 yards interval - Left for two hours during rain in field near Reninghelst. - Strength Effective 36 officers + 775 (19.6 hour later Strength) - Ration Strength 27 officers + 909 OR -	R.Meayall
ST.HUFERTVSHOEK				

June 30th 1917.

R. Meayall.
Captain Adjutant.
for O.C. 1st Batt. or Fusiliers.

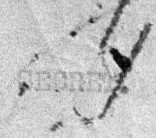

SECRET   COPY NO. 8

11TH NORTHUMBERLAND FUSILIERS ORDER No.16.

Ref.Map - Trench Map HILL 60.
ZILLEBEKE Trench Map, 1/10,000.   6th June 1917.

1. The Second Army will attack the MESSINES - WYTSCHAETE Ridge and its extension Northwards to KLEIN ZILLEBEKE on Z day.
    The task of the 23rd Division is to capture BATTLE WOOD and the KLEIN ZILLEBEKE SPUR and to cover the left flank of the Xth Corps by forming a defensive flank facing East.

2. The 204th (WURTTEMBURG) Division, consisting of 120th, 413th and 414th Infantry Regiments holds the front line from about opposite RAVINE WOOD I.34.d. to opposite OBSERVATORY RIDGE.

3. The frontage allotted for assault to the 69th Inf.Bde. is from WINDY CORNER to the SNOUT, both inclusive.
    The 70th Brigade will assault the enemy's position between I.30.c.50.75. and I.30.b.40.30.
    These attacks will converge so as to bring the inner flanks of Brigades in touch on the red objective about I.30.c.50.00.

4. Mines under HILL 60 and the CATERPILLAR will be fired at ZERO. The assaulting lines will move forward at ZERO plus 15 seconds whether the mines explode or not.

5. Objectives and dividing lines of assaulting units are laid down in 69th Brigade Instructions Nos. 1 & 2, contents of which have already been communicated to Company Commanders and to which further reference can be made if desired.

6. The capture and consolidation of the red and blue lines will be carried out by the 10th Duke of Wellington's on the right, 8th Yorks. in the centre, and 11th West Yorks on the left.
    The assault on the black line by the 9th Yorks on the right and the 12th D.L.I. on the left will be made at ZERO plus 3 hours 40 minutes.
    A new ZERO hour will be named after the capture of the BLACK LINE, and the artillery barrage will lift off the line OAF KEEP - IMPERFECT TRENCH at second ZERO hour plus 20 minutes.
    During the three hours pause of the barrage parties of this Battn. will probably be required to carry forward ammunition, etc., for the 12th D.L.I.

7. The 11th N.F. will be in Brigade Reserve and will be under the orders of G.O.C. 69th Brigade. With the exception of the two platoons of "B" Company attached to the 11th West Yorks, no personnel of this Battalion will be used for purposes of ~~counter attack~~ reinforcing without reference to the G.O.C. Brigade.

8. Places of assembly and subsequent moves of the 11th N.F. are laid down in 11th Northumberland Fusiliers Instructions No.1.
    All units will be in their assembly trenches at ZERO minus 30 minutes and reports will be sent by runners to Battn. H.Q. to this effect.

SHEET 2.   6th June 1917.

9. With reference to Instructions issued from this office re FIGHTING
    DRESS, O.C. Companies will send parties tonight as soon after dark as
    possible to the Battalion Forward Dump at I.29.a.3.0. just East of
    LARCH WOOD to draw the necessary tools, sandbags, bombs and flares,
    and will carry them direct to assembly trenches. The Regimental
    Sergeant Major will arrange to send up an N.C.O. early this evening to
    get the stores in the Dump divided and to issue them.

10. The Battalion will move to places of assembly on Y/Z night as
    follows:-
        "B" Coy will move off at   12.30 a.m.
        "D" "   "   "   "   12.45 a.m.
        "H.Q" "   "   "   "   1 a.m.
        " " "   "   "   "   1.5 a.m.
        " " "   "   "   "   1.20 a.m.

    Companies will move to their positions by the most direct route but
    there will be no movement East of the line I.22.central - BLAUWE POORT
    FARM until after 1a.m.

    The Platoons of "A" Coy for escorting prisoners, less their
    Lewis Gun and Bombing Sections, will proceed to their rendezvous
    independently.

11. Rations for consumption on Z day will be issued before leaving the
    BUND. Rations for consumption on "A" day are at the Forward Dump and
    will be drawn from there on the night Z/A.

    The Water Point for the Battalion is at SHRAPNEL CORNER.

12. Regimental Aid Post is at the WHITE HOUSE, ZILLEBEKE.

13. The Signal Officer will take two watches to 69th Brigade H.Q. to
    be synchronised at 10 p.m. on Y days.
    These watches will be sent down to the BUND by 11.45 p.m. and O.C.
    Companies will synchronise watches at the Headquarter Mess at 12 midnight

14. The S.O.S. Signal will be one RED Very Light.

15. ZERO hour will be notified later.

16. ACKNOWLEDGE.

                                              R.Mayah
                                              Capt. & Adjutant,
                                              11th Northd. Fusiliers.

    Copy No.1 - "A" Coy.   Copy No.5 - T.O. & Q.M.
     "   No.2 - "B" "   "   No.6 - Signal Officer.
     "   No.3 - "C" "   "   No.7 - R.S.M.
     "   No.4 - "D" "   "   No.8 - War Diary.

SECRET.   COPY NO.

11TH NORTHUMBERLAND FUSILIERS ORDER No.16.

Ref.Map – Trench Map HILL 60.
         ZILLEBEKE Trench Map, 1/10,000.   6th June 1917.

1. The Second Army will attack the MESSINES – WYTSCHAETE Ridge and its extension Northwards to KLEIN ZILLEBEKE on Z day.
    The task of the 23rd Division is to capture BATTLE WOOD and the KLEIN ZILLEBEKE SPUR and to cover the left flank of the Xth Corps by forming a defensive flank facing East.

2. The 204th (WURTEMBURG) Division, consisting of 120th, 413th and 414th Infantry Regiments holds the front line from about opposite RAVINE WOOD I.34.d. to opposite OBSERVATORY RIDGE.

3. The frontage allotted for assault to the 69th Inf.Bde. is from WINDY CORNER to the SNOUT, both inclusive.
    The 70th Brigade will assault the enemy's position between I.30.a.30.75 and I.27.b.30.50.
    These attacks will converge so as to bring the inner flanks of Brigades in touch on the red objective about I.30.c.50.00.

4. Mines under HILL 60 and the CATERPILLAR will be fired at ZERO. The assaulting lines will move forward at ZERO plus 15 seconds whether the mines explode or not.

5. Objectives and dividing lines of assaulting units are laid down in 69th Brigade Instructions Nos. 1 & 2, contents of which have already been communicated to Company Commanders and to which further reference can be made if desired.

6. The capture and consolidation of the red and blue lines will be carried out by the 10th Duke of Wellington's on the right, 8th Yorks. in the centre, and 11th West Yorks on the left.
    The assault on the black line by the 9th Yorks on the right and the 12th D.L.I. on the left will be made at ZERO plus 3 hours 40 minutes.
    A new ZERO hour will be named after the capture of the BLACK LINE, and the artillery barrage will lift off the line OAF KEEP – DEFENCE TRENCH at second ZERO hour plus 20 minutes.
    During the three hours pause of the barrage parties of this Battn. will probably be required to carry forward ammunition, etc., for the 12th D.L.I.

7. The 11th N.F. will be in Brigade Reserve and will be under the orders of G.O.C. 69th Brigade. With the exception of the two platoons of "B" Company attached to the 11th West Yorks. no personnel of this Battalion will be used for purposes of ~~counter attack~~ reinforcing without reference to the G.O.C. Brigade.

8. Places of assembly and subsequent moves of the 11th N.F. are laid down in 11th Northumberland Fusiliers Instructions No.1.
    All units will be in their assembly trenches at ZERO minus 30 minutes and reports will be sent by runners to Battn. H.Q. to this effect.

SHEET 2.   6th June 1917.

9.   With reference to Instructions issued from this office re FIGHTING DRESS, O.C. Companies will send parties tonight as soon after dark as possible to the Battalion Forward Dump at I.29.a.5.0. just East of LARCH WOOD to draw the necessary tools, sandbags, bombs and flares, and will carry them direct to assembly trenches. The Regimental Sergeant Major will arrange to send up an N.C.O. early this evening to get the stores in the Dump divided and to issue them.

10. The Battalion will move to places of assembly on Y/Z night as follows:-

   "A" Coy will move off at   12.30 a.m.
   "B" "   "   "   "   12.45 a.m.
   "C" "   "   "   "   1 a.m.
   "D" "   "   "   "   1.5 a.m.
   "S" "   "   "   "   1.30 a.m.

   Companies will move to their positions by the most direct route but there will be no movement East of the line I.22.central – BLAUWE POORT FARM until after dawn.

   The Platoons of "A" Coy for escorting Indian prisoners, less their Lewis Gun and Bombing Sections, will proceed to their rendezvous independently.

11. Rations for consumption on Z day will be issued before leaving the BUND. Rations for consumption on "A" day are at the Forward Dump and will be drawn from there on the night Z/A.

   The Water Point for the Battalion is at SUTHERN CORNER.

12. Regimental Aid Post is at the WHITE HOUSE, ZILLEBEKE.

13. The Signal Officer will take two watches to 69th Brigade H.Q. to be synchronised at 10 p.m. on Y day.
   These watches will be sent down to the BUND by 11.45 p.m. and O.C. Companies will synchronise watches at the Headquarter Mess at 12 midnight

14. The S.O.S. Signal will be one RED Very Light.

15. ZERO hour will be notified later.

16. ACKNOWLEDGE.

                                                R.C.Meyah
                                                Capt. & Adjutant,
                                                11th Northd. Fusiliers.

Copy No.1 = "A" Coy.   Copy No.5 = E.O. & Q.M.
  " No.2 = "B" "   " No.6 = Signal Officer.
  " No.3 = "C" "   " No.7 = R.S.M.
  " No.4 = "D" "   " No.8 = War Diary.

SECRET.   COPY NO. 9.

11TH NORTHUMBERLAND FUSILIERS - ORDER NO. 17.

1. "A" and "C" Coys, 11th N.F. under the command of Major R.H. Gill, are placed at the disposal of G.O.C. 69th Brigade from 6 p.m. tonight until further orders.

   They will remain in the BUND until such time as orders are received for them to proceed into the line.

2. "B" and "D" Coys and Battalion H.Q. will move off forthwith by platoons to Camp "O", G.24.a.7.7.

3. All kits, mess kits, etc., of "B", "D" Coys and H.Q. will be stacked at the usual Battalion Dump under a guard to be detailed by the Regimental Sergt. Major.
   The Transport Officer will arrange to collect these and convey them to the camp.
   Rations for these Companies and H.Q. will be taken direct to the camp.

   Rations for "A" and "C" Companies will be brought to the BUND as soon as possible, and if the Companies have moved up to the line before their arrival the Transport Officer will convey them to JACKSON'S DUMP.

4. Companies are responsible for cleaning up their dugouts before moving off.

5. The Brigade Major, 68th Brigade, will remain at RAILWAY DUGOUTS, and any urgent enquiries needing immediate attention will be sent direct to him.

6. The Qr.Mr. will proceed to the Camp forthwith. He will allot the accommodation to the Companies and H.Q. concerned and arrange for guides to meet the Companies.

                                                          R.C. Mayall.
                                                          Capt. & Adjutant,
10/6/17.   11th Northd. Fusiliers.

       Copy No.1 - Major Gill.   Copy No.6 - T.O.
         " No.2 - "A" Coy.   " No.7 - Qr.Mr.
         " No.3 - "B" "   " No.8 - R.S.M.
         " No.4 - "C" "   " No.9 - War Diary.
         " No.5 - "D" "

SECRET.   COPY NO. 8

11TH NORTHUMBERLAND FUSILIERS - ORDER NO.18.

1. "B" and "D" Coys and Battn. H.Q., 11th N.F. will move to THIEUSHOUK tomorrow 13th inst.

    These Units will parade, ready to move off at 4 a.m. Head of the column at 68th Brigade Reinforcement Camp. Order of march - "B", "D" Coys., H.Q., 1st Line Transport.
    ROUTE:- Via Southern Switch Road - BOESCHEPE.

2. The shelters in the present camp will be struck and placed under a guard to be detailed by the Regimental Sergt. Major, and handed over to a unit of the 24th Division tomorrow morning. List of all stores will be made out and a receipt obtained by the N.C.O. in charge of the guard.

3. Reveille - 2.30 a.m.

    Breakfasts - 3 a.m.

4. "A" and "C" Coys will proceed by train under orders issued by 69th Brigade.
    2nd.Lt. L.W. Ablett, with an approximate entraining state, will meet the Brigade Major at H.10.b.5.1. at 2 a.m. on 13th inst., and proceed to the new area by train with his Company.

5. 1 lorry will be available for the move and the Qr.Mr. will detail a guide to meet the lorry at Brigade Headquarters at 4 a.m. Lorries must be returned to lorry park as soon as possible.

6. All Officers' valises, stores, mess kit, etc., will be stacked under a loading party to be detailed by the Regimental Sergt. Major by 3.30 a.m.

    The valises and mess kit of Headquarter Officers will be stacked at the Brigade Reinforcement Camp.

    The Qr.Mr. will arrange for the collection of the stores and removal to the new area.

                                                            Capt. for Adjutant,
                                                            11th Northumberland Fusiliers.
12/6/17.

          Copy No.1 - C.O.   Copy No.5 - Qr.Mr.
          "   No.2 - "B" Coy.   "   No.6 - 2nd.Lt. Ablett.
          "   No.3 - "D" "   "   No.7 - R.S.M.
          "   No.4 - T.O.   "   No.8 - War Diary.

SECRET.

To/- O.C., " " Coy.

12th June 1917.

1. "B" and "D" Companies and Battalion H.Q. will not move to the BERTHEN Area until tomorrow 13th inst. Orders for this move will be issued later.

2. "A" and "C" Companies will, on relief in the line, proceed by train to GODEWAERSVELDE Station, under orders of 69th Brigade.

The Transport Officer will arrange to have one limber at JACKSONS DUMP at 11 p.m. tonight to convey Lewis Guns and Officers' bundles and mess kit to the Transport Lines.

The Qr.Mr. will arrange with the Transport Officer to send over to the New Area tonight the Field Kitchens of these Companies, one water cart and the Officers' valises and mess kit. As supply wagons are not available to take supplies delivered today over to the new area the Transport Officer will arrange for their conveyance.

One lorry will be available for the Battalion tomorrow. All Transport which is not actually required for the move tomorrow will move to the new area today under orders issued by the Transport Officer and will be clear of their lines by 6 p.m.

Capt. Blackett, with two runners, will proceed to the new area tonight, and will meet "A" and "C" Coys at GODEWAERSVELDE Station at 3 a.m. and guide them to their billets.

3. The Battalion and Transport will be billeted at THIEUSHOUK.

R.C. Mayall
Capt. & Adjutant,
11th Northd. Fusiliers.

12/6/17.

SECRET.   COPY NO. 8

11TH NORTHUMBERLAND FUSILIERS - ORDER NO.19.

1. The 12th D.L.I. with "B" Company 11th N.F. attached, will relieve the 10th N.F. in Camp at DICKEBUSCH H.34.a. tomorrow June 21st.

2. MY "B" Coy 11th N.F. will be attached to 12th D.L.I. for rations, accommodation and discipline, and will be prepared to find a daily working party of 100 men under orders of O.C. 12th D.L.I.

   Working parties will commence work on the night of 21st/22nd.

3. An Advance party consisting of 1 Officer and 4 N.C.O's, will be at Brigade Headquarters at 10 a.m. tomorrow, and will be conveyed to Camp by motor lorry.

4. The Company will parade in full marching order, ready to move off at 2.30 p.m. Lorries will be available to convey them to DICKEBUSCH.

5. O.C., "B" Coy will notify the Adjutant at once of the strength of Officers and other ranks whom he proposes to move to the new area, in order to find the required working party. As far as possible, he will leave Specialists under training behind, and these men will be attached to "A" Company.

6. The Qr.Mr. will be responsible for making arrangements with the Qr.Mr. of 12th D.L.I. for the rationing and water supply of this Company.

   Baggage wagons will be available for conveyance of Officers' valises, mess kit, Lewis Guns, etc., and the Qr.Mr. will issue the necessary detail for loading.

   The Transport Officer will arrange with the Transport Officer of 12th D.L.I. for the Baggage wagons and the cooker to travel by road with the Transport of 12th D.L.I.

7. A cycle will be drawn by O.C. "B" Company for use of the orderly whilst in the new area.

                                                    R.C. Mayall
                                                    Capt. & Adjutant,
                                                    11th Northd. Fusiliers.

Issued at 1 p.m. 20/6/18, by runner.

    Copy No.1 - C.O.   Copy No.5 - Qr.Mr.
     "   No.2 - "B" Coy.   "   No.6 - "A" Coy.
     "   No.3 - O.C. 12 D.L.I.   "   No.7 - R.S.M.
     "   No.4 - T.O.   "   No.8 - War Diary.

SECRET.   COPY NO. 10.
           11th NORTHUMBERLAND FUSILIERS ORDER NO.20.
           ───

Reference Map Sheet 27 and 28, 1/40,000.
                                                    28th June 1917.

1.   The Battalion will march to MICMAC CAMP, H.31.b., relieving a
      Battalion of 72nd Brigade, 24th Division, on the 30th instant.

2.   During the march an interval of 200 yards will be maintained
      between half Battalions.

3.   Reveille - 3.30 a.m.
              Breakfasts - 4 a.m.
      All Officers' kits, Company Stores, Qr.Mr's Stores etc., will be
4.   stacked ready for loading at 5 a.m.
      Dumps will be established as follows:-

         1. At Headquarters, for H.Q. Kits and stores.
         2. At the Camp, for kits and stores of "A", "B" and "C" Coys.
         3. At "D" Coy's billets for stores of that Company.

      1 N.C.O. and 3 men will be detailed by the Regimental Sergt. Major
      as a loading party for each dump, and no other personnel will travel
      on the lorry.

      The Qr.Mr. will arrange for the collection of the stores from
      each Dump.

      The Transport Officer will send the Mess cart round to collect the
      two mess boxes per Company at 5 a.m.   Any Mess boxes above this
      number will be stacked at the respective dumps.

      1 lorry will be available and the Qr.Mr. will detail a guide to
      meet this at Brigade H.Q. at 6 a.m.   No lorry will leave
      this area before 8 a.m. and they will be returned to Park as soon
      as the work is completed.

      The Battalion will parade ready to move off at 5.30 a.m. "A",
      "B" and "C" Coys and H.Q. in the field, "D" Company on the road.

      Transport will march in rear of the Battalion, and the Transport
      Officer will arrange for its collection in rear of Headquarters by
      5.30 a.m.   D Coy

      Baggage and Supply wagons will be left in the Square at
      GODEWAERSVELDE and will march from there under orders of O.C. 191
      Coy., A.S.C. at 7 a.m.

      Dinners on arrival.

4.   An Advance party consisting of 1 Officer to be detailed by O.C.
      "B" Coy and 1 N.C.O. per Coy., and 1 for H.Q. and Transport, will
      report at Brigade Headquarters at 10 a.m. tomorrow 29th inst.
      Camps will be allotted on arrival.   The Officer may take his
      kit.

      Receipts for all material taken over and handed over must be
      obtained and sent in to Orderly Room by 4 p.m. on 30th inst.
      Pumps and water troughs are to be included in any stores taken or
      handed over.

Sheet 2.   28th June 1917.

   The Advance party will relieve the Camp Guard in the new Camp on the morning of 30th inst., before the outgoing Battalion leaves.

   An Advance party of the 123rd Brigade will be taking over the Camp and billets in this area on 29th inst.

   Guides from the Advance party sent on to the new area will be at the Road junction G.30.d.2.9. at 9 a.m. on the morning of the 30th inst.

   All tents which have been moved whilst the Battalion has been in this camp will be re-pitched under arrangements to be made by the Qr.Mr., by 6 p.m. tomorrow 29th inst.

5.   The strictest march discipline will be maintained. No man will fall out of the ranks unless he is in possession of written permission of an Officer.
   This note will be retained by the man until after his arrival in camp.
   O.C. "D" Company will detail 1 Officer to march in rear of the Battalion to collect stragglers.

   Numbers of men who fall out and the hours at which they rejoin will be reported to Orderly Room as soon after arrival in camp as possible.

6.   ~~Acknowledge~~ ROUTE:- LEVEL CROSSING Q.12.d.6.5. – R.1.b.7.1. – CROSS ROADS L.33.c.1½.3. – Cross roads L.35.d.1½.3. – RENINGHELST
7 and ~~OUDERDOM~~

7.   Acknowledge.

                                           R.C. Mayall.
                                           Capt. & Adjutant,
Issued at 9 p.m. 28/6/17.   11th Northumberland Fusiliers.

Copy No.1 – C.O.   Copy No.6 – T.O.
  " No.2 – "A" Coy.   " No.7 – Qr.Mr.
  " No.3 – "B" "   " No.8 – R.S.M.
  " No.4 – "C" "   " No.9 – H.Q.Coy.
  " No.5 – "D" "   " No.10 – War Diary.

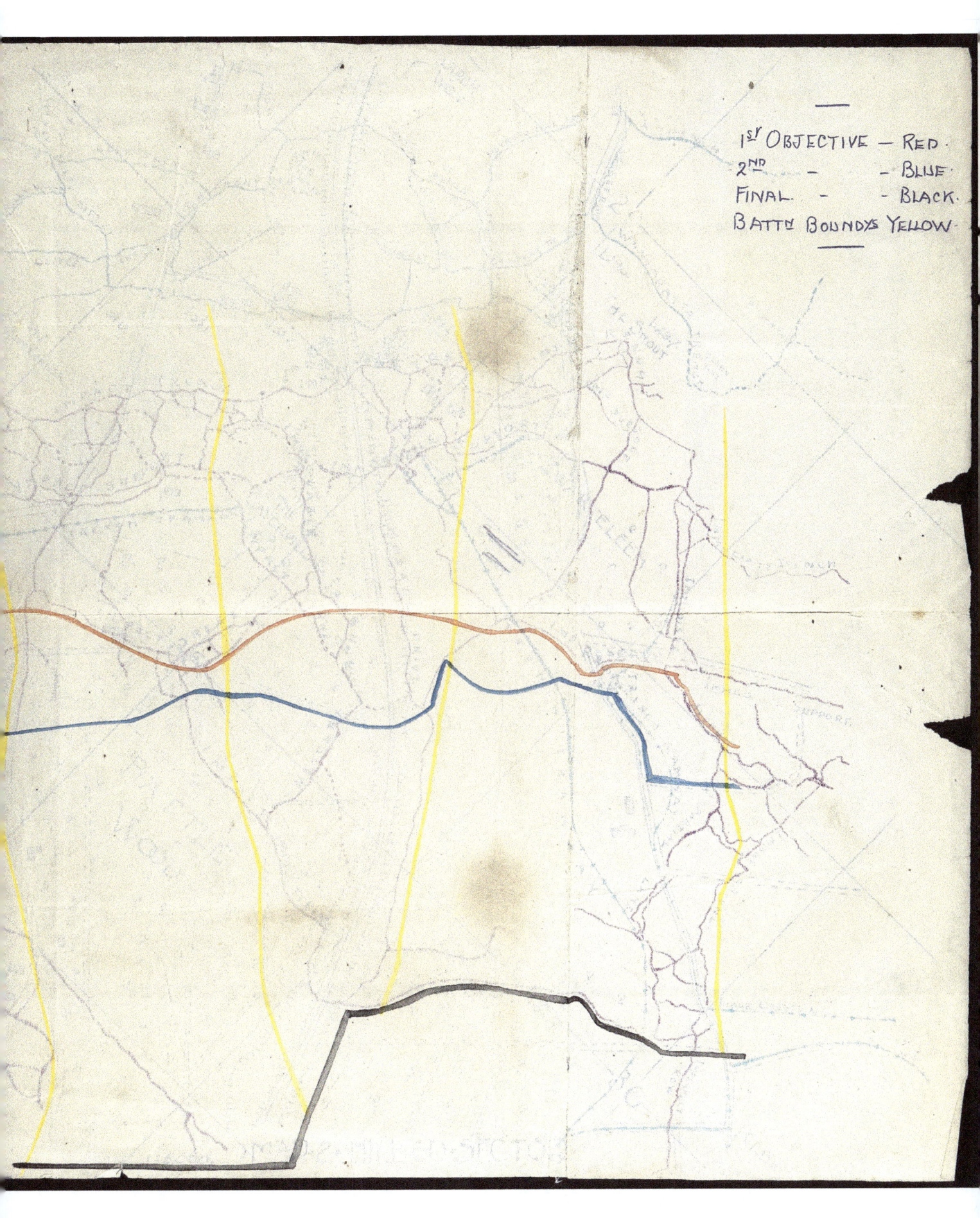

1ˢᵗ OBJECTIVE — RED.
2ⁿᵈ — — BLUE.
FINAL. — — BLACK.
BATTⁿ BOUNDYS YELLOW.

THE ATTACHED IS THE WAR DIARY OF THE 11TH (SERVICE) BATTALION NORTHUMBERLAND FUSILIERS FOR THE MONTH OF JULY 1917.

R C Mayall

Capt. & Adjutant,
for O.C. 11th(S)Bn. Northumberland Fusiliers.

31/7/17.

WAR DIARY or INTELLIGENCE SUMMARY

Army Form C. 2118.

XI NF Vol 22

Place	Date	Hour	Summary of Events and Information	Remarks and references to Appendices
MICMAC CAMP. H.31.c. Sheet 28 N.W.	1/7/17		Church Parade Service – enemy shelled in vicinity of camp during the afternoon. Training resumed of draft of 2 off. + 172 O.R.	Reninghelst
	2/7/17		Between 1 am and 3:30 am enemy shelled in vicinity of camp. Coy. Commander Batts. had the use of the baths at RENINGHELST. Capt. Adorian, 2/Lt. Stevens rejoined from leave. Lt. Clarkson arrived on the 2/4 inst. were inspected by Co. and M.O. – Draft of 1 off. 69 O.R. allotted: A Coy 30 – B Coy 45 – C Coy 30 – D Coy 65. – Advance parties from A.C. Coys proceeded up to the line.	Reninghelst Reninghelst
	3/7/17			
	14/4/17		A + D Coys moved up from MICMAC CAMP to support positions. B Coy were at RUSKIN HOUSE + B Coy HEDGE ST. TUNNELS. Other two Coys H.Q. stayed at MICMAC CAMP. Battn. checked Hun. the line on LACLYTTE RENINGHELST Rd. Casualties 3 killed 1 missing 6 others (killed) 30 wounded. A/L/E + A + C Coys + H.Q.	GW Mackell
LEFT BATTN DIV. FRONT	5/7/17		B + D Coys moved up to the front line. B on the right R on the L/E + A + C Coys R/H.Q. left Micmac Camp at 9 pm. A + C Coys up to the line. Disposition – D Coy left front Coy: B Coy Right front Coy; A Coy Support in CANADA ST. TUNNEL. Battn. H.Q. HEDGE ST TUNNEL. Casualties Nil	GW Mackell
H.Q. HEDGE ST.	6/7/17		Fair amount of MH fire during the day and enemy aeroplane very active and continually flying over our lines. Large working parties at night digging a new front line joining up the M/gun sentry post. A good deal of rolling at night had good work done. Casualties 4 killed 11 wounded.	GW Mackell
	7/7/17		Much quieter day + night. A lot of work was carried out on new front line at night. Casualties 4 wounded.	GW Mackell

WAR DIARY
or
INTELLIGENCE SUMMARY
(Erase heading not required.)

Army Form C. 2118.

Place	Date	Hour	Summary of Events and Information	Remarks and references to Appendices
[Eppy?]	8.7.17		Fairly [quiet] during daylight. RUDKIN HOUSE + MAPLE ST receiving flown wind strafing. Night fairly quiet out in front. About 100 yards of wire put up on extreme left of line. Also some put out towards Right Co. posts. Our Div. front line had cleared. 50 boxes of Mills bombs & 200 Rifle Grenades. Casualties up to left Co. Casualties Nil.	G.W.Machell
	9.7.17		Relieved by 10th N.F. + took over their positions. The Coens Stafford Batt. A Coy. METROPOLITAN LEFT + B Coy. CANADA ST + C. RUDKIN HOUSE + D. NEWFOUNDLAND. H.Q. — Scott H.Q. — SETBA DUGOUT. WINNIPEG ST. Casualties 5 wounded.	G.W.Machell
SUPPORT NAFFN.	10.7.17		Fairly quiet during day, except for his usual barrage at 3 pm & 10 pm. 4 Officers & 350 men working parties. Casualties 2 killed 9 wounded.	G.W.Machell
	11.7.17		Heavy shelling towards CANADA ST, HEDGE ST + RUDKIN HOUSE during day. 5 Officers & 336 men working parties at night. Casualties 4 wounded 1 Missing.	G.W.Machell
	12.7.17		Usual heavy shelling + a great deal of activity in the air on both sides. A.T.S. Coys here to be relieved by 8th Yorks (?) by 9th Yorks. Relief were late & did not arrive until morning of 13th. Casualties 4 wounded.	G.W.Machell
	13.7.17		12.15a.m. Started Canning fort at 1.30 am. Received 5 prisoners. Relieving Coys arrived between 2.30 am & 3.30 am. Relief Complete 4.30 am. Battalion reaches MICMAC CAMP by 7.30 am. After a quiet journey out. Casualties 1 killed 4 wounded.	G.W.Machell

WAR DIARY or INTELLIGENCE SUMMARY

Army Form C. 2118.

Place	Date	Hour	Summary of Events and Information	Remarks and references to Appendices
CAMP AL	14.7.17		Battalion moved to Camp located 4 10k West Reburp at N.1.a.7.8. Capt. Rogers. M.C. awarded a bar to his Military Cross. Lieut G.P. Sterling & 2nd Lt. G.O. Edwards awarded Military Cross. C.S.M. Smith & the Nephew Cpl. awarded Ft. D.C.M. General Salute for Districts 2nd Lt. Edwards with W. M.C.	Rebuilt
N.1.a.7.8. Rdk 28 sw	15.7.17		Church Parades in Camp. Battle at RENINGHELST from 8 am - 12 noon. 150 men fatigue. Two enemy aeroplanes over Camp during morning.	G.R. Rebuilt
	16.7.17		Companies carried out programme of work. Capt. R? Mayall returned from leave. Draft of 2 2. O.R. joined the Battalion and were posted to C. Coy.= Lieut 16 Officers by C.O.	Re Kueyser
	17.7.17		Companies paraded under their own arrangements - found 120 men for working parties.	Re Kueyser
	18.7.17		Capt. W.K. Maclachlan proceeded on leave. - Companies paraded under their own arrangements - 100 men found for working party. 2nd Lt. J. Watt joined for duty and was posted to C. Coy. - Orders received for move to THIESHOUK - Company parades - found 100 men for working parties.	Rebuiyer
	19.7.17		Companies paraded under their own arrangements - found 100 men for working parties - Officers traced plan of enemy's lines. The Batt. paraded at 6.30 am and marched to THIESHOUK -	Rebuiyer
	20.7.17			Rebuiyer
	21.7.17		11.15 am - Bn. fell out on the line of march Quiet parades - Capt. R.B. Mitchell	Rebuiyer
	22.7.17		Reported - Major M.R. Backhouse & General Mitchell & General Court Martial and Joined for duty	Rebuiyer
	23.7.17		Companies cleaned up - In inspection by G.O.C. Division - Companies emptied	Re Kuiyer

2449 Wt. W14957/M90 750,000 1/16 J.B.C. & A. Forms/C.2118/12.

Army Form C. 2118.

WAR DIARY
or
INTELLIGENCE SUMMARY

(Erase heading not required.)

Instructions regarding War Diaries and Intelligence Summaries are contained in "F. S. Regs., Part II. and the Staff Manual respectively. Title Pages will be prepared in manuscript.

Place	Date	Hour	Summary of Events and Information	Remarks and references to Appendices
THIEUSHOUK.	24/7/17		The Battalion and 1st Lin Transport was inspected by G.O.C. 23rd Division in fighting order – Major Batchmos joined the 12 D.L.I. (23rd Indiv.) – Capt. Blacklock and Mitchell proceeded on leave – Major Platt D.S.O. (V.R.) dined with HQ Mess.	R.E. Huayah
	25/7/17		Wet morning – A Coy had the use of the range in the afternoon – Lieut. Hunter returned from leave – 2/Lt. Smith S.H. Smith 2 – Read Joined – Sent	R.E. Huayah
	26/7/17		Conference paraded for the Range – 2/Lts. Smith S.H.: Smith 2. – Read Joined duty tactics – 3 — R.E. Conference had its was of the Range. – Brigade Cricket Trial Match. – Warning Order for move to ST OMER district received	R.E. Huayah
	27/7/17		Warning Order cancelled – Conference heated in close order work – Do A Conference had the use of the range – Gen. Babingtn visited the Coul.	R.E. Huayah
	28/7/17		Battalion R.E. Inspection in the morning – Brigade sports in the afternoon – Orders received for move to QUELMES Area.	R.E. Huayah
	29/7/17		Heavy storm in morning washed out Church Parade. The Transport of the Battalion started from THIESHOUK at 3.26 pm and proceeded by march route to ERBLINGHEM – Baln. had use of the baths – detailed to finish on the range.	R.E. Huayah
	30/7/17		Transport moved from ERBLINGHEM and marched to QUELMES arriving about 1pm – 1st Battn marched from THIESHOUK at 11.15 am. – entrained at CHESTRE 2.20 off 105 OR at 3pm – detrained at ST OMER at 5.15pm – marched to QUELMES arriving at 8pm – 6 men fell out on the line of march. The Batt. had the day for resting, refitting, clothing, etc. of training.	R.E. Huayah
QUELMES.	31/7/17		Reconnoitred training Areas – Strength of Batt: 39 officers + 959 O.R.	R.E. Huayah

31.7.17.

R.E. Huayah Capt. & Adjutant
for O.C. 11 Northd. Fusiliers

SECRET.   COPY NO. 10.

11TH NORTHUMBERLAND FUSILIERS - ORDER NO.21.

Reference Map Sheet 28 N.W. 1/20,000.
        ZILLEBEKE, 1/10,000.
        HILL 60, 1/5,000.   4th July 1917.

1.   The 68th Brigade will relieve the 70th Brigade in the MOUNT SORREL Sector on the nights 4/5th, 5/6th, 6/7th July.
       The Brigade front extends from OBSERVATORY Road exclusive, to KLEIN ZILLEBEKE I.36.a.86.42.

       The exact disposition of the 70th Brigade will be taken over and exact disposition reports will be rendered immediately after the relief on the night 5/6th.

2.   The Battalion reliefs will be as follows:-
        Night 4/5th July.

            "B" Coy 11th N.F. from MICMAC CAMP relieves 1 Company of
                8th York and Lancs in MAPLE STREET.

            1 guide per platoon will be at VALLEY COTTAGES at
            11 p.m.

            "D" Coy 11th N.F. from MICMAC CAMP relieve 1 Company of
            8th York and Lancs. in HEDGE STREET TUNNELS. 1 guide
            per platoon will be at VALLEY COTTAGES at 11 p.m.

       These two Coys will come under the orders of G.O.C. 70th Brigade from 11 p.m. 4th inst., and will be in support for the left front Battalion.

Night 5/6th July.

            "B" Coy 11th N.F. relieves Right front Company of 11th
            Sherwood Foresters. Guides for one per post and one per
            platoon will be at Company Headquarters at 9 p.m.

            "D" Coy 11th N.F. relieves left front Company of 11th
            Sherwood Foresters. Guides one per post and one per
            platoon will be at HEDGE STREET at 9 p.m.

            "A" Coy 11th N.F. from MICMAC CAMP relieves Support Company
            11th Sherwood Foresters in CANADA STREET Area.

            Battalion H.Q. and "C" Company 11th N.F. relieve H.Q. and
            Reserve Coy 11th Sherwood Foresters in HEDGE STREET TUNNELS.

            Guides, one per platoon for "A" and "C" Coys and one for
            H.Q., will be at VALLEY COTTAGES at 11 p.m.

       Companies will commence leaving the Camp two hours before the time at which guides have been arranged to meet them.
       At least 100 yards interval will be maintained between platoons.

3. ROUTES - Cross Country tracks will be used where possible. These must be reconnoitred by Companies at once. No further maps are available. The overland route to DICKEBUSCH is passable for troops and wheeled transport, the track from DICKEBUSCH to CONVENT LANE for troops and pack transport, DERBY ROAD (CORDUROY ROAD) passable for troops and wheeled transport.

SHEET 2.   4th July 1917.

4. All trench stores, air phots, maps, defence schemes, etc., will be taken over on the morning of relief days.   1 Officer and 1 N.C.O. per Company will be detailed to go in advance for this purpose.

5. All Officers' bundles, mess kit, Lewis Guns and stores for the trenches will be stacked on the road near the Farm, ready for loading, by 8.45 p.m. on the nights of relief.

Stores to be returned to Transport Lines will be stacked in separate heaps, in the same place, by the same hour.

Each Company will detail a small loading party under arrangements to be made by the Regimental Sergt. Major.

6. The Ration Dump when in the line will be at VALLEY COTTAGES.

Water will be drawn from Water Points at LARCH WOOD and FOSSE WOOD.

Cooking will be done in HEDGE STREET and CANADA STREET.

7. Completion of all reliefs will be reported as early as possible in code.

8. ACKNOWLEDGE.

R.C. Magall

Capt. & Adjutant,
Issued at 10 a.m. 4/7/17, by runner.   11th Northd. Fusiliers.

```
Copy No.1 - C.O.           Copy No.6 - T.O.
  "  No.2 - "A" Coy.         "  No.7 - Qr.Mr.
  "  No.3 - "B"  "           "  No.8 - R.S.M.
  "  No.4 - "C"  "           "  No.9 - H.Q.Coy.
  "  No.5 - "D"  "           "  No.10 - War Diary.
```

SECRET.   COPY NO. 10

11TH NORTHUMBERLAND FUSILIERS - ORDER NO. 21.(A.)

Ref. Map Sheet HILL 60, 1/5,000.   8th July 1917.
             28 N.W. 1/20,000.

1. The 10th N.F. will relieve 11th N.F. in the Left Battalion Sector tomorrow night, 11th N.F. taking over the dispositions of 10th N.F., and becoming the Support Battalion.

2. The following will be the disposition:-
    "A" Coy   - METROPOLITAN LEFT.
    "B" "   - CANADA STREET TUNNEL.
    "C" "   - RUDKIN HOUSE.
    "D" "   - HEDGE STREET TUNNEL.
    Headquarters - HEDGE STREET TUNNEL.

3. The following guards will be taken over and will be relieved by 3 p.m. in the afternoon:-
To be found by "A" Coy:-
1 N.C.O. and 4 men - Water guard at I.3.b.2.7.
1 N.C.O. and 2 men - Dump at S.P.9.
1 N.C.O. and 3 men - Water Point at STREAM CORNER.

To be found by "C" Coy:-
1 N.C.O. and 3 men - Guarding Iron Rations at VALLEY COTTAGES.
1 N.C.O. and 3 men - Water Point I.22.d.90.05.

4. 1 Officer & 2 N.C.O's per Company and 1 N.C.O. from Headquarters will proceed to take over during daylight tomorrow.

Detailed receipts for all stores, etc., taken and handed over will be sent to Battalion H.Q. by 10 a.m. on 10th inst.

5. No position will be vacated until occupied by relieving Unit.

6. Owing to Companies being so split up, O.C. Companies will arrange to carry their own rations from tomorrow night. The following will be the Ration Dumps:-
    "A" Coy - LONE TREE DUMP, near JACKSON'S DUMP.
    "B", "C", "D" Coys and H.Q. - VALLEY COTTAGES.

7. Completion of relief will be reported as early as possible.

8. ACKNOWLEDGE.

                                                       Capt. & A/Adjutant,
                                                       11th Northd. Fusiliers.

Issued by runner at 8 p.m. 8/7/17.

             Copy No.1 - C.O.   Copy No.6 - "D" Coy.
               " No.2 - Second-in-Command.   Copy No.7 - T.O.
               " No.3 - "A" Coy.   " No.8 - Qr.Mr.
               " No.4 - "B" "   " No.9 - R.S.M.
               " No.5 - "C" "   " No.10 - War Diary.

SECRET.   COPY NO. 10

11TH NORTHUMBERLAND FUSILIERS - ORDER NO.22.

Ref. Map HILL 60, 1/5,000.   12th July 1917.

1. The Brigade will be relieved in the MOUNT SORREL Sector on the nights of 12/13th, 13/14th, and 14/15th inst.
   11th N.F. will be relieved on the night of the 12/13th., "A" and "B" Coys by 8th Yorks., "C" and "D" Coys by 9th Yorks.

2. Each Company will send out 1 Officer and 4 N.C.O's to take over the Camps vacated by the Companies who are relieving them.

3. Usual Working Parties will be required from the 11th N.F. tonight.

   Work will cease by 12.30 a.m. 13th inst., before the raid of 12th D.L.I. takes place.

4. Arrangements must be made by Officers Commanding Companies for the men to clear their dugouts so that it will not be necessary for the working parties to return to the dugouts after work.

5. 1 guide per Platoon of "C" and "D" Coys., will be at VALLEY COTTAGES at 10.30 p.m.
   O.C. "D" Coy will detail an Officer to take charge of these guides.

   1 guide per Platoon of "A" and "B" Coys will be at the junction of VERBRANDEN ROAD and PANAMA CANAL at 10.30 p.m.
   O.C. "A" Coy will detail an Officer to take charge of these guides.

   O.C. "B" Coy will arrange to send his guides along to "A" Coy during the afternoon in order to go down with the Officer and prevent the possibility of mistake.

6. Two Limbers will come up tonight to VALLEY COTTAGES for carrying back stores. This will include any stores of "A" Coy to be taken back.
   Stores to be taken back will be at the Dump as early as possible after dusk.

7. Completion of relief will be reported to H.Q. as early as possible.

8. ACKNOWLEDGE.

                                                    [signature]
                                                    Capt. & A/Adjutant,
Issued by runner at 11.40 a.m.   11th Northd. Fusiliers.
          12/7/17.

          Copy No.1 - C.O.   Copy No.6 - "D" Coy.
           "   No.2 - 2nd-in-Command.   "   No.7 - T.O.
           "   No.3 - "A" Coy.   "   No.8 - Q.M.
           "   No.4 - "B" "   "   No.9 - R.S.M.
           "   No.5 - "C" "   "   No.10 - War Diary.

SECRET.   COPY NO. 10

11TH NORTHUMBERLAND FUSILIERS ORDER NO.23.

Ref. Sheets, 27 & 28, 1/40,000.   20th July 1917.

1. The 68th Infantry Brigade will proceed by march route to the BERTHEN Area on 21st July, the 11th N.F. taking over billets and camp at THIEUSHOUK.

2. The Battalion will parade ready to move off at 6.30 a.m. Order of march - "C", "D", "A", "B", Headquarters, 1st Line Transport. Head of column on the road at the entrance to the camp.

    An interval of 200 yards between Companies and 400 yards between Battalion will be maintained during the march.

    ROUTE:- Cross roads N.2.c.2½.2., LA CLYTTE, WESTOUTRE, BERTHEN. Guides from Advance parties will be at BERTHEN to meet Companies at 9.15 a.m.

    The Band will march for one hour with each Company in turn, commencing with the leading Company. The Bandmaster will arrange for the rifles and packs of the men to be labelled and stacked at the dump by 5.30 a.m.

3. The Regimental Sergt. Major will detail a Rear Party of 1 N.C.O. and 2 men to remain behind to hand over Camp to the incoming Battn. Recipts will be obtained for all tents, bivouac sheets and stores handed over and handed in to Orderly Room immediately the Rear party arrives at THIEUSHOUK.

4. Lorries will be available for the move. Detail will be issued to the Qr.Mr. as soon as received.

    All Officers' kits, mess kits, Stores, etc., will be stacked under near the road, under arrangements to be made by the Regimental Sergt. Major, by 5.30 a.m.

    The Qr.Mr. will arrange for the collection of the Stores from the Dump. Companies will detail 1 N.C.O. & 2 men per Company to remain behind as a loading party. These men will be selected in consultation with the Medical Officer.

    Lewis Guns and Lewis Gun Stores will be loaded on the limbers this afternoon.

5.   Reveillé - 4 a.m.
                   Breakfasts - 4.45 a.m.
                   Dinners on arrival.

6. The strictest march discipline will be maintained. No man will be allowed to fall out without written permission from an Officer, and the names of the men who fall out will be reported to Orderly Room on arrival.

                                                              R.C. Mayall.
                                                           Capt. & Adjutant,
Issued at 12.30 a.m. 20/7/17,   11th Northd. Fusiliers.
by runner.

SECRET. COPY NO. 10

11TH NORTHUMBERLAND FUSILIERS ORDER NO. 24.

Ref. Maps 27, 1/40,000 &
HAZEBROUCK 5a.   28th July 1917.

1. The Transport of the 68th Brigade Group will move to the QUELMES area by road, under the orders of Capt. Haddon A.S.C., on July 29th.

2. The Transport Officer will detail a mounted orderly to report at Brigade Headquarters at 9.30 a.m. on July 29th.

3. Order of march of transport will be:- 191st Coy. A.S.C., B.H.Q., 12th D.L.I., 10th N.F., 11th N.F., 13th D.L.I., 68th M.G.Coy., 71st F.A.

    The 11th N.F. will be at the junction of roads Q.35.b.4.4. at 3.26 p.m.

    ROUTE - THIEUSHOUK, CAESTRE, LE PENPLIER, LONGUE CROIX, Cross Roads U.22.b.5.0., - U.19.c.4.8. An interval of 200 yards will be maintained between the Transport of Units.

    On July 30th the order of march will be:- 11th N.F., 191st Coy., A.S.C., etc. etc.

    11th N.F. to be at U.19.c.4.8. at 5 a.m. and to march to billets in QUELMES. ROUTE:- EBBLINGHEM, RENESCURE, ARQUES.
    Transport will make its own way from ARQUES to their billets.

4. The Qr.Mr. will arrange for the cooking and supply of water for the Battalion after the departure of the Transport. Lorries will be available for the move on the 30th.

5. The Transport Officer will arrange to have all Officers' Riding horses at ST. OMER Station at 4.30 p.m. on 30th inst.

6. All Officers' kits will proceed by lorry on 30th inst., but all Company Stores and any spare Officers' kits must be at Q.M. Stores by 11 a.m. on 29th inst.

    The two mess boxes per Coy may be retained until 30th. All mess kit over and above this will be at the Qr.Mr's Stores by 11 a.m. tomorrow.

                                            R.C. Mayall Capt. & Adjutant,
                                                  11th Northd. Fusiliers.

        Copy No.1 - T.O.   Copy No.6 - T.O.
         "   No.2 - "A" Coy.   "   No.7 - Qr.Mr.
         "   No.3 - "B" "   "   No.8 - R.S.M.
         "   No.4 - "C" "   "   No.9 - H.Q.Coy.
         "   No.5 - "D" "   "   No.10 - War Diary.

SECRET.   COPY NO. 10.

11TH NORTHUMBERLAND FUSILIERS ORDER NO. 25.

Ref. Map Sheet 27. 1/40,000
and HAZEBROUCK 5a.   29th July 1917.

1. The 68th Brigade Group, less Transport, will move to QUELMES area on July 30th., 11th N.F. proceeding to billets in QUELMES.

2. 2nd.Lt. E.G.Simons, 1/N.C.O. per Coy., and 1 N.C.O. from H.Q., will parade at Brigade Headquarters at 8 a.m. on July 30th as advance party.

3. The Regimental Sergt. Major will detail 1 L/Cpl. and 1 man to remain behind as a rear party in charge of camp. The Qr.Mr. will arrange for this party to have 4 days rations.
   The Qr.Mr. will arrange for all tents in the Transport Field to be struck and handed in to the camp forthwith. He will make out a list of camp equipment and stores to be handed over and leave it with the N.C.O. i/c Rear party.

4.   Reveillé - 6 a.m.
              Breakfasts - 7.45 a.m.

5X   All Officers' kits and mess kits will be stacked as follows by 9 a.m.:-

    "A", "B" & "C" Coys - At the entrance to the Camp.
         "D" Coy   - Entrance to their billet.
         H.Q. "   - Qr.Mr's Stores.

   The packs and rifles of the band, properly labelled, will be handed in to the Qr.Mr's Stores by the same hour.

   The Regimental Sergt. Major will issue the necessary detail for loading parties.

   The Battalion will parade, ready to move off at 11.15 a.m. "A", "B", "C" Coys and H.Q. will be formed up in the camp, and "D" Coy will join the column at the road junction Q.35.c.4.9. Men will carry haversack rations.

              12.30 p.m. Entrain at CAESTRE.
              4 p.m.   Detrain at ST. OMER.

   2nd.Lt. J.Moffat is appointed Battalion Entraining Officer and will report to Lieut. GREEN, at CAESTRE Station, 3/4 hour before the departure of the train. He will take a copy of the entraining state.

5. Lorries will be available for the move. Details will be issued to the Qr.Mr.

                                              R.C. Mayall.
                                              Capt. & Adjutant,
29/7/17. Issued by runner at 4.45 p.m.   11th Northd. Fusiliers.

        Copy No.1 - C.O.   Copy No.6 - Qr.Mr.
         "   No.2 - "A" Coy.   "   No.7 - R.S.M.
         "   No.3 - "B" "   "   No.8 - H.Q. Coy.
         "   No.4 - "C" "   "   No.9 - Entraining Officer.
         "   No.5 - "D" "   "   No.10 - War Diary.

Army Form C. 2118.

WAR DIARY
or
INTELLIGENCE SUMMARY.
(Erase heading not required.)

Instructions regarding War Diaries and Intelligence Summaries are contained in F.S. Regs., Part II. and the Staff Manual respectively. Title pages will be prepared in manuscript.

XI Inf / 23 £

Place	Date	Hour	Summary of Events and Information	Remarks and references to Appendices
QUELMES W.B.R.	1/8/17		It poured with rain all day so that all work had to be done in billets - the Commanding Officer visited billets in the morning and gave a lecture to all officers in the afternoon	R.C. Wayall
Moly 27 A.S.F.	2/8/17		The G.O.C. Division visited the battalion in the morning. The Battn. was allotted 'C' Range at Q.35 central and this was given to 'B' Company but owing to rain it could not be used all day - all Companies had lectures etc. during the morning and in the afternoon 2 hours route march	R.C. Wayall
	3/8/17		C. Range was allotted to A & B Companies but only 1 hour's firing could be done owing to rain - C & D Companies on the training area	R.C. Wayall
	4/8/17		C Range allotted to C & D Companies but very little firing possible - A & B Companies on the training area - C & D Companies each completed three practices	R.C. Wayall
	5/8/17		Church parade in the morning for C & D Companies - A & B Companies had the use of the Range at Q.35 central and fired five practices each	R.C. Wayall
	6/8/17		A Battalion Attack on the Training area in the morning - Officers leave Staff and all Officers recalled from leave - 2/Lt. Abbott Edgar length to regiment	R.C. Wayall
	7/8/17		In the morning Companies prepared for inspection by G.O.C. 2nd Army - G.O.C. 2nd Army inspected the battalion at work - Orders received for move or distant but cancelled a postponed until given	R.C. Wayall

WAR DIARY
or
INTELLIGENCE SUMMARY.
(Erase heading not required.)

Army Form C. 2118.

Place	Date	Hour	Summary of Events and Information	Remarks and references to Appendices
QUELMES	8/8/17		C & D Companies had the use of the Range at Q.35 central - "B" baths at St. Omer were allotted to the battalion and to arts lorries transported its parties	Relwayall
SERQUES	9/8/17		Battalion paraded at 10.15 a.m. and marched to the SERQUES sub-area arriving at 12.15 p.m. - 5 men fell out on the line of march - Batt HQ Q.17.d.7.5 - Companies very much scattered	Relwayall
	10/8/17		Conference of C.O.'s at Bde HQ in morning and Coy Commanders at Bn HQ at 4 pm. Companies paraded under their own arrangements - leave for officers reopened	Relwayall
	11/8/17		Companies paraded on the training area in the morning - in the afternoon the Corps Commander Sir Ivor Maxse lectured all Company Commanders & C.o.s	Relwayall
	12/8/17		Church Parades this morning - in the afternoon "B" Range was allotted to "C" Coy and the Miniature Range to "D" Coy.	Relwayall
	13/8/17		In the morning all officers went out on to manoeuvre area to prepare tonight of operations. Conference of Adjutants at Bde HQ - night of operations were carried out	Relwayall
	14/8/17		Major R.H. Gill rejoined from leave - Companies only did 2 hours work in the morning Commander-in-Chief passed through village	Relwayall
	15/8/17		Company Commanders & 1 other officer per Coy went on Special Course - Company parades in billet	Relwayall

Army Form C. 2118.

WAR DIARY
or
INTELLIGENCE SUMMARY.
(Erase heading not required.)

Instructions regarding War Diaries and Intelligence Summaries are contained in F. S. Regs., Part II. and the Staff Manual respectively. Title pages will be prepared in manuscript.

Place	Date	Hour	Summary of Events and Information	Remarks and references to Appendices
SERQUES	16/8/17		A Coy had the use of the Shell Firing Range at GUEMY - Other 3 companies on Training area - Capt R Lindsay proceeded to join RFC ('i') & Capt E.G. Bowers HE took over Command of A Coy - 2 Lt. Spiers joined for duty (15") - A Coy were not allowed to use the range.	R. Lusgall
	17/8/17		A Coy paraded near Gillets - B.C.D Coys on training area all day - Gun demonstration by Gas Officer at Eperlecques	R. Lusgall R. Lusgall
	18/8/17		Battalion had the use of "B" Range in the afternoon and all had shots fired - had the use of the Baths in the afternoon - Company Commanders Course ended	R. Lusgall
	19/8/17		Church Parades in the morning - Company Commanders' Conference in the afternoon	R. Lusgall
	20/8/17		The Battalion practised the attack on its training area from 9am - 1.15 pm	R. Lusgall
	21/8/17		Warning Order received for move to RHENIGHEST area on 24" inst and for transfer of Division to II Corps - Company parades all day - Capt A Lowry SE left the Bn to Brigade Exercises on Training Area all day - Practice for ceremonial attack on XVIII Corps front - Orders for move of transport etc received at 10.35pm and at 11 pm.	R. Lusgall
	22/8/17			R. Lusgall
	23/8/17		B & C Companies proceeded in lorries for the GUEMY Firing Range at 9.30 am - Transport left at 8.45 am and Lantern W&G Coys at 3.40 pm - No firing on range possible - 11th N.F. Order No 27 issued at 6.30 pm for move to new area.	R. Lusgall

WAR DIARY
or
INTELLIGENCE SUMMARY.

(Erase heading not required.)

Army Form C. 2118.

Place	Date	Hour	Summary of Events and Information	Remarks and references to Appendices
MICMAC CAMP	24/8/17		Battalion paraded at 7.30am and marched to WATTEN Station entraining there at 11.30am – detrained at RHENIGHEST siding at 4.30pm and marched to MICMAC CAMP at 6pm – transport arrived at 2pm	R. Mayall
	25/8/17		This day being the second anniversary of the arrival of the battalion overseas the following officers & other ranks who originally came overseas with the battalion are still serving with it: Capt. R.C. Mayall (Adjutant); Capt. W.K. MacLachlan (O.C. D. Coy); Capt. G.H. Blackett (A/o Lajt) – Capt H.M.P. West (O.C. B. Coy) – Lt. W.A. Henri (Transport Off.) 2nd-Lt J.B.W. Robertson (att. T.M.B.) — 243 other ranks. Actually with the battalion. All ranks under Company arrangements – Officers visited hostel of HOOGE Sector. Warning orders received that the Brigade will probably go into action on 29th	R. Mayall
	26/8/17		C.O. & 2 other officers went up the line in morning – Church Parades	R. Mayall
	27/8/17		Two officers & two NCOs of A.C. Coys went up the line to see left sector of Air Front. Company Commanders Conferences – Company Parades	R. Mayall
	28/8/17		Capt. Westcott Stirling went up the line to see left sector – Company parades – Instruction & Fighting Kit issued for Brigade to companies – Conference at Brigade to re-Battalion moved at 5.30pm to DICKEBUSCH	R. Mayall
H.33.a.7.3	29/8/17		Capt. Channer & Lt Bonner went up the line relieving 7" R.B. in Camp.	R. Mayall

WAR DIARY
or
INTELLIGENCE SUMMARY.
(Erase heading not required.)

Army Form C. 2118.

Place	Date	Hour	Summary of Events and Information	Remarks and references to Appendices
DICKEBUSCH	30/8/17		62nd Brigade Plan of Operations for for the coming operations received - 11th Northd Order No 29 issued - 2nd Lt W R Bell + party proceeded to MILLAM as Staff to Corps Reinforcement Camp	Relmsgo/
H.33.a.7.3.	31/8/17		11th North Fus Instructions No 4 issued - enemy barrel the vicinity of the camp during the afternoon but caused no casualties to this battalion - Strength fighting 40 Officers + 954 OR - Ration strength 30 Officers + 779 OR - Travel Strength 27 Officers + 69 OR.	Relmsgo/

31.8.17.

R. Keogh.
Captain & Adjutant.
for O.C. 11 Northd Fusiliers

SECRET. COPY NO. 10.

11TH NORTHUMBERLAND FUSILIERS ORDER NO.26.

Ref. Map HAZEBROUCK, 5a.
and 27A., S.E., 1/20,000. 8th August 1917.

1. The 68th Infantry Brigade Group will proceed by march route to the EPERLEQUES Area on August 9th, the 11th N.F. being billeted in SERQUES.

2. The Battalion will parade, ready to move off, on the Battalion field, at 10.15 a.m. Order of march - Band, B, C, D, A, HqQ., 200 yards interval will be maintained between Companies, and the Band will march with each Company in turn for one hour.

   ROUTE:- QUELMES, Q.34.c.3.9., ZUDAUSQUES, CORMETTE, by road through Q.28.d.& b., to cross roads at Q.18.c.4.9.
   Guides for the Battalion will be at the cross roads Q.18.c.4.9. at 11.30 a.m.

   1st Line Transport will accompany the Battalion and will be formed up on the road outside the Battalion field by 10.15 a.m. After the Battalion has passed the point W.3.a.5.5. all the Brigade Transport will follow in rear of 11th N.F. Transport.

3. The strictest march discipline will be maintained. No man will be allowed to fall out without written permission of an Officer, and numbers of men falling out will be reported to Orderly Room on arrival in billets.

4. There will be no long halts, but the usual hourly halts will be observed.

5. Dumps for stacking Officers' valises, extra mess kit, stores, etc., will be established as follows:-

   Road junction by "A" Coy's Mess - For H.Q. Officers and "A" Coy.
   Orderly Room - For Headquarters, "B" and "C" Coys.
   Qr.Mr's Stores - For "A", "D" Coys and Transport.

   Everything will be stacked by 8 a.m. and the Regimental Sergt. Major will detail loading parties to be at the dumps by that hour.

   The Qr.Mr. will arrange for collection of the stores.

   1 lorry is allotted to the Battalion and the Qr.Mr. will arrange for a guide to be at Brigade H.Q. at 7 a.m. to meet it.

   The Mess cart will collect the two mess boxes per Company at 9.30 a.m.

   R.C. Mayall.
   Capt. & Adjutant,
   11th Northd. Fusiliers.

Issued by runner at 9.45 p.m.

   Copy No.1 - C.O.   Copy No.6 - T.O.
   "   No.2 - "A" Coy.   "   No.7 - Q.M.
   "   No.3 - "B" "   "   No.8 - R.S.M.
   "   No.4 - "C" "   "   No.9 - H.Q. Coy.
   "   No.5 - "D" "   "   No.10 - War Diary.

SECRET. COPY NO. 3

11th NORTHUMBERLAND FUSILIERS - ORDER NO. X.

Ref. Map Sheet FRANCE, 27A., S.E.,
1/20,000. 13th August 1917.

1. The enemy is entrenched on the high ground between OUERCAMP, V.1.b.7.7. and a point about Q.a.8.

   The English Army has established a line of outposts BOISDINGHEM - CUBLINGHEM - INGLINGHEM - and then along a line to Q.9. central.

2. The Commander of the English force has decided to attack the enemy's position during the night Aug. 13/14th.
   The 68th Infantry Brigade will attack the enemy's position between Q.13.b.7.9. and Q.13.a.2.3.

   The 11th Northd. Fusiliers will be the right assaulting Battalion, with the 13th D.L.I. on their left.

   The 11th N.F. will attack the enemy's front, support and reserve line between Q.13.b.7.9. and Q.13.a.9.7.

3. The Battalion will be formed up on the line Q.14.c.0.7. and Q.14.a.4.0. before ZERO hour.
   The advance will be made with "C" Company (right) and "B" Company (left) in the front line, and "A" Company (right) and "D" Company (left) in support. Each Company will form two waves which will advance 50 yards behind each other.

   The objective of the right Company will be the enemy's position from Q.13.b.7.9. to Q.13.b.3.7½. and the objective of the left Company will be from Q.13.b.3.7½. to Q.13.a.9.7.

   The first wave will advance at ZERO, and will be by a bearing of 320°, direction being by the left.

   Battalions will not advance as far as the objective, but will reform on the INGLINGHEM - LE BROUET Road and return to billets by platoons.

   The Battalion will move to the position of assembly by platoons at 200 yards interval. Order of march - B, C, D, A, Headquarters, leading platoon to pass the point Q.17.b.6.5. at 9.15 p.m.

4. Watch, synchronised by Brigade, will be sent round to Companies before 6 p.m.

5. ZERO hour will be 10.30 p.m.

6. Regimental Aid Post will be at Q.14.c.3.7.

7. ACKNOWLEDGE.

8. Reports to be sent to Q.14.c.4.5.

R.C.Mayall
Capt. & Adjutant,
11th Northd. Fusiliers.

Issued by runner at 2.30 p.m.

Copy No.1 - 68th Bde. Copy No.6 - "C" Coy.
"   No.2 - O.C., 13 D.L.I. "   No.7 - "D" "
"   No.3 - C.O. "   No.8 - Intelligence Officer.
"   No.4 - "A" Coy. "   No.9 - Signal Officer.
"   No.5 - "B" " "   No.10 - War Diary.

SECRET.   BRIGADE EXERCISE.   COPY NO. 15.

11TH NORTHUMBERLAND FUSILIERS - ORDER NO. Y.

Ref. Map 27A., S.E. and
POELCAPPELLE, Ed.1., 1/10,000.   20th August 1917.

1. On Wednesday August 22nd., the 68th Infantry Brigade will practise an attack over a piece of ground to represent an area (Map POELCAPPELLE, 1/10,000), with the following boundaries. D.7.central to D.1.c.0.0. - County cross roads - V.21.a.9.4. - V.28.a.1.6. - WELLINGTON FARM (inclusive) - D.7.central.

   This area is a level piece of ground dotted with farms intersected by hedges. It is crossed by the STROOMBEEK, which is no obstruction.

   The 69th Brigade will attack on the left and X Brigade on the right.

   The piece of ground on which the practice attack will take place is (Map 27A., S.E.) on the TILQUES Training Area.

2. The 11th N.F. will attack the first objective (BLUE LINE). 6 guns of 68th M.G. Coy. will be attached.

   The 12th D.L.I. will attack the second objective (RED LINE).

   The 13th D.L.I. and 10th N.F. will attack the third objective (BLACK LINE).

   The first objective (BLUE) is the ground between Q.13.a.central - P.18.d.6.2. It represents a line on the POELCAPPELLE Map approximately from WELLINGTON FARM to V.26.c.0.0.

3. The attack on the BLUE LINE will be carried out by the 11th N.F. with three Companies in the firing line, D., A., C., and B Company in reserve for carrying.

   The jumping off line will be divided as follows :-

   "D" Coy - Q.14.c.8.3. - Q.14.c.6.0.
   "A" " - Q.14.c.6.0. - Q.20.a.3.6.
   "C" " - Q.20.a.3.6. - Q.20.a.0.3.
   "B" " - In Quarry Q.20.b.8.2.

4. The Objectives will be as follows :-

   "D" Coy - WELLINGTON FARM (inclusive). - STOKES FARM (inclusive).
   "A" " - STOKES FARM (exclusive) to YORK FARM (exclusive).
   "C" " - YORK FARM (inclusive) - P.18.d.6.2.

   The general bearing of the line of Advance is 320° (45° on POELCAPPELLE Map).

   The boundaries of the Companies will be imaginary lines running from the flanks of the jumping off points to the flanks of the objectives.

   O.C. Companies will ensure that proper direction is kept and that they do not encroach on each other's area. All farms, strong points, and entrenchments within these areas will be dealt with by the Companies concerned.

   Companies will move to the attack with 3 Platoons in the firing line and supports and 1 platoon in local reserve (only to be used in case of urgent necessity). Moppers-up will be detailed by O.C. Companies in sufficient numbers for their own Company areas.

SHEET 2.   20th August 1917.

4. CONTINUED :-

The barrage will lift at the rate of 100 yards in five minutes and will rest 150 yards beyond the BLUE LINE for one hour.

Immediately the objective has been reached, Companies will consolidate their positions and intensive digging will be started. For this purpose 20 shovels and 10 picks will be carried by each Company.

5. The 12th D.L.I. will pass through our objective at ZERO plus 2 hours 5 minutes.

The 13th D.L.I. and 10th N.F. will pass through our objective at about ZERO plus 3 hours 30 minutes.

6. O.C. 68th M.G. Coy will detail 2 guns to take up a position for covering fire in the vicinity of VON TIRPITZ FARM as soon as this position has been captured. The remaining 4 guns will remain in reserve at Q.14.c.6.0. until the BLUE LINE is captured when they will move forward as follows :-

1 to vicinity of WELLINGTON FARM - 1 to vicinity of STOKES FARM -
1 to vicinity of WINCHESTER FARM - 1 to vicinity of YORK FARM.

O.C. 68th M.G. Coy will arrange for an Officer to be attached to Battn. H.Q. to receive the necessary orders to advance.

7. The Regimental Aid Post will be established at Q.14.c.6.0. and a Forward Dressing Station at Q.13.d.4.4. as soon as the objective (BLUE) is taken. O.C. Companies will arrange to fall out 10% of their men as casualties and the Medical Officer will make the necessary arrangements for collection of wounded.

8. The Transport Officer will arrange for the Pack animals to carry ammunition, rations and water to the Brigade Forward Dump at Q.21.a. central.

O.C. "B" Coy will be responsible for taking over these loads and sending them up to the firing line by means of the YUKON PACKS.

9. All troops will march to their positions of assembly independently and will be formed up, ready to jump off, half an hour before ZERO.

10. Watches will be synchronised at Battalion H.Q. at 9 p.m. on 21st inst.

11. ZERO hour will be at 9 a.m.

12. ACKNOWLEDGE.

13. Reports to Q.20.~~a.5.6~~ b.0.3. A Forward Command Post will be established at Q.13.d.4.4. to which Battalion H.Q. will move as the advance proceeds.

Q.20.a.2.7.

R.C. Mayall
Capt. & Adjutant,
11th Northd. Fusiliers.

Issued by runner at 11 p.m. 20/8/17.

Copy No.1 - Bde. H.Q.	Copy No.6 - "A" Coy.	Copy No.11 - M.O.
" No.2 - O.C., 12th D.L.I.	" No.7 - "B" "	" No.12 - Sig.Off.
" No.3 - O.C., 68 M.G.C.	" No.8 - "C" "	" No.13 - I.O.
" No.4 -- C.O.	" No.9 - "D" "	" No.14 - R.S.M.
" No.5 - 2nd-in-Command.	" No.10- T.O. "	" No.15 - War Diary

SECRET.

AMENDMENT TO PARA. 4 OF 11TH NORTHD. FUSILIERS ORDER NO. Y.

With reference to the above paragraph, in accordance with the instructions of the G.O.C. Brigade the Platoon in reserve of the centre Company will now remain in Battalion reserve under the orders of the O.C., 11th N.F.

R C Mayall

Capt. & Adjutant,
11th Northd. Fusiliers.

21:8:17.

SECRET.   COPY NO. 10

11TH NORTHUMBERLAND FUSILIERS ORDER NO. 27.

Ref. Map 27, 28, 1/40,000.   23rd August 1917.

1. The 68th Brigade Group, less transport, will move to the OUDERDOM Area on August 24th, the 11th N.F. proceeding to MICMAC CAMP, H.31.B.5.5.

2. The Brigade will come under the II Corps from 10 a.m. on 24th August.

3. The following intervals will be maintained on the march in the IInd Corps area :-
   (a) East of RENINGHELST - POPERINGHE Road - 200 yards between Companies.
   (b) West of above road - 500 yards between Battalions.

4.   Reveille - 5 a.m.
                 Breakfasts - 6 a.m.
   All Officers' kits, mess kits, camp kettles, etc., will be stacked as follows by 7 a.m :-
       Headquarters & "C" Coy - Orderly Room.
       "A", "B" & "D" Coys --- Qr.Mr's Stores.

The Regimental Sergt. Major will detail loading parties for both dumps.

The Acting Q.M.S. will detail a guide to report to the Brigade Q.M.S. at Brigade H.Q. at 7 a.m. to guide 1 lorry to the Battalion Dumps.

Capt. G.H. Blackett will be in charge of the loading arrangements and will proceed with the lorry.

The lorry will be returned to its Park as soon as possible after its duties are completed.

Rations for consumption on the 24th will be issued today and carried on the man. Rations for consumption on the 25th will be issued on arrival in new area.

   The Battalion will move to the entraining station - WATTEN - as follows :-

   Headquarters and "C" Coy - Parade ready to move off from Orderly Room at 7.30 a.m.

   The Band, "A", "B" & "D" Coys - To join column at the Church in SERCQUES at 7.50 a.m.

The Battalion will entrain at WATTEN at 10 a.m. and detrain at RENINGHELST at 1.50 p.m.

2nd.Lt. J. Moffat is appointed Battalion Entraining Officer and will report to Captain E.E. Dorman-Smith, M.C., at WATTEN Station at 9.15 a.m.

The N.C.O. i/c Band will arrange for the packs and rifles of the bandsmen to be stacked at the Qr.Mr's Stores by 7 a.m.

                                                           continued :-

Sheet 2.

Lewis Guns of "B" and "C" Coys will be man handled to the Entraining Station.

5. ACKNOWLEDGE.

R.C. Mayah

Capt. & Adjutant,
11th Northd. Fusiliers.

Issued by runner at 6.30 p.m.
23/8/17.

Copy No.1 = C.O.	Copy No.6 = Entraining Officer.
" No.2 = "A" Coy.	" No.7 = Q.M.
" No.3 = "B" "	" No.8 = R.S.M.
" No.4 = "C" "	" No.9 = H.Q.Coy.
" No.5 = "D" "	" No.10 = War Diary.

SECRET.   COPY NO. 10.

11TH NORTHUMBERLAND FUSILIERS ORDER NO. 28.

Ref. Map Sheet 28 N.W., 1/20,000.   29th August 1917.

1. The 68th Infantry Brigade will move by march route today, 29th August, to the DICKEBUSCH Area, the 11th N.F. proceeding to Camp at H.33.a.7.3., vacated by 7th R.B.

2. Companies will move to the new camp independently, passing the Orderly Room at the following times :-

    Band & Headquarters — 5.30 p.m.
    "A" Company   ——— 5.32 p.m.
    "B"   "   ——— 5.34 p.m.
    "C"   "   ——— 5.36 p.m.
    "D"   "   ——— 5.38 p.m.
    1st Line Transport   ——— 5.40 p.m.

3. All Officers' kits, mess kits, Company Stores, etc., will be stacked at the Qr.Mr's Stores by 5 p.m. The Regimental Sergt. Major will detail a loading party of 1 N.C.O. & 5 men.
    The Qr.Mr. will arrange for the stores to be transferred to the new camp by lorry.

4. ACKNOWLEDGE.

                                                    R C Mayah
                                                    Capt. & Adjutant,
Issued by runner at 3.35 p.m.   11th Northd. Fusiliers.

    Copy No.1 — C.O.   Copy No.6 — T.O.
    "   No.2 — "A" Coy.   "   No.7 — Q.M.
    "   No.3 — "B" "   "   No.8 — R.S.M.
    "   No.4 — "C" "   "   No.9 — H.Q.Coy.
    "   No.5 — "D" "   "   No.10 — War Diary.

CONFIDENTIAL.

WAR DIARY.

of

11th (S) BATTALION, NORTHUMBERLAND FUSILIERS.

From Sept. 1st 1917.

To. Sept. 30th 1917.

WAR DIARY
or
INTELLIGENCE SUMMARY.
(Erase heading not required.)

Army Form C. 2118.

Place	Date	Hour	Summary of Events and Information	Remarks and references to Appendices
DICKEBUSCH H.33.a.7.3	1.9.17		Orders were received for the relief of the 23rd Division by the 25th Division - Officers and 3 OR of 1st Australian Division attached for 48 hours - orders received at 9.45 to proceed to STEENVOORDE Area - Reinforcements went to OUDERZEELE (II Corps)	Relwayall
DALLINGTON CAMP	2.9.17		Battalion paraded at 8.45am and marched via Reninghelst & Abeele - arrived 15 STEENVOORDE Batt.n was turned back and sent back to DALLINGTON CAMP	Relwayall
L.35.a.9.9		at L.35.a.9.9 - 31 men fell out on the line of march - considerable aerial activity all night	
STEENVOORDE Area.	3.9.17		Advance party proceeded to STEENVOORDE the morning - Battalion paraded at 5.45pm and marched to billets in farms near STEENVOORDE - 12 men fell out on the line of march	Relwayall
	4.9.17		Battalion had the use of the Baths but no clean clothing available - training Orders for II Corps Offensive received - Orders for move received	Relwayall
NORDPEENE Area.	5.9.17		Battalion marched off at 7.12 am to billets in NORD PEENE area - 35 men fell out on the line of march - reinforcements arrived from OUDERZEELE - 2/Lt MARTINDALE joined for duty	Relwayall
	6.9.17		Parades under Company arrangements - 2nd Lt. W. Newton joined for duty	Relwayall

WAR DIARY or INTELLIGENCE SUMMARY

Army Form C. 2118.

Place	Date	Hour	Summary of Events and Information	Remarks and references to Appendices
NOORDPEENE Area	7.9.17		The G.O.C. Brigade inspected "C" Company marching order and also practical the billets etc. of the battalion. — Lecture by A.D.M.S.	Reheayall
	8.9.17		Parades under company arrangements. 2/Lt Moffatt & Officer of A Coy & NCO. A Coy went up to the line — 2/Lt Newton went to hospital — 2/Lt Nelson & Petrie joined.	Reheayall
	9.9.17		Church Parades in morning — Orders for X Corps Offensive prepared.	Reheayall
	10.9.17		11th N.F. Order No 32 issued for Thursday operations — Company parades in the morning and in the evening Battalion practised forming up on tapes	Reheayall
	11.9.17		Company parades — Battalion practised moving in go modes by night	Reheayall
	12.9.17		Brigade practised the attack over flagged course — Orders received for move and advance party proceeded to STEENVORDE area	Reheayall
STEENVORDE	13.9.17		Battalion paraded at 12.25p.m. and marched to STEENVORDE area being billetted in farms — 9 men fell out but all rejoined on march	Reheayall
MURRUMBIDGE CAMP	14.9.17		Battalion paraded at 8.30 p.m. and marched to No 5 Area being in camp at MURRUMBIDGE Camp on the LA CLYTTE road arriving at 1.30 p.m — 10 men fell out but all rejoined on the line of march	Reheayall
	15.9.17		Conferences for officers in morning — Congrada to 11th N.F. Order No 32 issued instructions	Reheayall

WAR DIARY
or
INTELLIGENCE SUMMARY.

(Erase heading not required.)

Army Form C. 2118.

Place	Date	Hour	Summary of Events and Information	Remarks and references to Appendices
T. Camp H.28.d.55	16/9/17		Battalion paraded at 9.15am and marched to T. Camp arriving at 10.30am – a fleet of 14 aeroplanes including Gothas flew over the Camp at 10.45am – Orders received that operations are altered – enemy shelled camp intermittently all night – men wounded	Rehayalt
	17/9/17		2nd Lt. M. Lyons and 2/4 RH Penney with 16 men of A+B Coys carried out a fighting patrol at dawn on ground between our jumping off line and DUMBARTON LAKES, capturing 1 prisoner and killing 2 Germans in addition to rendering a very useful report (attached) – our casualties were 1 killed – 1 wounded – Enemy shelled vicinity of camp all day – 11 NF Order No 32 issued.	Rehayalt
TERR TOP TUNNELS	18/9/17		The Battalion paraded at 10am and marched to TARR TOP TUNNELS relieving the 2 ROYAL in the front line sector on the night of the Divisional front – B Coy took over front line, D Company in support and A and C Company in reserve – Sec. Lt. C.S. BOWMAN killed + 7 O.R. wounded. At 9pm the Battalion moved to three battle positions in tapes in front of DUMBARTON LAKES – quiet day on the line.	Rehayalt
Front Line	19/9/17			Rehayan

Army Form C. 2118.

WAR DIARY
or
INTELLIGENCE SUMMARY.
(Erase heading not required.)

Instructions regarding War Diaries and Intelligence Summaries are contained in F. S. Regs., Part II. and the Staff Manual respectively. Title pages will be prepared in manuscript.

Place	Date	Hour	Summary of Events and Information	Remarks and references to Appendices
The Battle of the MENIN ROAD	20.9.17		By 3.30 am the battalion was in position on a tape line in front of DUMBARTON LAKES - No casualty was caused without attack or a casualty. At 5.40 am the barrage opened and the battalion with A and C Companies in the firing line - B Company in close support and D Company in Reserve moved to the attack of the RED LINE, the 1st Objective. The attack met with was very heavy at first from Machine Gun fire especially from J.20.a.1.1 where an enemy M.G. post held out for a considerable period causing heavy casualties. After heavy hand to hand fighting A and C Companies reinforced by B Coy reached their Objective and dug in. D Company carried up materials for consolidation and the line was held and consolidated in its 10th N.P.16 paid during to their attack in the BLUE LINE. Many of the enemy were killed and many Taken prisoners also 1 M.G. Captured by C Coy. Our casualties were A Coy 2nd Lt A. M. Lynn wounded seriously - O.R. 14 killed, 42 wounded 3 missing; B Coy Capt H.M.P.Nest, 2nd Lt. G.O.Edwards M.C. killed, 2nd Lt. E.G. Smith wounded - O.R. 16 killed 37 wounded, 9 missing ; C Coy Capt C.T.H. Coleman killed, 2nd Lt G. Watt wounded, 2nd Lt W. Holt wounded at duty - O.R. 10 killed, 43 wounded 7 missing	

WAR DIARY
or
INTELLIGENCE SUMMARY.
(Erase heading not required.)

Army Form C. 2118.

Place	Date	Hour	Summary of Events and Information	Remarks and references to Appendices
			D Company 2nd Lt S. Brewer - OR 2 killed, 16 wounded, 1 missing	
			Total casualties Officers 4 killed, 5 wounded - OR 42 killed, 138 wounded	
			20 missing. - Grand Total 9 Officers & OR 200	
			Enemy shelled our position intermittently throughout the day but owing	
			to the success of the 10 N.F. and 13 DLI in capturing its BLUE and GREEN	
			lines our battalion position became Support (Orders & Appen attached)	
	22/9/17		Battalion remained in the line all day - heavy enemy activity to the	Renewal
			against the 41st Div succeeded in breaking their line and endangered	—
			our flank - At 12 midnight A Coy was withdrawn to Battle Lucky	
			Dugout J.19.b.81 and D. Coy went into position facing S in its	
			DUMBARTON WOODS - Casualties included in 20"	
			At 7am A and C Companies were withdrawn to JAM SUPPORT and at 7pm	Renewal
	22/9/17		the whole Battalion was relieved by 12 DLI (2 Companies) and outreliefs	—
			to BEDFORD HOUSE - Casualties included in 20".	
T.Camp	23/9/17		Battalion marched at 9am to T.Camp DICKEBUSCH - Reinforcements	Renewal
DICKEBUSCH			arrived - orders received for move to WESTOUTRE area.	

Army Form C. 2118.

WAR DIARY
or
INTELLIGENCE SUMMARY.
(Erase heading not required.)

Instructions regarding War Diaries and Intelligence Summaries are contained in F.S. Regs., Part II. and the Staff Manual respectively. Title pages will be prepared in manuscript.

Place	Date	Hour	Summary of Events and Information	Remarks and references to Appendices
NESTOURER	24/9/17		Battalion marched to THUNDERER CAMP arriving at 11.30 a.m. No men fell out on the line of march. 2/Lt A.N. Lyne awarded M.C. to read on 17th	R@Chuayall
THUNDERER CAMP M.8.a.3.2	25/9/17		G.O.C. Division inspected the Battalion in the morning. A draft of 229 OR. arrived. 2nd Lt J. Ridley joined for duty and was posted to B. Coy.	R@Chuayall
	26/9/17		The Commanding Officer redistributed the draft and it was posted as under as follows:- 80 to A; 60 to B; 60 to C; 29 to D. Coy. Effective strength 36 officers + 1027 OR; Return 32 off + 916 OR. Trench Strength 29 off + 601 OR. (exclusive of Draft of 229 OR.)	R@Chuayall
	27/9/17		Gen C.N. Colville resigned command of the Brigade and Col Barker of 11 West Yorks took over. Orders received for Battn to move up on 28th inst	R@Chuayall
RIDGE WOOD CAMP	28/9/17		Battn paraded at 8.30 a.m. and marched to RIDGE WOOD CAMP arriving at 11.45 a.m. Draft of 229 proceeded to X Corps Reinforcement Camp Abele	R@Chuayall
N.5 Central	29/9/17		Major R.H. Gill inspected kits of A. Coy. Battn found 130 men for carrying fatigue	R@Chuayall
	30/9/17		Church Parades. Battn found 100 men for carrying fatigue. Effective Strength 38 off + 1020 OR; Ration 338 off + 894 OR; Trench 27 off + 577 OR (does not include draft).	R@Chuayall

R@Chuayall
Capt/Adjt
for O.C. 11 N.F.

30. 9. 17.

SECRET.   COPY NO. 10

11TH NORTHUMBERLAND FUSILIERS – ORDER NO. 30.

Ref. Map Sheets 27 & 28, 1/40,000.   1st Septr. 1917.

1. The 68th Infantry Brigade will move by march route tomorrow 2nd Septr. to Back Areas, the 11th N.F. proceeding to billets in the STEENVOORDE Area.

2. 2nd.Lt. J.Moffat and 1 N.C.O. per Company will report at the Orderly Room at 6.30 a.m. to proceed as Advance party. They will be at Brigade H.Q. at 7 a.m.

3.   Reveille   –   6 a.m.
            Breakfasts – 6.45 a.m.
All Officers' kits, mess kits, Company Stores etc., will be stacked at the Qr.Mr's Stores by 7.30 a.m. The Regimental Sergt. Major will detail a party of 1 N.C.O. and 3 men for loading purposes.
The Qr.Mr. will detail a guide to meet a lorry (time and place will be notified later) and will be responsible for conveying all stores to the new area.

    Companies will parade on their own parade grounds, ready to move off at 8.45 a.m. Order of march – D, C, B, A, H.Q., 1st Line Transport.
    East of RENINGHELST 200 yards will be maintained between Companies. West of RENINGHELST no interval.

ROUTE:– Cross roads OUDERDOM, RENINGHELST, ABEELE.

    The Transport Officer will arrange for 1st Line Transport to be drawn up on the road outside the Camp by 8.45 a.m.

    Haversack rations will be carried.   Dinners on arrival.

4. All tent shelters will be struck and stacked at the Qr.Mr's Stores by 6.45 a.m. The Regimental Sergt. Major will detail an N.C.O. to remain behind to hand over camp and obtain receipts.

5. ACKNOWLEDGE.

R.C. Mayall.
Capt. & Adjutant,
11th Northd. Fusiliers.

Issued by runner at 10.20 p.m.
1/9/17.

    Copy No.1 – C.O.   Copy No.6 – T.O.
       "   No.2 – "A" Coy.   "   No.7 – Q.M.
       "   No.3 – "B" "   "   No.8 – 2nd.Lt.J.Moffat.
       "   No.4 – "C" "   "   No.9 – A/R.S.M.
       "   No.5 – "D" "   "   No.10 – War Diary.

SECRET.   COPY NO. 10

11TH NORTHUMBERLAND FUSILIERS – ORDER NO.31.

1.   The 68th Brigade Group will move by march route tomorrow 5th inst., to the NOORDPEENE Area, the 11th N.F. proceeding to billets in N.W. NOORDPEENE.

2.   Reveille – 4 a.m.
                Breakfasts – 5 a.m.

   All Officers' kits, mess kits, stores etc., will be dumped as follows by 6 a.m.:-
   H.Q., "A" & "B" Coys – H.Q. Mess Farm.
   "C" and "D" Companies – On road by "C" Coy's billet.

   Only 1 man per Coy will be left at each dump.

   The Qr.Mr. will detail a guide to report at 68th Brigade H.Q. in the SQUARE, STEENVOORDE, at 6 a.m. for lorries.

   The Battalion will parade, ready to move off, at 7.12 a.m. Order of march – "B", "A", "D", "C", Headquarters. Head of the column to be at road junction K.32.d.4.0.
   O.C. Companies will arrange to arrive at the Starting Point punctually, as it will be a Brigade column.

   Dinners on arrival.

   The Qr.Mr. will arrange to collect all stores from the Dumps and to convey them to the new area.

3.   Transport will move separately under the Command of Capt. H. Haddon, A.S.C. The 11th N.F. will follow the 10th N.F. and will be at road junction K.32.d.4.0. at 8.40 a.m. The Transport Officer will make his own arrangements for collecting the field kitchens and watercarts.

4.   ROUTE:- OXELAERE, BAVINCOVE.

5.   ACKNOWLEDGE.

                                                               R C Mayall
                                                               Capt. & Adjutant,
Issued by runner at 10.15 p.m.   11th Northd. Fusiliers.

         Copy No.1 – C.O.   Copy No.6 – T.O.
            " No.2 – "A" Coy.   "   No.7 – Q.M.
            " No.3 – "B" "   "   No.8 – R.S.M.
            " No.4 – "C" "   "   No.9 – H.Q. Coy.
            " No.5 – "D" "   "   No.10 – War Diary.

COPY NO. 10

11TH NORTHUMBERLAND FUSILIERS - ORDER NO. 32.

Ref. Map - Trench Operation Map A.1/5,000.   9th Septr. 1917.

1.   The enemy is occupying a position running North and South through INVERNESS COPSE and DUMBARTON LAKES.   His troops are distributed in depth, the foremost line consisting of a series of Strong Points, fortified shell holes and portions of destroyed trenches.

   68th Brigade will attack the enemy's position on the front from JAVA AVENUE J.19.b.6.½. to junction JASPER DRIVE and GREEN JACKET RIDE J.19.b.7.7. with X Brigade (41st Division) on its right and the 69th Brigade on its left.

   70th Infantry Brigade will be in Divisional Reserve.

2.   The objectives of the 68th Brigade are shown on map A as follows :

   First Objective - RED LINE.
   Second Objective - BLUE LINE.
   Third Objective - GREEN LINE.

   The attack on the RED and BLUE Lines will be carried out by the 11th N.F. on the right and the 10th N.F. on the left, the dividing line between Battalions being shown by a green line.

   The attack on the GREEN LINE will be carried out by the 13th D.L.I.

   12th D.L.I. will be in Brigade Reserve.

3.   The approximate assembly positions for the 11th N.F. at ZERO hour on "ATTACK DAY" will be on a taped line in trenches in J.19.b.

   The general bearing of the line of advance is 90°.

   "A" Company, 11th N.F. will advance at ZERO hour, and capture and consolidate the portion of the RED LINE allotted to the Battalion, establishing a Strong Point (A) at J.20.a.8.1.   O.C. "A" Company will detail a special party under the command of 2nd Lieut. A.M.Lyone to meet a party of the 41st Division at J.20.a.8.1.

   "B" and "C" Companies, 11th N.F. will advance through "A" Coy at ZERO plus ---- (time to be notified later) and attack, capture and consolidate the portion of the BLUE LINE allotted to the Battalion.

   "B" Company will be on the right and "C" Company on the left.

   Strong Point (D) at J.20.d.7.7. will be established by "B" Coy.

   O.C. "B" Company will detail a special party under the command of 2nd Lieut. R.H.Penney, to meet a party of the 41st Division at J.20.d.2.9.   This party will carry a pigeon in order that a report of touch being obtained may be sent at once.

   O.C. "C" Company will arrange meeting places to keep touch with the 10th N.F. on his left.

   The dividing line between "B" and "C" Companies is shown by a Black line on Map "A".

   "D" Company will carry all material necessary for the consolidation of the Objectives, and the R.E's and Pioneers will assist in the construction of the Strong Points.

3. - CONTINUED -

"O".C. Companies will ensure that proper direction is kept and will afford one another mutual support in the advance.

All Strong Points within their areas will be dealt with by the Companies concerned.

Each Platoon and Section must be given a special task, a special objective, and special work to do on reaching it.

4. Moppers-up will be detailed by Officers Commanding Companies, with the exception of "C" Company, in sufficient numbers for their Company areas. "B" Company will be responsible for the mopping-up of the whole area between the RED and BLUE LINES.

Definite units will be detailed to mop up specific areas, with instructions to search thoroughly for machine guns, and to make sure that no German capable of using his arms is overlooked.

5. The Attack will be covered by an Artillery, Machine gun and STOKES Mortar barrage.

The Field Artillery barrage will commence 150 yards in advance of the front line of infantry and will move forward at the following rates :-

To the RED LINE -- at the rate of 100 yards in six minutes.
From RED to BLUE LINE -- at the rate of 100 yards in eight minutes.
From BLUE to GREEN LINE -- at the rate of 100 yards in ten minutes.

A pause of 30 minutes will be made after the RED objective has been reached, and a pause of 1 hour and 30 minutes after the BLUE objective has been reached.

6. Pioneers will mark out tracks "V" and "W" shown on map A with posts marked with two white rings.

7. The Battalion Signal Officer will arrange for runner routes to be marked out from Battalion Headquarters to Companies as soon as possible after the objectives have been gained. These will be marked with small pieces of wood painted "RUNNER" at frequent intervals.

Brigade Signal Officer is arranging to mark out runner routes from Brigade Headquarters to Battalion Headquarters. For this purpose flags 2 feet square, half white, half yellow, will be used.

8. The Regimental Aid Post will be established near Strong Point at J.19.c.7.9.
After the Objectives have been taken a Forward Dressing Station will be established approximately at J.20.b.3.2.

9. "ATTACK DAY" and ZERO hour will be notified later.

10. No papers dealing with this operation will on any account be taken up to the line.

11. Instructions on the following subjects will be issued separately :

    1. Fighting kit.
    2. Artillery.
    3. Strong Points (including allotment of machine guns and trench mortars for garrison).
    4. Signals and communication.
    5. Administrative arrangements, including location of dumps.

12. O.C. Companies will forward plan of their operations to Battalion Headquarters as soon as possible.

13. ACKNOWLEDGE.

14. Reports to Strong Point at J.19.c.7.9.

R.C.Mayall
Capt. & Adjutant.
11th (S) Bn. Northumberland Fusiliers.

Issued by runner at 11 a.m.
10/9/17.

Copy No. 1 - H.Q., 68th Bde. ✓
  ,, No. 2 - C.O.
  ,, No. 3 - 2nd-in-Command. ✓
  ,, No. 4 - "A" Coy. ✓
  ,, No. 5 - "B" Coy. ✓
  ,, No. 6 - "C" Coy. ✓
Copy No. 7 - "D" Coy. ✓
  ,, No. 8 - Signal Officer.
  ,, No. 9 - Medical Officer.
  ,, No.10 - War Diary.
  ,, No.11 - File.
Copies 12 - 15 - Retained.

12. O.C. 68. M.G. ✓
13. O.C. B. Coy n II ✓

XTH CORPS OFFENSIVE.

CORRIGENDA TO 11TH NORTHUMBERLAND FUSILIERS ORDER NO.32.

Para.3, first sentence, please substitute the following :-

"The approximate assembly positions of the 11th N.F. at ZERO hour on "ATTACK DAY" will be on jumping-off tapes in J.19.b. The Intelligence Officer will be responsible for laying out the tapes.
The tapes will be laid out parallel to one another at intervals of 50 yards in the following manner:-

J19.b.7.1.
J.19.b.85.75

← Direction of Advance

"A" Coy.
─────────────────────────

50x

XXXXXXXX
"D" Coy.
─────────────────────────

50x

"C" Coy.   "B" Coy.
─────────────────────────

50x

"B" Coy.
12th D.L.I.
─────────────────────────

Ac Coys frontage 200
B&D Coys 400

Each Company will have an approximate frontage of 200 yards on the assembly position, with the exception of "B" and "C" Coys., 11th N.F. and "B" Coy. 12th D.L.I., who will each have 100 yards.

1 Section 68th M.G.Coy will assemble in the vicinity of Battalion Headquarters, LUCKY DUGOUT, J.19.b.7.1.

Companies will adopt the formations already practised and will be in position ½ hours before ZERO.

Fourth sentence, please substitute the following :-

"The attack on the BLUE LINE will be carried out by :-

"B" and "C" Companies 11th N.F. in the Firing line.

"B" Company 12th D.L.I. in close support (not to be used without reference to O.C. Battalion).

1 Section 68th M.G. Coy.

(2)

At ZERO hour "B" and "C" Coys will move forward from the jumping-off position so as to avoid the enemy's barrage.

They will move up as close as possible to our barrage in front of the RED LINE in sufficient time to advance to their objectives when the barrage lifts in its advance to the BLUE LINE.

They will attack, capture and consolidate the portion of the BLUE LINE allotted to the Battalion.

At ZERO hour "B" Coy 12th D.L.I. will move forward in rear of "C" Coy 11th N.F. until they reach the road running from J.20.a.55.45 - J.20.a.50.10. where they will remain and await orders from O.C. 11th N.F. O.C. "B" Coy 12th D.L.I. will arrange communication with Battalion Headquarters as soon as he gets into position on the above line. He will detail an Officer to be at Battalion Headquarters as LIAISON Officer.

The Section of 68th M.G. Coy will remain in its assembly position until orders are issued for 2 Guns to move forward to Strong Point A and 2 Guns to Strong Point D by O.C. 11th N.F. The Commander of the Section will make arrangements to use his guns for the purpose of providing covering fire for the attack from the vicinity of his assembly position.

Tenth sentence, please add :-

"D" Company will follow close behind "A" Coy, carrying all materials necessary for consolidation and will establish a Forward Dump in the vicinity of the RED LINE. From this Dump parties will be sent forward to "B" and "C" Coys 11th N.F. carrying materials, when the BLUE LINE has been taken.
On no account will any man of "D" Company return from the Forward Dump until the assaulting Companies of 11th N.F. have passed through to their objectives.
The four Lewis Guns of "D" Company will advance with their Company as escort, and will remain in reserve at the RED LINE.

Para.4, please substitute :-

"Moppers-up will be detailed by Officers Commanding Companies in sufficient numbers for their Company Areas.
Two sections of "B" Company will be attached to "C" Company for this purpose."

Para.5 is cancelled by Artillery and Machine Gun Instructions issued separately.

Para.6, please delete and substitute the following :-

"The following parties will assist O.C. "B" Company in the construction of Strong Point D at J.20.d.7.7. (This point is not a Strong Point at present, but is the site selected for one as a support for the right flank of the Division):-

1 Section R.E's, 1 Platoon Pioneers, and 2 Platoons of attached Infantry for carrying parties.

These parties will not form part of the garrison but will return on completion of the work.

The 9th South Staffs will construct the following tracks :-

"V" Track.   J.19.central - Strong Point A, J.20.a.75.10. - Strong Point D.

"W" Track.   Junction of JASPER DRIVE - GREEN JACKET RIDE - Strong Point E.

Para.7, first sentence, please substitute :-

"These will be marked by sticks, 3 feet long, painted red and white."

Para.8, please substitute :-

"The Regimental Aid Post will be established at J.19.a.5.5. Junction of Jam Row and Jam Support.

Para.14, please substitute :-

"Reports to LUCKY DUGOUT, J.19.b.7.1."

R.C. Mayall

Capt. & Adjutant,
11th Northd. Fusiliers.

15/9/17.

XTH CORPS OFFENSIVE.　　　　　　　COPY NO. 11.

11TH NORTHUMBERLAND FUSILIERS - ORDER NO. 32.

Reference Map - Trench Operation Map A 1/5,000.　　17th Sept. 1917.

1. Information and Objectives as detailed in paras. 1 and 2 of 11th N.F. Order No. 32, dated 10/9/17.

2. The attack will be carried out as follows :-

    RED LINE   -   11th N.F.
    BLUE LINE -   10th N.F. plus 2 Coys 12th D.L.I.
    GREEN LINE -   13th D.L.I. plus 2 Coys 12th D.L.I.

3. The approximate assembly positions of the 11th N.F. at ZERO hour on "ATTACK DAY" will be on Jumping-off Tapes running from J.19.b.7.1. to J.19.b.85.75.
   The Battalion will form up in accordance with the attached plan.
   1 Section of the 68th M.G. Coy. will assemble in the vicinity of Battalion Headquarters, LUCKY DUGOUT, J.19.b.7.1.

   Companies will adopt the formations already practiced and will be in position half-an-hour before ZERO.

   At ZERO hour "A" Coy (right) and "C" Company (left) will advance, capture and consolidate the RED LINE.

   O.C. "A" Company will detail a Special Party under the command of 2nd Lieut. A.M. LYONE to meet a party of the 15th Hants Regt. at J.20.a.8.1.

   O.C. "A" Company will detail a Special Unit to capture, consolidate and garrison Strong Point A.

   O.C. "B" Company will detail 1 Platoon under 2nd Lieut. L.W. Ablett to procedd with the 11th West Yorks., as far as the RED LINE where it will rejoin its Company.

   O.C. "C" Company will arrange Liaison with the 11th West Yorks on the RED LINE.

   The dividing line between "A" and "C" Companies is as shewn on Map A.

   "B" Company will be in close support and at ZERO hour will advance close behind "A" and "C" Companies.

   "D" Company will carry all necessary materials for the consolidation of the RED LINE. Special parties will be detailed to follow close in rear of "B" Company with materials necessary for immediate requirements of "A" and "C" Companies.

   The four Lewis Guns of "B" Company will remain in reserve.

   The Section of the 68th M.G. Coy. attached to the Battalion will remain in its assembly position until orders are issued by O.C. 11th N.F. for two guns to move forward to Strong Point A and two guns to a dugout at J.20.a.2.15. where they will support the attack by covering fire.

   All Companies will move forward from the Jumping-off positions as

(2)

soon after ZERO as possible so as to avoid the enemy's barrage.

O.C. Companies will ensure that proper direction is kept and will afford one another mutual support in the advance.

All Strong Points within their Areas will be dealt with by the Companies concerned.

Each Platoon and Section must be given a special task, a special objective and special work to do on reaching it.

4. Moppers-up will be detailed by O.C. "A" and "C" Companies in sufficient numbers for their Company areas. Definite Units will be detailed to mop up specific areas, with instructions to search thoroughly for machine guns and to make sure that no German capable of using his arms is overlooked.

5. Owing to the apparently boggy nature of the ground in the DUMBARTON LAKE Area the 10th N.F. and 13th D.L.I. will pass round the flanks of the RED LINE to form up for the attack on their respective objectives.

6. The 9th S. Staffs will construct the following tracks :-

"V" Track. J.19.central - Strong Point A - Strong Point D.

"W" Track. Junction of JASPER DRIVE - GREEN JACKET RIDE - Strong Point E.

7. The Regimental Aid Post will be established at J.19.a.5.5., Junction of JAM ROW and JAM SUPPORT.

8. "ATTACK DAY" and ZERO hour will be notified later.

9. No papers dealing with this Operation will on any account be taken up to the Line.

10. Instructions on the following subjects have been issued separately :-

      1. Fighting Kit.
      2. Artillery.
      3. Cancelled.
      4. Signals.
      5. Administrative arrangements.
      6. Reinforcements.
      7. Contact Aeroplane.
      8. Machine Guns.

11. With the exception of paras 1 and 2, 11th N.F. Order No. 32 dated 10/9/17 and Corrigenda dated 15/9/17 are hereby cancelled.

12. Reports to LUCKY DUGOUT, J.19.b.7.1.

R.C. Mayall.
Capt. and Adjutant.
11th (S) Bn. Northumberland Fusiliers.

17/9/17. Issued by runner at 7 p.m.

PLAN OF ASSEMBLY AT ZERO HOUR.

Left.		Right.
"C" 200 yards.		"A" 200 yards.

50↑ 50↑

"B" 400 yards.

50↑

"D" 400 yards.

The tapes will be laid out parallel to one another at 50 yards interval. "A" and "C" Companies will each have an approximate frontage of 200 yards and "B" and "D" Companies 400 yards each.

The Battalion Intelligence Officer will be responsible for laying out the tapes.

SECRET.   COPY NO. 10

11TH NORTHUMBERLAND FUSILIERS ORDER NO.33.

Ref. Map Sheet 27.   12th Septr. 1917.

1. The 68th Brigade Group will move by march route to the STEENVOORDE Area on Septr. 13th., the 11th N.F. proceeding to billets in STEENVOORDE Central.

2. The Battalion will parade ready to move off at 1 p.m. Head of column at "B" Coy's billet. Order of march – Band, Signallers and Headquarters, A, B, C, D.

   ROUTE:- Via BAVINCHOVE.

3. 1st Line Transport will move independently under the command of Capt. H. Haddon, A.S.C.
   The Transport Officer will make his own arrangements for collecting the Transport and will be at Road Junction ZUYTPEENE at 1 p.m., following transport of 10th N.F.

4. All Officers' kits, mess kits, Company Stores, packs and rifles of the bandsmen, etc., will be stacked at the following dumps by 8.30 a.m.:-

   Headquarter billet – For Headquarters and "A" Coy.
   "B" Company's billet – For "B" Company.
   "C" Company's billet – For "C" and "D" Companies.

   Lorries will be available for the move and the Qr.Mr. will detail a guide to be at Brigade Headquarters by 8 a.m.

   1 N.C.O. and 3 men for each dump will be detailed by the Regimental Sergt. Major for loading duty.

   The Qr.Mr. will be responsible for collecting the stores from the dumps and conveying them to the new area.

   Companies may each retain two mess boxes, which will be collected by the Mess cart at 10.30 a.m.

   The Transport Officer will arrange for collection of the Lewis Guns this afternoon.

   A haversack ration will be consumed before starting, and dinners on arrival.

5. The Qr.Mr. will arrange for the handing over of billets and area stores.

6. The 68th Brigade will move on Septr. 14th to No.5 Area. Orders will be issued later.

                                                       RC Mayall
                                                       Capt. & Adjutant,
12/9/17.   11th Northumberland Fusiliers.

         Copy No.1 – C.O.   Copy No.6 – T.O.
          "   No.2 – "A" Coy.   "   No.7 – Q.M.
          "   No.3 – "B" "   "   No.8 – A/R.S.M.
          "   No.4 – "C" "   "   No.9 – H.Q. Coy.
          "   No.5 – "D" "   "   No.10 – War Diary.

SECRET. COPY NO. 10

11TH NORTHUMBERLAND FUSILIERS - ORDER No.34.

Ref. Map Sheet 27 & 28, 13th Septr. 1917.
1/40,000.

1. The 68th Brigade Group will move by march route tomorrow 14th inst., to No.5 Area, MURRUMBIDGE, 11th N.F./ proceeding to Camp in that Area.

2.   Reveille - 5.45 a.m.
        Breakfasts - 6.30 a.m.

All Officers' kits, mess kits, Company stores etc., will be stacked at the following dumps by 7.30 a.m. :-
"A" Coy - Dump to be arranged by Qr.Mr. who will notify O.C. "A" Coy.
"B" " - On the road by billet.
"C" " - On the road by billet.
"D" " - At the point where kits were dumped today.
H.Q. Officers - H.Q. Mess.
Headquarter Coy - Q.M. Stores.

Only 1 man will be left at each Dump. The Qr.Mr. will send a guide to Brigade H.Q. to meet lorry at 7 a.m., and will be responsible for collecting and conveying the stores to the new Area.

Tents and bivouac sheets issued tonight will be stacked at the Dumps and handed over by the Qr.Mr. to the Area Commandant, receipt being obtained and rendered to Orderly Room.

The Battalion will parade, ready to move off, at 8.30 a.m. Order of march - Band, H.Q., D, C, B, A, 1st Line Transport. (1st Line Transport will move with the Battalion tomorrow). Head of the column will be at road junction K.32.d.4.0.

Haversack rations will be carried - Dinners on arrival.

Packs of the bandsmen will be stacked at the dumps.

3. The Medical Officer will see men whom Company Commanders consider absolutely unfit to march tomorrow, at the Transport Lines at 6 a.m. The daily sick parade will be held on arrival in new area.

4. 1 N.C.O. per Company and 1 for H.Q. to be detailed by the R.S.M., will report to 2nd.Lt. J.Moffat, on the road by the Transport Lines, at 4.30 a.m. to proceed as Advance party.

R.C. Heayall
Capt. & Adjutant,
11th Northd. Fusiliers.

Issued by runner at 10 p.m.

Copy No.1 - C.O. Copy No.6 - T.O.
" No.2 - "A" Coy. " No.7 - Q.M.
" No.3 - "B" " " No.8 - A/R.S.M.
" No.4 - "C" " " No.9 - H.Q.Coy.
" No.5 - "D" " " No.10 - War Diary.

XTH CORPS OFFENSIVE.

11TH NORTHUMBERLAND FUSILIERS INSTRUCTIONS NO.1.

FIGHTING KIT.

In the forthcoming Operations the following Fighting Kit will be worn by all ranks of the Battalion :-

Clothing as issued.
Arms as issued.
Pack on back, slung.
Equipment as issued, with the exception of the haversack, which will not be carried.
Steel helmet.
Waterbottle filled, in sling.
Waterproof sheet.
1 large tool on the back of every other man of "A", "B" & "C" Coys - 5 shovels to 2 picks.
Tube helmet.
Box respirator.
Field dressing.
2 sandbags per man of "A", "B" & "C" Coys.
2 grenades (Mills No.5) of "A", "B" & "C" Coys. One to be carried in each top pocket and be collected on reaching the objective and to be used as a reserve.
Moppers-up will carry grenades in quantities to be arranged by O.C. Companies.
S.A.A. - 170 rounds per man, with the exception of Signallers, Runners, Lewis Gunners and Bombers, who will each carry 50 rounds.
2 Red flares every other man of "A", "B" & "C" Coys - 1 to be carried in each bottom pocket.
1 Iron Ration.
1 day's Preserved Meat and Biscuit.
The small entrenching tool will not be carried.

All Officers will be dressed exactly the same as their men.
Sticks will not be carried.

Specialists will be equipped as laid down in S.S.143, Part I, para.3.

Wire cutters, Very Pistols, S.O.S.Rockets, Very Lights, and distinguishing marks to be carried as laid down in Sections XXXI and XXXII of S.S.135.

All tools, bombs, flares and rations, will be issued to the men before leaving their Camps.

R.C. Mayall

Capt. & Adjutant,
11th Northd. Fusiliers.

14/9/17.

XTH CORPS OFFENSIVE.

11TH NORTHUMBERLAND FUSILIERS INSTRUCTIONS NO. 2.

ARTILLERY ARRANGEMENTS.

1. The 68th Brigade Front will be covered by the Right Group of the Artillery allotted to the 23rd Division, consisting of the following Batteries :-

   A.156, B.156, C.156, C.162, D.315, D.156.

   The Centre Group of Divisional Artillery is so arranged as to be able to cover the whole of the Divisional Front. The O.C. Centre Group will detail two batteries so as to act during the attack as Brigade Liaison Batteries. The G.O.C. 68th Infantry Brigade will have a direct call on one battery, and may withdraw it from barrage work to deal with any special object.

   The O.P. of the Right Group will be at J.19.b.30.75.

2. The Infantry will halt on the RED objective for three quarters of an hour (45 minutes) and on the BLUE objective for two hours approximately. Infantry posts will be pushed forward on both objectives to a maximum distance of 100 yards in front of the final line selected for consolidation. These posts will be responsible for warning the troops consolidating of impending counter-attack, and also for mopping-up any shell holes or dugouts between the objectives and the barrage.

   This cancels the last sentence of para.5 in 11th N.F. Order No. 32.

3. The movements of the barrage will be as follows :-

   To RED LINE.

   At ZERO the barrage will come down at the safety limit (about 150 yards) in front of our front line where it will remain until ZERO plus 3 minutes whilst the Infantry close up to it.
   At ZERO plus 3 minutes the barrage moves forward, covering the first 200 yards at 100 yards in four minutes, and then slowing down to 100 yards in six minutes till it is 200 yards beyond the RED LINE, where it pauses.

   To BLUE LINE.

   The barrage will advance at the rate of 100 yards in eight minutes.

4. The dividing line for barrage purposes between the 23rd Division and the 41st Division is a straight line through J.21.d.10.78. - J.19.b.60.06.

   The creeping 18 pdr. barrage nearest the Infantry known as Barrage "A", will reach and pause beyond the successive objectives on the line given above as follows :-

4. - CONTINUED -

BEYOND RED LINE.

Points.	Barrage reaches and pauses.	Barrage resumes advance.
Line c J.20.d.20.92.	ZERO plus 35 mins.	ZERO plus 1 hr. 20 mins.
" d J.14.d.93.86.	" " 35 "	" " ½ hr. 20 mins.

BEYOND BLUE LINE.

Line c J.21.c.10.86.	ZERO plus 1 hr. 52 mins.	" " 3 hrs. 52 mins
d J.15.c.83.80.	" " 1 hr. 52 mins.	" " 3 hrs. 52 mins

5. The Infantry will be notified when they reach the RED and BLUE LINES respectively by firing a proportion of smoke shells in the barrage.

6. ~~Thisxexxssxs~~ These instructions cancel para.5 of 11th N.F. Order No.32.

R.C.Mayall

Capt. & Adjutant,
11th(S)Bn.Northumberland Fusiliers.

14/9/17.

To/- O.C., " " Coy.

14/9/17.

With reference to 11th N.F. Instructions No.1 :-

1. Indents for rations, tools, grenades, S.O.S. Rockets, Very Lights, flares & S.A.A. will be submitted to Orderly Room by 12 noon tomorrow. Care must be taken to calculate the quantities on the number of men going into action.

2. Number of Very Lights is left to discretion of O.C. Coys.

3. Indents for distinguishing marks for Moppers-up, Carrying parties, etc., will be submitted to the Qr.Mr. forthwith.

4. Orders for dumping greatcoats and haversacks will be issued later.

R C Mayall

Capt. & Adjutant,
11th Northd. Fusiliers.

SECRET. COPY NO. 10

11TH NORTHUMBERLAND FUSILIERS - ORDER NO. 35.

Ref. Map Sheet 28, 1/40,000. 15th Septr. 1917.

1. The 68th Infantry Brigade will move to No.1 Area by march route tomorrow 16th inst., 11th N.F. proceeding to "J" Camp, H.28.d.5.6.

2. An Advance party consisting of 2nd.Lt. J.Moffat, 1 N.C.O. per Company, 1 from H.Q. and 1 from Transport, will parade at the Orderly Room at 8 a.m. They will proceed to the camp on cycles and return to HALLEBAST CORNER to meet their Companies and guide them to the camp.

3. The Battalion will parade, ready to move off, on the ground where they fell out yesterday, at 9.15 a.m. First Line Transport will be drawn up on the road outside the camp and will accompany the Battalion on the march.

   100 yards interval will be maintained between Companies on the march.

4. Lorry will be available for the move. The Qr.Mr. will detail a guide to be at Brigade H.Q. at 7 a.m.

   All Officers' kits, xxxxxxxxx Company Stores, etc., will be stacked by the Qr.Mr's tent near the road, by 8 a.m.

   The Qr.Mr. will arrange to convey them to the new area by lorry.

   Officers' Mess boxes will be dumped at the same place by 9 a.m., where they will be collected by the Mess cart.

   All Tents and bivouac sheets will be struck and dumped near the Qr.Mr's tent by 8 a.m. The Qr.Mr. will arrange to convey these to the Area Commandant's stores by the first lorry and obtain receipt.

R.C. Mayall
Capt. & Adjutant,
11th Northd. Fusiliers.

Issued by runner at 9.45 p.m.

```
Copy No.1 - C.O.           Copy No.6 - T.O.
 "   No.2 - "A" Coy.        "   No.7 - Q.M.
 "   No.3 - "B"  "          "   No.8 - A/R.S.M.
 "   No.4 - "C"  "          "   No.9 - H.Q.Coy.
 "   No.5 - "D"  "          "   No.10 - War Diary.
```

XTH CORPS OFFENSIVE.
———————————

11TH NORTHUMBERLAND FUSILIERS INSTRUCTIONS NO 4.
- -

S I G N A L S.

1. **POSITIONS OF HEADQUARTERS.**

    68th Brigade H.Q.   -   TORR TOP SUBWAY.
    68th Adv.   "   -   J.19.b.10.25.
    11th N.F.   -   J.19.b.7.1.

2. **COMMUNICATION BEFORE ZERO.**

    (a) Between Brigade H.Q. and Battalion H.Q.

        By overland cable.
        By runner.

    (b) Between Advanced Brigade H.Q. and Battalion H.Q.

        By overland cable.
        By runner.

    (c) From Battn. H.Q. to Companies.

        By runner.   Any route.

3. **COMMUNICATION AFTER ZERO.**

    (a) From Advanced Brigade H.Q. to Battn. H.Q.

        By overland cable.
        By visual, from Battn. H.Q. and from Companies. (There is a
            Central Visual Station at J.19.b.10.25).
        By runner.   The Battalion Signal Officer is responsible for
            laying out a runner route from Battn. H.Q. to Advanced
            Brigade H.Q. by means of the red and white sticks.

    (b) From Battn. H.Q. to Companies and vice versa.

        By runner. O.C. "A" and "C" Coys will arrange for their
            runners to lay out a runner route back to Battn. H.Q. as
            soon after the objective is taken as possible.   Red and
            white sticks will be issued to Companies by the Signal
            Officer before leaving the camp.

    All Runners will work in pairs, a distance of about 50 yards
will be maintained between the two men.   Both men if possible
will carry copies of the message, but if time does not permit of this
the first man will carry the message in the right hand breast
pocket.   The message will be removed and carried on by the second
man in the event of the first becoming a casualty.   If relay
posts are established, on reaching a relay post the runners will
hand over their messages to the runners already there who will take
them to the next place.   Runners will remain at the relay post
until others relieve them in like manner.

(2)

By Pigeon. To be used in case of emergency. Two Pigeons each will be issued to "A" and "C" Coys. and two to Headquarters.

Pigeons will be released singly and copies of the message sent by next pigeon or runner. Each pair of pigeons will be issued with an envelope containing two clips and three message forms. On no account will pigeons be fed, but they should be given a supply of water.

By visual, if the nature of the ground permits. One daylight lamp will be issued to each of "A", "B" and "C" Coys. and two to Headquarters. All messages sent by visual unless the urgency of the message warrants it being sent in clear, should be sent in code.

4. SYNCHRONISATION OF WATCHES.

The Battalion Signal Officer will make his own arrangements for synchronising at least two watches per Company each day until "ATTACK DAY".

RC Mayall
Captain and Adjutant.
11th Northumberland Fusiliers.

17.9.17.

XTH CORPS OFFENSIVE.

11TH NORTHUMBERLAND FUSILIERS INSTRUCTIONS NO.5.

1. **DUMPS.**   The following Dumps have been established :-

    (a) DIVISIONAL AMMUNITION DUMP — CAMBRIDGE SIDING, N.1.central.

    (b) ADV. BRIGADE DUMP ———————— OBSERVATORY DUMP, I.24.d.1.4.

    (c) BATTALION FORWARD DUMP ———— JEFFREY DUMP, J.19.c.5.9.

    These Dumps contain S.A.A., Grenades No.27, No.24, Mills Hand, "P" Bombs, K.J. Bombs, Very Lights, Red Flares, and Petrol tins. Amounts at each Dump have been given to O.C. "D" Company.
    The Dumps are marked with Illuminated Signs.
    On "ATTACK DAY" Brigade will arrange to send forward further supplies to the Battalion Forward Dump, and establishment of ammunition in First Line Transport will be complete with personnel standing by in case of emergency.

2. **RATIONS.**   On the morning of "ATTACK DAY" minus 2, Companies will draw from the Qr.Mr. before leaving Camp to proceed to the Line, the following rations :-

    Rations for "ATTACK DAY" minus 1.
    Rations for "ATTACK DAY".

    In addition every man will carry his Iron Ration.
    Rations for "ATTACK DAY" plus 1 have already been dumped at the Battalion Forward Dump and will be issued by Ration Parties from "D" Company on the night of "ATTACK DAY".   The Qr.Mr. will be responsible for arranging for the distribution and issue of these rations.

    SOLIDIFIED ALCOHOL.   On the morning of "ATTACK DAY" minus 2 Companies will draw from the Qr.Mr. Tommy Cookers as follows :-

    "A", "B" and "C" Coys — 40 tins each.
    "D" Coy — 25 tins.
    H.Q.   "   — 5 tins.

    This will be used for providing a hot meal for the men before ZERO hour on "ATTACK DAY" and also for cooking throughout "ATTACK DAY".   There are eight men's rations in one tin.

    On the night of "ATTACK DAY" minus 1, the Qr.Mr. will arrange to convey up to Companies cooked meat and an issue of rum for the meal before ZERO hour on "ATTACK DAY", Tommy Cookers being used for the purpose of warming up the meat.

    A gift of two packets of cigarettes and some chewing gum will be issued to Companies on the morning of "ATTACK DAY" minus 2, for use on "ATTACK DAY".

3. **WATER.**   In addition to the water bottles already in possession of the men, Companies will draw the following extra bottles :-

    "A" and "C" Coys — 85 each.
    "B" Coy — 80.

    O.C. Companies will be responsible that all waterbottles are filled, both before leaving Camp on "ATTACK DAY" minus 2, and also before ZERO hour on "ATTACK DAY".

(2)

There are two hundred filled petrol tins dumped at JEFFREY DUMP, for use on "ATTACK DAY".
There are further dumps of filled petrol tins at TORR TOP TUNNELS and at OBSERVATORY DUMP.
Petrol tins may be filled at TORR TOP and at any of the following Water Points :-

    Tank No. 111, - I.21.c.2.9.
    " No. 116, - I.21.d.8.9.
    Pump, house at I.21.b.4.1.
    " " at I.21.d.8.9.

O.C. "D" Coy will have men specially detailed for filling tins from one or more of these places on "ATTACK DAY".

The Qr.Mr. will arrange to send up at least 30 tins of fresh water nightly to the Battalion Ration Dump. (The Transport Officer will arrange the Battalion Ration Dump). "D" Company will be responsible for conveying the water from the Battalion Ration Dump to the Battn. Forward Dump.

All ranks are to be impressed with the necessity for returning without delay all empty petrol tins to the Battalion Forward Dump, as the water supply entirely depends on this.

4. SOUP KITCHENS. Soup kitchens have been established at the following points :-
    VERBRANDENMOLEN Collecting Post.
    WOODCOTE HOUSE.
    BRIDGE 20A (Canal Bank) near HOME FARM.

5. FIGHTING KIT. The tools, grenades, ammunition, flares, etc., laid down in 11th N.F. Instructions No.1, will be drawn from the Qr.Mr., and issued to the men on the morning of "ATTACK DAY" minus 2.

6. TRANSPORT. The SHRAPNEL CORNER - VERBRANDEN - ZILLEBEKE Road is not to be used by Transport on the day or night preceding and the day or night of "ATTACK DAY". No Transport except what is absolutely necessary is to move East of the KRUISSTRAATHOEK - VIERSTRAAT Road on these two days and nights.

Any Transport which has to proceed North of the Canal during the above period is to return by the MIDDLESEX ROAD.

Traffic Map is issued herewith to the Transport Officer.

7. REINFORCEMENTS. All Reinforcements laid down in 11th N.F. Instructions No.6, para.3, will proceed to the Battalion Transport Lines at OTTAWA CAMP before the Battalion proceeds up to the line on "ATTACK DAY" minus 2.

8. R.E. STORES. Battle Dumps of Consolidation Stores are located at:-

    J.19.c.4.6., J.19.b.1.7., J.13.d.1.2., J.13.d.8.8.

9. CASUALTIES. As soon as possible after reaching the Objective, Companies will forward an estimated Casualty Report to Headquarters. This will be followed as early as possible by the daily accurate casualty report.
    After "ATTACK DAY" the daily accurate casualty report will be furnished to Headquarters by 1 p.m. daily.

(3)

9. — CONTINUED @

The detailed casualty report will be sent back each night by O.C. Companies by their Company Qr.Mr. Sergts. to Battalion Rear Headquarters at the Transport Lines.

10. PRISONERS OF WAR. Companies will be responsible for sending back Prisoners to Battalion Headquarters, where they will be taken over by escorts provided by O.C. "D" Company.

They will be conducted to TORR TOP East Side, where they will be taken over by escorts of the 12th D.L.I. and sent to the Divisional Cage.

On no account will prisoners be searched or documents taken from them.

Receipts will be obtained by O.C. "D" Company for all prisoners handed over.

11. INTELLIGENCE. O.C. "B" and "D" Companies will each detail one reliable N.C.O. to search the captured ground for documents, maps, etc. They will wear brassards marked "INTELLIGENCE" and will be attached to Battalion Headquarters under the orders of the Intelligence Officer.

12. STRAGGLERS. All Stragglers of the Battalion will be detained at the Brigade Stragglers' Post, TORR TOP, and after Medical examination will be sent to rejoin their Units. Any stragglers found medically unfit to rejoin will be sent to the Battalion Transport Lines with a certificate from the Medical Officer.

13. CLEARING THE BATTLEFIELD. The eight Stretcher Bearers per Company are responsible for clearing the battlefield between the Objective and the Jumping-off Line. If it is found during the battle that the number of stretcher bearers is insufficient to deal with the situation application will be made to Battalion Headquarters for additional bearers. The application must be accompanied by a guide.

14. SALVAGE. There will be a Salvage Dump at Battalion Headquarters. All ranks are to be warned that they are not to return from any part of the battlefield without bringing an article of salvage with them. All salvaged articles will be carried from the Battalion Salvage Dump to the Battalion Ration Dump by parties to be detailed by O.C. "D" Company, and thence by Regimental First Line Transport to the Divisional Salvage Dump.

All ranks of the Transport will be warned that the A.P.M. has orders to take the names of any drivers of vehicles returning empty from the Forward Area.

15. BURIAL ARRANGEMENTS. The Battalion is responsible for burying all dead on the Brigade Front between the present front line and the RED Objective. As soon as possible after the battle O.C. "D" Coy will be called upon to furnish a party of 20 N.C.O's and men under an Officer to collect all bodies into one or more central places where graves will be dug.

Details of routine to be observed will be issued to the Officer concerned.

R. Mayall
Capt. & Adjutant,
11th Northd. Fusiliers.

17/9/17.

XTH CORPS OFFENSIVE.

11TH NORTHUMBERLAND FUSILIERS INSTRUCTIONS No.6.

REINFORCEMENT ARRANGEMENTS.

1. The following Officers will go into action with the Battalion in the forthcoming offensive :-

Headquarters.

Lt. Colonel A.A. St. Hill.
Capt. & Adjt. R.C. Mayall.
2nd. Lieut. J. Moffat.
2nd. Lieut. J.H. Dunn-Yarker.
Capt. H.C.A. Haynes, R.A.M.C. - Attached.

"A" Company.

Lieut. C.S. Bowman.
3 other Officers.

"B" Company.

Capt. H.M.P. West.
3 other Officers.

"C" Company.

Capt. C.J.H. Adamson.
3 other Officers.

"D" Company.

Capt. J.W. Hunter.
3 other Officers.

O.C. Companies will submit the names of the Officers going into action, as early as possible.

2. The Assistant Adjutant, Orderly Room Staff, and men likely to proceed on leave between Septr. 18th and 25th, when the Battalion proceeds into the line will be left at the Transport Lines. Names of the probable men for leave will be circulated to Coys today.

3. All other personnel, in accordance with the instructions issued on 26/8/17, will be sent to the Brigade Depot Battalion, on a date to be notified later.

   The Band will proceed with these details.

4. Names of the personnel to be left behind in accordance with para. 3 above will be rendered to this office by 6 p.m. today.

R.C. Mayall.

Capt. & Adjutant,
11th (S) Bn. Northumberland Fusiliers.

15/9/17.

XTH CORPS OFFENSIVE.

11TH NORTHUMBERLAND FUSILIERS INSTRUCTIONS NO.7.

CONTACT AEROPLANES.

1. Arrangements for communication between Advanced Troops and Aeroplanes will be as follows :-

    (a) A Contact Aeroplane will be maintained in the air from ZERO (if light enough) till ZERO plus 5 hours 15 minutes.

    (b) Aeroplanes of the Xth Corps Squadron are distinguished by three broad white bands on the fuselage and by the attachment of a black board on the left lower plane. (Diagram can be seen on application)..

    (c) These machines will be furnished with wireless but will only use it for the purpose of reporting a counter-attack or transmitting an Infantry signal message calling for a barrage.

2. (a) Contact Aeroplanes will call for flares by firing a White light and sounding a KLAXON Horn. Leading Infantry will light flares approximately at the following times :-

    On the RED LINE, - ZERO plus 45 minutes.
    On the BLUE LINE - ZERO plus 2 hours 5 minutes.

    Infantry must, however, ensure that the aeroplane is calling for flares before lighting up, and must realise that the presence of an aeroplane at a given time is dependent on the light.

    (b) It is recognised that during confused fighting it is difficult for bodies of troops to know if they are actually the leading troops, and it must not be assumed that flares show that there are no other troops in front. Isolated bodies of troops out of touch on their flanks should light flares when called on to do so by aeroplane.

    (c) The colour of the flares will be Red.

    (d) The lighting of flares should be supplemented by waving helmets, handkerchiefs, maps, papers, mess tins, or any light coloured object. Troops who display no movement when the aeroplane is over them render themselves liable to be mistaken for the enemy, who would thus try to avoid being observed.

    (e) Flares should be lit in groups of three or four flares. Care must be taken not to use all the flares at one time.

3. The wireless aeroplane will be up throughout the day for the purpose of looking out for counter-attacks and for transmitting Infantry messages calling for barrage.

R.C. Mayall.
Capt. & Adjutant,
11th Northd. Fusiliers.

15/9/17.

XTH CORPS OFFENSIVE.

11TH NORTHUMBERLAND FUSILIERS INSTRUCTIONS NO. 8.

MACHINE GUNS.

1. The attack of the 68th Brigade will be supported by a Machine Gun barrage, the front being covered by the 19th and 248th Machine Gun Companies.

2. The rate of fire will be as follows :-

    (a) While supporting the attack - One belt per gun per four minutes.

    (b) During intervening periods - One belt per gun per eight minutes.

    (c) For S.O.S. Signals ---- One belt per gun per two minutes for ten minutes, and afterwards until situation is clear 20 rounds per minute.

    Tracings and tables shewing barrage can be seen on application.

3. All Guns employed on the Divisional barrage can be turned on any part of the front. If it is required to bring concentrated fire fire on a given point it is only necessary to give the map reference (for this purpose the five hundred yard squares on the map are sub-divided into four parts and numbered 1 to 4.).

    1 Gun in each Battery is allotted for Anti-Aircraft work. It will fire in the barrage but will be withdrawn as required.

4. Four Guns of the 68th Machine Gun Company are allotted to the 11th N.F. Position of assembly and subsequent disposition for these guns are detailed in para. 3 of 11th N.F. Order No. 32.

R.C. Mayall.

Capt. & Adjutant,
11th Northd. Fusiliers.

15/9/17.

To/- O.C., " " Coy.

17/9/17.

1. Please cancel all paras. of 11th N.F. Instructions Nos. 1 to 8, which referred to the capture, consolidation and garrison of the BLUE LINE by "B" and "C" Coys, 11th N.F.

2. Please make following amendment to para. 4 (top of page 2) of 11th N.F. Instructions No. 2 :-

BEYOND THE RED LINE.

For "Zero plus 1 hr. 20 mins."

read

Zero plus 1 hr. 28 mins.

For all subsequent barrage times advance time 21 minutes. The time of barrage to resume advance from BLUE LINE will thus be 4 hrs. 13 mins. instead 3 hrs. 52 mins.

3. With reference to para. 5 of 11th N.F. Instructions No. 5, Companies will draw the battle stores from the Qr.Mr. at the following hours tomorrow morning :-

"A" Coy - 9 a.m.
"B" " - 9.30 a.m.
"C" " - 10 a.m.
"D" " - 10.30 a.m.
H.Q. " - 10.45 a.m.

Companies will dump greatcoats, haversacks, and small entrenching tools (where necessary) at the Qr.Mr's Stores at 11 a.m. Reinforcements will not be included.

RC Mayall

Capt. & Adjutant,
11th Northd. Fusiliers.

Map Reference: ZILLEBEKE 1/10000.

REPORT ON RECONNAISSANCE OF GROUND IN J.20.a. CARRIED OUT BY

A PATROL UNDER 2ND LIEUT. LYONE ON THE MORNING OF 17TH SEPT.1917.

At 5.25 a.m. I formed my party up in front of the S.P. at J.19.b.7.7. on the right of the raiding party. At 5.30 a.m. when the barrage started, we advanced keeping to the right of and a little behind the raiding party. Accompanying the raiding party, we proceeded to that part of the wood about J.20.a.19.49, and from there direct to the dug-out at J.20.a.21.20.

The raiding party fired into the dug-out, secured a prisoner, and then gave the signal for the withdrawal which they carried out at once.

We could see a large number of the enemy retiring at the double in the direction of J.20.c.35.75. My party immediately got down and opened rapid fire on them. The light was not clear enough to see whether we inflicted any casualties, and we had not time enough to wait and see where they were going.

We then proceeded towards that part of the lake at J.20.a.50.40. crossing JASPER DRIVE while doing so. We found that trench in fair condition and not knocked about much.

t J.20.a.50.40. 2nd Lieut. PENNEY and I captured a prisoner.

The narrow part of the lake was found to be a ditch easily traversed with very little water in it. The upper part of the lake was from 4" to 10" deep with about one foot of water in places.

By this time it was getting lighter, and 2nd Lieut. PENNEY and I decided to withdraw. We withdrew and proceeded towards the western edge of the wood down the north side of the lake.

While we were at the lake shots were fired at us from the western edge of the wood.

On arriving at J.20.a.19.49, we discovered a small dug-out not concreted, out of which the enemy had fired at us. He was called upon to come out but did not do so. We bombed the dug-out and fired some shots into the doorway. From there we made our way to our own line. It was then about 6.10 a.m. and fairly light.

During all the above operations, 2nd Lieut. PENNEY was close to me and we were working together.

I consider the ground that we went over quite passable. The wood is easily defined as the trees were still standing.

Known casualties inflicted on the enemy by my section :-
2 killed and two others hit.

My casualties were 1 L/Cpl. killed, 1 Private wounded.

A.H.Lyone

2nd Lieut.
"A" Coy., 11th Northd. Fus.

SECRET. COPY NO. 1.

11TH NORTHUMBERLAND FUSILIERS — ORDER NO. 36.

Ref. Map Sheet 28 N.W., 1/20,000.   18th Septr. 1917.

1. The 68th Infantry Brigade will take over their Battle front from 70th Infantry Brigade on the night of 18/19th Septr., the 11th N.F. relieving 70th Infantry Brigade in the front line.

2. The 11th N.F. will proceed to TORR TOP on the morning of the 18th, preparatory to taking over the line in the evening. Companies will leave this Camp at the following times :-

    "D" Coy — 10 a.m.
    "B" " — 10.5 a.m.
    "C" " — 10.10 a.m.
    "A" " — 10.15 a.m.
    H.Q. " — 10.20 a.m.

    ROUTE:- SHERWOOD CAMP H.33.c. — SCOTTISH WOOD — BRIDGE 21 — ZILLEBEKE HALT (VALLEY COTTAGES TRACK).

    All movement East of the DICKEBUSCH — LA CLYTTE Road will be by platoons at 200 yards interval, with 400 yards interval between Companies. East of the line BEDFORD HOUSE — RAILWAY DUGOUTS, movement during daylight will be by sections at one hundred yards interval, four hundred yards between Companies.

    Each Company will send an Officer to reconnoitre the road and tracks and to meet their Companies. Tracks are marked with posts with two white rings and notice boards giving the destinations.

3. 1 N.C.O. per Company and 1 from H.Q. to be detailed by the R.S.M., under the Battalion Signal Officer, will parade at Orderly Room at 6 a.m., to proceed in advance to take over accommodation from the Town Major at TORR TOP.

4. Details for taking over the line will be issued after arrival at TORR TOP.

5. Companies will move from this Camp equipped and prepared to go into action. The Battle stores and dumping of greatcoats, haversacks and entrenching tools will take place three hours earlier than the times notified yesterday.

6. Reinforcements and personnel left out of action will remain behind under the command of Major R.H.Gill and will proceed to the Transport Lines at an hour to be notified later.
    Each Company will furnish to Orderly Room by 9 a.m. a nominal roll of all details left behind.

                                            R C Mayall
1.30 am 18/9/17   Capt. & Adjutant,
18/9/17.   11th Northd. Fusiliers.

        Copy No.1 — C.O.   Copy No.6 — T.O.
         "   No.2 — "A" Coy.   "   No.7 — Q.M.
         "   No.3 — "B" "   "   No.8 — Signal Officer.
         "   No.4 — "C" "   "   No.9 — A/R.S.M.
         "   No.5 — "D" "   "   No.10 — War Diary.

The O.C.
11th Northumberland Fusiliers

I have never been able to come & see you but I must write to say how much we wish you the very best of good luck on going out, & how much we all admire the splendid work of your gallant & excellent people.

I hope you will go out thinking of the 33rd D.A. half the

nice things that we think of the gallant 11th N.F. whom we are all so proud to have helped to win your success.

(Bernard Butler.
Lt. Col. R.+A.
Cdg. 156 Brigade R.F.A.
& Right Group 23rd D.A.

23.9.17

SECRET.   COPY NO. 10

             11TH NORTHUMBERLAND FUSILIERS - ORDER NO. 37.

Ref. Maps, Sheet 28, 1/40,000.   23rd Septr. 1917.

1.   The Battalion will move to THUNDERER Camp, M.8.a.3.2., tomorrow
   24th Septr. 1917.

2.   Reveille   - 6 a.m.
                      Breakfasts - 6.45 a.m.

   All Officers' kits, Company Stores etc., will be stacked near the
   entrance to the Camp by 7.30 a.m.   The Qr.Mr. will detail two G.S.
   wagons to report at the Camp at that hour for conveyance of these
   stores.   The A/R.S.M. will detail 1 N.C.O. & 4 men as loading
   party.

   Mess boxes will be stacked at the same place by 8.15 a.m. and the
   Transport Officer will arrange for the mess cart to collect them.

   The Qr.Mr. will detail a guide to be at Brigade Headquarters by
   6.30 a.m. for lorry.   The lorry will first call at the Camp to
   pick up the Orderly Room boxes and will then proceed to the Qr.Mr's
   Stores.   Four G.S. Wagons will also be available for the move.

        The Battalion will parade in the Company Lines, ready to move
   off at 9 a.m.   Order of march - B, C, D, A, H.Q.   The Transport
   Officer will arrange for the Transport to join the column at
   HALLEBAST CORNER.
        The Band will march with each Company in turn, commencing with
   "B" Coy.   The packs of the band will be stacked by 6.30 a.m.,
   ready to go on the lorry.

        Dinners on arrival.

        ROUTE :- LA CLYTTE & RENINGHELST.   100 yards interval will be
   maintained between Companies.

3.   2nd.Lieut. Edgar will arrange for guides from the advance party
   to meet the Battalion at the Cross Roads in HEKSKEN, M.3.c.1.1.

                                                 G.M.Hackett
                                              Capt. & A/Adjutant,
Issued at 10.15 p.m. by runner.   11th Northd. Fusiliers.
23/9/17.

          Copy No.1 - C.O.   Copy No.6 - T.O.
           "   No.2 - "A" Coy.   "   No.7 - Q.M.
           "   No.3 - "B" "   "   No.8 - R.S.M.
           "   No.4 - "C" "   "   No.9 - H.Q.Coy.
           "   No.5 - "D" "   "   No.10 - War Diary.

SECRET.   COPY NO. 10

11TH NORTHUMBERLAND FUSILIERS - ORDER NO.38.

Ref. Map Sheet 28.   27th Septr. 1917.

1.   The 11th N.F. will move to RIDGE WOOD CAMP, N.5.central, tomorrow 28th inst.

2.   2nd.Lt. E.G.Simons, 1 N.C.O. per Company and 1 from H.Q., will parade at Orderly Room at 7 a.m. to proceed in advance.   A guide provided by this party will meet the Battalion at the Cross Roads N.2.b.8.9., HALLEBAST CORNER.   The Transport Officer will make his own arrangements for advance party and for meeting the column.

3.   The Battalion will parade, ready to move off, at 8.30 a.m. To be formed up in mass, facing the Orderly Room, by that hour.

    All Transport will march in rear of the Battalion.   A distance of 200 yards will be maintained between Companies throughout the march. ROUTE :- M.3.c.2.3. - RENINGHELST - OUDERDOM - Cross Roads N.2.b.8.9. - Cross roads N.10.c.8.5.

    The band will parade as a Unit.

4.   All Officers' kits, mess kits with the exception of the two boxes per Company, Company stores and packs of the band, will be stacked at the Qr.Mr's Stores by 7.30 a.m.   The Transport Officer will arrange to collect the two mess boxes per Company by 8.15 a.m.

    The Qr.Mr. will detail a guide to report at Brigade Headquarters by 7 a.m. for a lorry.

5.   The new draft will accompany the Battalion, unless otherwise ordered.

                                                            R.C. Mayall.
                                                            Capt. & Adjutant,
Issued at 10.15 p.m. by runner.   11th Northd. Fusiliers.

        Copy No.1 - C.O.   Copy No.6 - T.O.
         "   No.2 - "A" Coy.   "   No.7 - Q.M.
         "   No.3 - "B" "   "   No.8 - A/R.S.M.
         "   No.4 - "C" "   "   No.9 - H.Q.Coy.
         "   No.5 - "D" "   "   No.10 - War Diary.

SECRET.   COPY NO. 1

11TH NORTHUMBERLAND FUSILIERS – ORDER NO. 39.

Ref. Map Sheets 27 & 28.   30th Septr. 1917.

1. The 68th Brigade Group will march to billets in the BERTHEN Area on October 1st. The 11th N.F. will be conveyed by busses from RIDGE WOOD to WESTOUTRE on the morning of 1st Octr., and Companies will fall in, on their Company parade grounds, ready to embus at 8 a.m. Each Company will send an Officer to report to the Adjutant for instructions at 7.45 a.m.

    The 11th N.F. will start from Cross roads M.8.c.0.6. at 2.40 p.m. and march via Cross roads R.16.c. – BERTHEN to the BERTHEN Area.

    Dinners will be served on arrival at WESTOUTRE.

2. The Transport will move independently to WESTOUTRE to arrive there by 11 a.m. The T.O. will make his own arrangements for collecting water carts, field kitchens etc. from RIDGE WOOD Camp.
    The Transport will be formed up in rear of the Battalion, ready to march off at 2.40 p.m.
    The Qr.Mr. will arrange for the field kitchens to prepare the midday meal for consumption at WESTOUTRE by noon.

3. 2nd.Lt. E.G. Simons & 1 N.C.O. per Company will report at Orderly Room by 6 a.m. to proceed as advance party. They will proceed by cycle and report to the Staff Captain at Brigade Headquarters, WESTOUTRE, KEMPTON CAMP M.14.b.9.8. at 8 a.m. 2nd.Lt. Simons will detail guides to meet the Battalion at BERTHEN Cross roads R.22.a.0.4.

4. All Officers' kits, mess kits, Company stores etc. and packs of the band will be stacked by the side of the road near Orderly Room by 7.45 a.m. The Regimental Sergt. Major will arrange the dump and detail a guard as loading party.
    The Qr.Mr. will detail a guide to report at Brigade H.Q., WESTOUTRE, for a lorry at 11 a.m. and will be responsible for collecting the stores at RIDGE WOOD Camp and conveying them to the new area.
    The Transport Officer will arrange to collect the Lewis Guns in sufficient time to move with the Transport Column.

5. The Signal Officer will send a representative to Brigade Headquarters at 12 noon tomorrow to synchronise watches.

6. All working parties with the exception of 1 Officer and 50 men of "C" Coy detailed to report to the C.E., Corps, are cancelled.

7. O.C. Companies will render return showing the number of men who fell out, immediately on arrival in billets.

                                            R. Chayah
                                            Capt. & Adjutant,
                                            11th Northd. Fusiliers.

Issued at 11.50 p.m. by runner.

    Copy No.1 – C.O.   Copy No.6 – T.O.
    "   No.2 – "A" Coy.   "   No.7 – Q.M.
    "   No.3 – "B" "   "   No.8 – A/R.S.M.
    "   No.4 – "C" "   "   No.9 – H.Q. Coy.
    "   No.5 – "D" "   "   No.10 – War Diary.

SPECIAL ORDER.

The Divisional Commander desires to convey to all ranks his most sincere congratulations on, and warmest appreciation of, their excellent work and gallant conduct during the late operations.

The marked success which attended their efforts is largely due to the excellent relations which exist between all ranks, arms and services of the Division, and to that readiness to co-operate with one another which they have at all times shown.

So long as this spirit continues, the Divisional Commander is confident that the 23rd Division will successfully carry out any task which may be assigned to it.

THE ATTACHED IS THE WAR DIARY OF THE 11TH(SERVICE) BATTALION,

NORTHUMBERLAND FUSILIERS, FOR THE MONTH OF OCTOBER 1917.

A. Hill Lt.Colonel,
Commanding
31/10/17.   11th(S)Bn. Northumberland Fusiliers.

WAR DIARY or INTELLIGENCE SUMMARY

Army Form C. 2118.

XI NF Vol 25

Place	Date	Hour	Summary of Events and Information	Remarks and references to Appendices
PHINEBOOM X 8 Central	1.10.17		W/o fuir orders had been issued and cancelled the Battn was finally ordered at 12 noon to entrus at RIDGE WOOD CAMP and proceed to METEREN Area — the Battn entrained at 1 pm and was transacked under canvas at PHINEBOOM by 3 pm — 1st Line Transport proceeded independently by road but two mules had to be left at DICKEBUSCH owing to 6 horses being hit by aerial bomb.	Relinquish
THIEUSHOUK 1917 Q.35.d.3.3	2.10.17		Battalion marched at 12.45 pm and proceeded to hutts near THIEUSHOUK arriving at 1.40 pm — 1st Line Transport convoyed stores as lorries available	Relinquish
	3.10.17		Companies paraded under their own arrangements all day	Relinquish
	4.10.17		Warning order received for battalion to be ready to move at 2 hours notice from 12 noon — Range allotted to B Coy in morning and C Coy in afternoon Company Commanders Conference at 3 pm.	Relinquish
	5.10.17		At 8 pm a party of 300 O.R. under Major R.H. Gill from B and D Companies with stretcher bearers from A & C Companies attached to Bde. H.Q. & or proceeded to BURR X Roads to be attached to 21st Division as stretcher bearers.	Relinquish

WAR DIARY or INTELLIGENCE SUMMARY

Army Form C. 2118.

Place	Date	Hour	Summary of Events and Information	Remarks and references to Appendices
THIEUSHOCK	6.10.17		Capt. W.K. MacLachlan and other members officers reported from forward area — Company arrangements for parade.	Re. royal
	7.10.17		A.O.C. Companies had the baths at THINGBOOM — Church Parade cancelled owing to wet weather — orders for were issued.	Re. royal
CURRAGH Camp.	8.10.17		The Batt'n paraded at 6.15am and marched to CURRAGH Camp arriving at 11.45am — "S" Coy of "C" Coy under 2/Lt W.R. Bell arrived from CRE & Coys — 300 men of B.D. Coys under Major Gill arrived after finishing attachment to 2nd Divison ecottotation pieneers — Battn had no any casualties.	Re. royal
ONTARIO	9.10.17		At 3pm the Battalion received orders to march to ONTARIO CAMP near ZEVECOTEN — the Battn marched at 4pm, arriving at 4.50pm.	Re. royal
DICKEBUSCH CAMP	10.10.17		At 12 noon the Battalion received orders to march to camp at DICKEBUSCH — marched at 1pm arriving at 2.30pm.	Re. royal
N.2, 6.6.S.	11.10.17		The whole battalion paraded at camp in DICKEBUSCH at 11am and marched to RAILWAY DUGOUTS where a halt was made at 1pm, followed — at 3pm A. "C" Companies under Major R.H. Gill proceeded up to TOIST FARM in support	Re. royal

WAR DIARY
or
INTELLIGENCE SUMMARY.

(Erase heading not required.)

Army Form C. 2118.

Place	Date	Hour	Summary of Events and Information	Remarks and references to Appendices
			1st 13th DLI relief being carried out at 8.30 pm – A Coy was in dug outs at T.10.c.9.6 and C Company in trench at T.10.c.9.4 – Maj & Coy HQ were at T.10.c.5.5 Batt. HQ. B & D Companies remained in the BUND.	
Front Line	13.10.17		Advance patrols proceeded up the line 16 Take over from the 13th DLI – 2nd Lieut W.R.B & 2nd Lieut T.B.W. Roberts wounded "C" Coy was killed on the MOUND T.10.a.6.8 and Sjt T.B.W. Roberts wounded at duty – The Battalion relieved the 13th DLI in the right sector of the Brigade front at night, dispositions being – Right front company "A" in trench from T.11.c.o.3 to T.11.c.3.3 – Centre front company "B" in trench from T.11.c.3.3 to T.11.c.5.3 – Left front company "A" from T.11.c.5.3 to T.11.d.1.3 C Company Support in trench from T.11.c.6.3 to T.11.c.6.7 – Battn HQ at T.10.c.5.5. – Very heavy shelling throughout the relief – relief complete 6.30 am (13)	Relingue
	13.10.17		A Coy got heavily shelled in the early morning – Battn HQ shelled heavily 2nd Lt J.W. STEVENS A Coy wounded.	Relingue
	14.10.17		C Coy. Very heavily shelled in early morning – 2 Lt S.W. ABLETT and 2 Lt E.D. BRUTY C Coy killed – Battn HQ Shelled heavily	Relingue
	15.10.17		Advance parties arrived from 8th Yorks – very heavy shelling all day.	Relingue

WAR DIARY or INTELLIGENCE SUMMARY

Army Form C. 2118.

Place	Date	Hour	Summary of Events and Information	Remarks and references to Appendices
			Companies were all relieved by 8/Yorks and proceeded to bivouacs at Jacob.	
			RAILWAY DUGOUTS arriving in small parties throughout the night - very heavily shelled - Capt F. Harris Jones found duty.	
BREWERY	6.10.17		Batt: HQ was relieved by HQ 8th Yorks and proceeded at 6.30am to bivouacs	Relayed
CAMP			at RAILWAY DUGOUTS - The battalion proceeded by platoons to Camp O	
H.28.d.9.5.			Brewery Camp DICKEBUSCH all being in by 3pm. Casualties for the tour	
			were - Officers Killed 2nd Lt W.R BELL, L.N ABLETT, E.D BRUTY - wounded	
			2nd Lt T.W STEVENS - 2nd Lt A.C MARTINGDALE (at duty) - 2nd Lt J.R.W ROBERTON	
			at duty - Other Ranks Killed 19 - wounded 64 (4 remain at duty) - 9 missing	
			Total Casualties for tour 98	
	7.10.17		Enemy's aeroplane brought down at 10.30am in vicinity of DICKEBUSCH.	Relayed
			VLAMERTINGHE CHURCH - G.O.C. Division presented Military Medals	
			to men - Batt: parade.	
	8.10.17		Enemy arrangements - enemy bombed from aeroplanes at 7.30pm in vicinity	Relayed
			of camp but caused no casualties - one man and one horse wounded	
			at Railway track 15 yards of line.	

WAR DIARY
or
INTELLIGENCE SUMMARY.
(Erase heading not required.)

Army Form C. 2118.

Place	Date	Hour	Summary of Events and Information	Remarks and references to Appendices
	19-10-17		Orders received and issued for the Battalion to move back to ST. MARTIN Au-LAERT Area on the 20th inst. as part of a composite Brigade under GOC 70th Bde - Part of 1st Line Transport started by road, moving to EECKE	Renvoyal
ST MARTIN	20-10-17		The dismounted personnel of the battalion entrained at DICKEBUSCH at 11:30am and detrained at WIZERNES at 4:30 pm, marching to billets in ST MARTIN	Renvoyal
Au LAERT			Au LAERT arriving at 6:15 pm - the transport entrained at VLAMERTINGHE at 8:30am and 3:35 pm and arrived in billets at 5 pm and 6 am (21st)	
	21-10-17		The companies spent the day in cleaning up and reorganization.	Renvoyal
	22-10-17		Classes for training specialists commenced including Lewis Gunners - Stokes Mortar Bombers - Runners - Signallers - Stretcher Bearers - other parades were carried out under company arrangements - the following awards appeared - The Military Cross - Capt. R.C. Mayall, 2nd Lt. W. Hall, 2nd Lt. S. Brown, 2nd Lt. H. Mellon, 2nd Lt. J. Moffatt, 2nd Lt. E. Smith - the Distinguished Conduct Medal - No 12011 R.Q.M.S. R.L. Parker, No 14893 Sergt. F. Rhodes and No 4359 40 Pte J. Allen - the Military Medal, 7898 Sergt. B.H. Watts - 3 bars to Military Medal and 29 Military Medals. (R.O. 15/10/17)	Renvoyal
	23-10-17		Lt. Col. Og. St. Hill proceeded on leave - Battalion had the use of the baths - Major. R.H. Gill assumed command of batt'n.	Renvoya.

WAR DIARY
or
INTELLIGENCE SUMMARY.

(Erase heading not required.)

Army Form C. 2118.

Place	Date	Hour	Summary of Events and Information	Remarks and references to Appendices
ST. MARTIN AU-LAERT	24/10/17		Company training and specialist classes - No 64196 Sergt Lightowlers awarded the D.C.M. - Lecture to Officers by A.D.M.S. on Sanitation	Reletuayals
	25/10/17		Company training - provided a working party of 300 O.R. for evening G.O.C. Division inspected billets in afternoon.	Reletuayals —
	26.10.17		G.O.C. Division presented ribbons to recipients of rewards at Brigade H.Q. at 10.30 a.m. - all other parades cancelled owing to rain	Reletuayals —
	27-10-17		Battalion ceremonial drill in the morning in preparation for Commander in Chief's inspection	Reletuayals —
	28-10-17		Church Parades in the morning - warning order received for move by rail - all officers and men recalled from leave including Lt. Col. A.A. St Hill	Reletuayals —
	29-10-17		The Brigade was inspected by G.O.C. Division in ceremonial drill - understrents submitted for everything to complete the Battalion - draft of 225 O.R. reported from the Cape Reinforcement Camp	Reletuayals —
	30-10-17		Staff fired elementary practices on "C" Range but owing to a complete lack of previous training in musketry practices, its shooting was bad - All Officers kits inspected and weighed - equipment, stores and clothing had to be reduced to scale and everything in excess of establishment	Reletuayals

Army Form C. 2118.

WAR DIARY
or
INTELLIGENCE SUMMARY.
(Erase heading not required.)

Place	Date	Hour	Summary of Events and Information	Remarks and references to Appendices
ST. MARTIN AU-LAERT.	31-10-17		The Battalion paraded 31 Officers + 633 OR for inspection by Sir Douglas Haig Commander in Chief – After the General Salute, the Battalion was inspected formed up in line and then marched past in column of route – Col A. A. St Hill rejoined from leave – 1st Line Transport was inspected by G.O.C. Brigade – The draft (180) had the use of the Battn. Battalion route march in afternoon – Effective Strength 38 Officers + 933 OR – Ration Strength 36 + 883 OR – General Strength 29 Off + 800 OR.	Russell

(Countersigned)

R. Russell
Captain Adjutant
11 Notts + Derbyshire

A. O. Hill Lt. Colonel
Commanding,
11 Notts + Derbyshire

To /-

2/10/17.

Officers' kits, Company stores, etc., and mess boxes over and above the two per Company, will be stacked by 10.30 a.m. this morning as follows :-

Headquarters, "B" and "C" Coys — Near the entrance to their billet.

"A" and "D" Companies — Near the road at the entrance to their billet.

The Regimental Sergt. Major will detail a guard of 1 N.C.O. and 3 men for each dump. This guard will also act as loading party.

The Qr.Mr. will be responsible for the collection and removal of the stores to the new area with such transport as is available.
There is no lorry available for the move.

Capt. & Adjutant,
11th Northd. Fusiliers.

SECRET. COPY NO. 10

11TH NORTHUMBERLAND FUSILIERS - ORDER NO. 40.

Ref. Map Sheet 27, 1/40,000.   2nd October 1917.

1. The 68th Brigade Group will move today to the THIEUSHOUK Area, the 11th N.F. proceeding to billets near THIEUSHOUK in Q.34 and 35.

2. The Battalion will parade, ready to move off, at 12.45 p.m. Order of march - D, A, B, C, Headquarters, 1st Line Transport, Head of column at Battalion Headquarters, X.8.central.
ROUTE - Cross roads X.7.d., FLETRE, THIEUSHOUK.

3. The Transport Officer will arrange to collect the two mess boxes per Company by 12.15 p.m.

   Transport Officer in conjunction with the Qr.Mr. will arrange for the conveyance of all Battalion stores and kits by regimental transport to the new area.

4. The Packs of the band will be stacked at the respective dumps by 10.30 a.m. The band will parade at Headquarters at 12.30 p.m.

R.C. Mayall
Capt. & Adjutant,
11th Northd. Fusiliers.

Issued by runner at 9.45 a.m.

```
Copy No.1 - C.O.           Copy No.6 - T.O.
   " No.2 - "A" Coy.          " No.7 - Q.M.
   " No.3 - "B"  "            " No.8 - A/R.S.M.
   " No.4 - "C"  "            " No.9 - H.Q.Coy.
   " No.5 - "D"  "            " No.10 - War Diary.
```

SECRET. COPY NO. 10

11TH NORTHUMBERLAND FUSILIERS - ORDER NO. 41.

Ref, Map Sheets 28 & 27, 1/40,000. 7th October 1917.

1. The 68th Brigade Group will move to No.8 Area tomorrow 8th inst., 11th N.F. proceeding to a Camp in WESTOUTRE S.W.

2. The Battalion will parade, ready to move off at 8.15 a.m. Order of march - A, C, H.Q., Details of "B" and "D" Coys., 1st Line Transport. Head of column to be at Road junction by Brigade Headquarters.
ROUTE - Road junction R.27.a.2.8., BERTHEN, Cross roads R.16.c., M.14.a.4.9., WESTOUTRE.

3. All Officers' kits, mess kits with the exception of the two boxes per Company, and stores will be stacked at each Company Headquarters by 7.15 a.m.: 1 man will be left in charge of each dump.
Lorry will be available for the move, and the Qr.Mr. will arrange to collect the stores and move them to the new area.

The two mess boxes per Company to be collected by the mess cart will be ready for loading by 7.45 a.m.

4. 1 N.C.O. per Company, under 2nd.Lieut. G.L. Whitehurst, will parade at Orderly Room at 7 a.m. to proceed in advance to the new area. This party will meet the Battalion on the road at M.14.a.4.9.

5. The Signal Officer will detail an orderly to report to Brigade Headquarters at 8 a.m. tomorrow morning to synchronise watches.

R.C. Mayall.
Capt. & Adjutant,
11th Northd. Fusiliers.

Issued by runner at 3.30 p.m.

Copy No.1 - C.O.   Copy No.6 - T.O.
"   No.2 - "A" Coy.   "   No.7 - Q.M.
"   No.3 - "B" "   "   No.8 - A/R.S.M.
"   No.4 - "C" "   "   No.9 - H.Q.Coy.
"   No.5 - "D" "   "   No.10 - War Diary.

SECRET. COPY NO. 10.

11TH NORTHUMBERLAND FUSILIERS — ORDER NO. 42.

Ref. Map Sheet 28. 1/40,000.   9th October 1917.

1.   The 11th N.F. will move to No.6 Area; ZEVECOTEN, today.

       The Battalion will parade on the road outside the Camp ready to move off at 4 p.m. Order of march — A, B, C, D, Headquarters. The Band will parade with their Companies and 1st Line Transport will move independently to new area. Head of the column at road junction M.17.c.5.6. (i.e. between the Camp and CANADA CORNER).

2.   The advance party will meet the Battalion on arrival in new area.

3.   The Qr.Mr. will arrange for the conveyance of all kits and stores to the new area.

4.   Teas will be consumed on arrival in new area.

                                               R C Mayall.
                                               Capt. & Adjutant,
Issued by runner at 3.25 p.m.   11th Northd. Fusiliers.

```
          Copy No.1 - C.O.              Copy No.6 - T.O.
           "  No.2 - "A" Coy.            "  No.7 - Q.M.
           "  No.3 - "B"  "              "  No.8 - R.S.M.
           "  No.4 - "C"  "              "  No.9 - H.Q. Coy.
           "  No.5 - "D"  "              "  No.10 - War Diary.
```

SECRET.   COPY NO. 12

11TH NORTHUMBERLAND FUSILIERS - ORDER NO. 43.

Ref. Map Sheet GHELUVELT, 28 N.E.3, 1/10,000 and
     Sheet 28, 1/40,000.   10th October 1917.

1. The 23rd Division will relieve the 7th Division on the front REUTELBEEK J.10.d.8.0. to J.5.b.5.1. on the night of the 10/11th inst.

    The 68th Brigade will hold the right sub-sector from J.12.a.2.2. to J.17.a.2.5.

    Brigade Headquarters will be at HOOGE TUNNELS.

    10th N.F. and 13th D.L.I. will be in the front line. The line runs approximately from J.12.a.2.2. to J.17.a.2.5.

2. On October 11th, the 11th N.F. will move as follows :-

    (i) "A" and "C" Coys, under Major R.H.Gill, to Support position at JOIST FARM J.10.d.2.1.

    (ii) Battalion Headquarters, "B" and "D" Coys, to Reserve position in RAILWAY DUGOUTS.

3. "A" and "C" Coys will move as follows :-

    Parade in Camp, ready to move off, at 11 a.m. Order of march - "A", "C". (Field kitchens and 1 water cart to follow this column). Form up outside RAILWAY DUGOUTS for dinners.
    ROUTE:- DICKEBUSCH, CAFE BELGE, KRUISSTRAATHOEK, SHRAPNEL CORNER, TRANSPORT FARM.
    Parade ready to move off at 2 p.m. Order of march - "A", "C". Move to Support position at JOIST FARM J.10.d.2.1., via WARRINGTON ROAD and HOOGE TUNNELS. Guides will meet each Platoon at HOOGE TUNNELS at 4 p.m. Field kitchens and water carts will remain at RAILWAY DUGOUTS.

4. Battalion Headquarters, "B" and "D" Coys will move as follows :-

    Parade in the Camp, ready to move off, at 11.10 a.m. Order of march - Headquarters, "B" and "D" Coys. Field kitchens and 1 water cart to follow this column. Dinners on arrival.
    ROUTE:- Same as in para.3 above.

5. An Advance Party of 1 Officer & 4 N.C.O's per Company will leave this camp at 8 a.m. to reconnoitre their Company positions. 2nd.Lt. J.Moffat and 1 N.C.O. to be detailed by the R.S.M. for Headquarters will proceed at the same hour.
    The Advance parties of "A" and "C" Coys will make arrangements for the allotment of accommodation between themselves, allowing for Forward Battalion Headquarters. They will return to HOOGE TUNNELS to guide up their Companies by 4 p.m.
    1 Officer each of "A" and "C" Coys will accompany the above party to reconnoitre the route from RAILWAY DUGOUTS to HOOGE TUNNELS and will return to their Companies at RAILWAY DUGOUTS by 2 p.m.
    2nd.Lieut. J.Moffat will allot the accommodation for the Companies remaining in RAILWAY DUGOUTS.

(2)

6. A distance of 200 yards will be maintained between Companies between this Camp and RAILWAY DUGOUTS.

   A distance of 200 yards between Platoons will be maintained between RAILWAY DUGOUTS and HOOGE TUNNELS.

   Movement East of HOOGE TUNNELS will be made in small parties during daylight.

7. Rations for consumption on 11th and 12th inst. have been issued to Coys already, and will be carried up to the line on the man.

   The Qr.Mr. will arrange to convey water nightly, commencing tomorrow, in petrol tins on limbers, for consumption in the line by "A" and "C" Coys. The water carts will supply the water required by H.Q., "B" and "D" Coys in RAILWAY DUGOUTS.

   The Forward Dump of "A" and "C" Coys will be CLAPHAM JUNCTION. Water will be there at 10 p.m. and Major R.H. Gill will detail the necessary carrying party.

8. Lewis Guns will be conveyed as far as HOOGE TUNNELS for "A" and "C" Coys and to RAILWAY DUGOUTS for "B" and "D" Coys, by Regimental transport. Limbers will follow their Companies and return to the Transport Lines on completion of duty.

9. Officers' Trench kits of Adv. Bn. H.Q., "A" and "C" Coys will be conveyed by limber to be at CLAPHAM JUNCTION by 10 p.m. tomorrow night. Major R.H. Gill will arrange to have them met there.

   Officers' Trench kits, Orderly Room Stores and Medical Stores will be conveyed by limber to RAILWAY DUGOUTS and will follow immediately in rear of "D" Coy.

   All Officers' valises, stores, etc., not to be taken into the line will be stacked at the Qr.Mr's Stores by 10 a.m.

   Officers' Trench kits of Adv.Bn.H.Q., "A" and "C" Coys will be stacked separately at the Qr.Mr's Stores by 10 a.m.

   The Mess cart will carry the two boxes per Coy as far as RAILWAY DUGOUTS and will follow in rear of "C" Coy.

10. The Band will proceed into the line with their Companies.

11. O.C. "A" and "C" Coys will endeavour to get into touch with the troops they are supporting as soon as possible after arrival at JOIST FARM.

12. O.C. "A" and "C" Coys will report arrival in their position as early as possible to Major R.H. Gill, who in turn will report to Battalion Headquarters.

13. These orders will not be taken further forward than RAILWAY DUGOUTS.

14. Only 1 Officer per Platoon, plus O.C. Coy and Second-in-Command will be taken into the line. The remainder will stay at the Transport Lines.

R.C. Mayall

Capt. & Adjutant,
11th Northd. Fusiliers.

Issued by runner at 9.30 p.m.

SECRET.   COPY NO. 10

                11TH NORTHUMBERLAND FUSILIERS - ORDER NO.44.
                ───

Ref.Map Sheets 27, 28, and
        HAZEBROUCK, 5a.   19th Octr. 1917.

1.   The Battalion will move tomorrow 20th October to the WIZERNES
        Area by train, proceeding to billets in LONGUENESSE.

2.   The Battalion will entrain at DICKEBUSCH at 11.30 a.m. tomorrow,
        arriving at WIZERNES at 3.43 p.m.
                Companies must be ready to fall in by 10 a.m. The actual hour
        of parade will be issued in the morning.

3.   The Transport, less that which has proceeded by road today, will
        entrain at VLAMERTINGHE Station as follows :-

        First train. Entraining at VLAMERTINGHE at 8.5 a.m. and detraining
                      at WIZERNES at 10.53 a.m.

                      4 Limbered G.S. wagons.
                      "A" and "C" Coy's Field kitchens.
                      Officers' Mess cart.
                      Maltese cart.

                      Personnel - 1 Officer and 13 other ranks of the transport.

        Second train. Entrain at VLAMERTINGHE at 6.35 p.m. Detrain at
                      WIZERNES at 9.18 p.m.

                      2 Limbered G.S. wagons.
                      "B" Coy's (half) and "D" Coy's kitchen.
                      2 water carts.
                      18 other ranks of the transport personnel.

        The accommodation for personnel and wagons, as detailed above, will
        on no account be exceeded.

        The Transport will report at VLAMERTINGHE Station 3 hours before the
        departure of each train. Head collars and breast ropes must be
        taken for horses. Water carts will be entrained full.

4.   2nd.Lieut. C.B.Longbotham is detailed as Entraining Officer at
        VLAMERTINGHE Station. He will report to the R.T.O. 4 hours before
        the first train is due to leave and will travel by the last train.

5.   Breakfasts, with the exception of "D" Coy., will be cooked on
        trench fires, and the camp kettles used, will be carried on the lorry.
                Dinners for the whole Battalion will be cooked on "A" and "C"
        Companies' Field kitchens on the train and will be ready for consumption
        when the Battalion arrives about 5 p.m.
                A haversack ration will be carried by all ranks for consumption
        on the train.
                The Qr.Mr. will make all necessary arrangements.

6.   All Officers' valises, stores, etc. will be stacked at the entrance
        to the camp under arrangements to be made by the Qr.Mr., by 8 a.m.
                The Qr.Mr. will detail a guide to report to 70th Brigade H.Q. at
        6 a.m. for any lorries that may be available at that hour. He will
        also detail guides to report at 8 a.m. in accordance with instructions
        issued to him by the Staff Captain this afternoon.

(2)

The Qr.Mr. will be responsible for conveying all kits and stores to the new area.

The A/R.S.M. will detail a loading party of 1 N.C.O. and 6 men to be at the Dump by 8 a.m.

7. All Transport to move on the first train will be loaded tonight. The Transport Officer will send down the Officers' Mess cart and Maltese cart tonight and will be responsible for collecting them in the morning in time to be at VLAMERTINGHE Station by 5.5 a.m.
O.C. Companies will be responsible that the mess boxes are put on the mess cart tonight. One mess box per Company for breakfast may be retained and carried on the lorry.

8. 2nd.Lieut. H.E. Cowling is appointed Battalion Entraining Officer and will be at the entraining point one hour before the departure of the train.

9. The A/R.S.M. will detail a guard of 1 N.C.O. & 5 men to remain behind to hand over camp. A receipt for tentage, latrines, etc., handed over will be obtained and handed in to Orderly Room when the guard rejoins the Battalion.

10. The strictest march and entraining discipline will be observed tomorrow.

R C Mayall

Capt. & Adjutant,
11th Northd. Fusiliers.

Issued by runner at 9.45 p.m.

Copy No.1 - C.O.   Copy No.6 - T.O.
"   No.2 - "A" Coy.   "   No.7 - Q.M.
"   No.3 - "B" "   "   No.8 - A/R.S.M.
"   No.4 - "C" "   "   No.9 - H.Q. Coy.
"   No.5 - "D" "   "   No.10 - War Diary.

www.ingramcontent.com/pod-product-compliance
Lightning Source LLC
Chambersburg PA
CBHW080925230426
43668CB00014B/2198